W9-CBA-702

The Music of
E.J. MOERAN

THE MUSIC OF
E.J. MOERAN

GEOFFREY SELF

With a Preface by
VERNON HANDLEY

TOCCATA
PRESS

First published in 1986 by Toccata Press.
© 1986 Geoffrey Self and Vernon Handley.

Music examples drawn by Harry Dinsdale.
A grant from the British Academy towards the costs
of preparing the music examples is gratefully acknowledged.

British Library Cataloguing in Publication Data

Self, Geoffrey
    The music of E.J. Moeran.
    1. Moeran, E.J. — Criticism and interpretation
    I. Title
    780'.92'4   ML410.M/

    ISBN 0-907689-17-5
    ISBN 0-907689-18-3 Pbk

Set in 11 on 12 point Baskerville by Bookmag,
13 Henderson Road, Inverness
Printed and bound in Great Britain by
Short Run Press Ltd., Exeter

Contents

FOR BERYL

PREFACE

Vernon Handley

There was a time when criticism was expected to inform an interested but not knowledgeable public of the strengths of works of art as yet unappreciated. In our time criticism has too often denigrated and dismissed, rather than introduced and expounded. An expression of prejudice and preference does nothing to further the work of an inquiring mind. A typical assessment insists that 'the music of Bartók or Stravinsky is immensely strengthened by having its roots firmly in the soil of Hungarian or Russian folk music' but that 'the music of Holst or Vaughan Williams is immeasurably weakened by being rooted firmly in the soil of English folk music'. The richness and variety of 20th-century music has placed a heavy burden on critics and musicologists, with the result that there are now many composers who have been misunderstood or wrongly assessed.

But we performers tend to have more open minds. We may at first take on a work because we have been requested to do so. We have all of us had the experience of having such a work come back to our minds maybe months later, demanding to be heard in our heads. This is particularly so with the works of E.J. Moeran: no conductor who has been in the presence of the energy of the *Sinfonietta* goes away completely unmoved, and will probably seize the chance – if offered – to conduct it again. Orchestral players always remember their occasional performances of the G minor Symphony. Countless members of choirs sing their parts of the *Songs of Springtime* in the bath or in the garden.

Indeed, with the exception of the enthusiastic scholar the performer has to be the temporary life-support-system for works which are due for a thorough revival. Occasionally someone in orchestral management or a broadcasting service will feel duty-bound to give the composer an airing. But it will usually be the enthusiasm engendered in the artist by that airing which will lead to further performances and the implanting in listeners' minds of just enough seeds of repetition to demand that the works will resound in other heads than those of the lucky performers.

As Moeran died in 1950 a sympathetic assessment of his output is timely, and Geoffrey Self, though plainly enthusiastic about his subject, is a model researcher. He makes claims for Moeran's abilities only when he can substantiate them, and his knowledge of the music is so deep that such substantiations are easy.

There is nowadays a fashion when writing about an artist to confuse the man and the work. Elgar's loves may have inspired him and given him energy, but since his capacity to love had been with him for almost all of his life, comment on any particular one of them probably has little light to shed on the overall development of his symphonic procedure. Geoffrey Self has not been ensnared by the easy attractions which too much emphasis on a man's arcane inner life will add to the book. Personal details are not excluded – indeed, a picture of Moeran's personality has never been more clearly presented – but the author has entitled his book *The Music of E.J. Moeran* and it is this subject that he puts clearly before us.

Three features of Mr Self's approach will recommend themselves to those who, like myself, have been angered by descriptions of Moeran's music as chromatic meandering without intellectual or structural strength: his close analyses of harmonic schemes, his ability to trace the long gestation of a work, and a firm grasp of the importance (or lack of it) of derivativeness. An example of the first is his understanding of *The Overture for a Masque*; of the second, his tracing of the influence of *The Shooting of his Dear* on the second movement of the Symphony; and of the third, his placing in perspective the influence of Ravel on the Piano Rhapsody. To complain of the influence of Ravel as an unabsorbed one in Moeran's writing is like complaining that Spanish music was incompletely absorbed by Ravel – both influences are clear without impairing the individuality of either composer.

When scholarship is spurred by enthusiasm and the two guided by unquestionable integrity, the result is always exciting for those of us who find sanity spectacular and spectacle a touch insane. In its sanity this is a deeply exciting book, its rejection of the spectacular (Moeran's relationship with Peter Warlock could have been blown up out of all proportion) coming at a time when the intimate sides of artists' lives are being investigated with 19th-century prurience. This book should hold our attention as completely as Moeran's music has held its author's.

Vernon Handley

List of Illustrations

INTRODUCTION

E.J. Moeran died on 1 December 1950. He had written a symphony, two concertos, some chamber music, many songs and several piano compositions. Much of his music would seem to have all the elements which make for popular appeal: it is colourful in sound, lively in rhythm and lyrical in melody. Yet, nearly four decades after his death at the age of 56, Moeran is still one of the least known and understood British composers of the first half of the 20th century.

He was highly regarded by those best placed to know – his fellow musicians. As early as June 1924, Philip Heseltine wrote:[1]

> there is no British composer from whom we may more confidently expect work of sound and enduring quality in the next ten years than from Jack Moeran; there is certainly no one of his years who has yet achieved so much.

A few years later, in 1935, Vaughan Williams could write to Moeran: 'Many thanks for the copy of the Nocturne – I thought it beautiful'.[2] A few weeks later, Sir Hamilton Harty (enquiring anxiously about the Symphony for which he had been hoping over the past ten years) wrote: 'All your friends, like myself, are steadfast in this trust of your gifts'.[3] And Arthur Bliss could even sign himself, in a letter: 'My affectionate congratulations from your inferior colleague'.[4]

Here, clearly, was an admired figure from whom much was expected. Many of these expectations were fulfilled with the first performance, under Leslie Heward in 1938, of the Symphony in G minor. With this work, Moeran emerged in full maturity as a composer able to work on a large scale, and

[1] 'Introductions – XVIII: E.J. Moeran', *Music Bulletin*, June 1924, pp.170–174.
[2] In a letter dated 8 February 1935.
[3] In a letter dated 29 March 1935.
[4] Undated; addressed from the Savile Club.

11

thereafter much of his work was in the larger forms. His progress was matched by growing public interest, coming to a peak, perhaps, during the 1939–45 War (although it must be allowed that most British composers benefited from understandable patriotism during this War). But the cold dawn of the post-War age was a withering time for the pastoral romanticism of Moeran, Bax and their like. New people were sought; Moeran's brief spell in the sun was over almost before it had begun. He had been born out of his time. He was a generation too young for the kind of music he had to offer. Moreover, complete mastery of style and technique came to him late in life – too late, for his personal disintegration accelerated shortly after the completion of the Cello Concerto, *Sinfonietta* and Cello Sonata.

Two criticisms tend to recur in comment on Moeran's work. First, his work is held to be derivative in the sense that influences are not absorbed and are thus readily identifiable. Secondly, his compositional technique and, in particular, his ability to create large-scale structures are held to be faulty. Moeran was a composer who responded to stimuli from other composers and in much of his work such influences *are* readily apparent. I believe, however, that there did emerge an authentic, individual voice, and further, that the works by which Moeran is known, insofar as he is known at all, are not necessarily representative of his finest achievement. He tends to be known by a handful of songs, piano pieces and part-songs, but it can, I think, be shown that he was one of the few British composers of his time able to fill a large canvas, and that, despite his own feeling of technical inadequacy, he eventually acquired a formidable technique, well able to meet the demands of large-scale composition.

While his music appears all too rarely in concert programmes there is a steady trickle of broadcasts, and much of his finest work is at present available on record. It will prove richly rewarding for those prepared to explore.

ACKNOWLEDGEMENTS

I gratefully acknowledge the help given to me in writing this study by the following: Martin Apeldoorn, Miss Gwendolen Beckett, Christopher Bornet, Michael Bowles, Ian Copley, Anthony Crossland, the late Lord Clark, Professor Peter Dickinson, Lewis Foreman, Dr Eric Fenby, Professor Aloys Fleischmann, Professor David Greer, Leon Goossens, Lionel Hill, Michael Holroyd, Denise Hooker, Professor A.J.B. Hutchings, Lyndon Jenkins, Jack Lindsay, Anne Macnaghten, Rhoderick McNeill, Fowke Mangeot, Henry Mills, Roger Nicholls, James Peschek, John Rippin, Colin Scott-Sutherland, the late Freda Swain, the late Mrs R. Sterndale Bennett, Adrian Thomas, Fred Tomlinson, Dr E.H. Williams, and Gonville Williams.

My thanks go also to Walter Knott and Peter Todd not only for their assistance but also for making available to me much correspondence without which the book would simply not have been possible; to Dr Jim Samson for his continual encouragement and practical help; to the staff of the library of Cornwall College of Further and Higher Education (and in particular Mrs G. Robinson) for their zeal in obtaining documents; and to Mrs Margaret Bunt for valuable help and advice in setting out the typescript. The British Institute of Recorded Sound (now the National Sound Archive), The English Folk Dance and Song Society, the Cornwall County Music Library and the Ministry of Defence also gave invaluable assistance. Stalwart help in proof-reading was given by David Brown and Guy Rickards. Nor should I leave unmentioned the help and expertise that Martin Anderson of Toccata Press brought to the style of the text and presentation of the book.

Permission to quote from correspondence is acknowledged with gratitude to: Mrs Ursula Vaughan Williams (Ralph Vaughan Williams to Moeran and to Holst); Professor David Greer (Sir Hamilton Harty to Moeran and Greer to the author); Dr E.H. Williams (to the author); Michael Bowles (to the author); Walter Knott (Moeran's letters to Peers Coetmore, Arnold Dowbiggin, Philip Heseltine, Sir Hamilton Harty, Tilly Fleischmann, Douglas Gibson, Lionel Hill, Harriet Cohen, and the *Musical Times*; also the correspondence between Peers Coetmore and Arnold Dowbiggin and Graham Moeran); Dr Eric Fenby (to the author); Anne Macnaghten (to the author); Chester Music (Douglas Gibson to Moeran); Freda Swain (to the author).

Thanks are due to the following copyright holders for giving permission to quote from their material: to the Headmaster of Uppingham School for passages from *Uppingham School Magazine*; to Penguin Books for permission to reprint extracts from *British Music of Our Time* (ed. A.L. Bacharach); to Duckworth for those from Christopher Palmer's *Delius: Portrait of a Cosmopolitan*; to The English Folk Dance and Song Society for the passages from Moeran's contributions to *The Folksong Journal*; to Professor A.J.B. Hutchings for the extracts from his BBC *Music Magazine* talk; to Novello and Co. for the use of the prefaces to the Moeran orchestral piece *Lonely Waters* and to his Second String Quartet and for the extracts from *The Compositions of E.J. Moeran* by Hubert Foss; to John Murray for Lord Clark's recollections of Philip Heseltine in his autobiography *Another Part of the Wood*; to Jonathan Cape for extracts from Augustus John's *Chiaroscuro*; to Jonathan Cape and the Society of Authors for two lines from *Loveliest of Trees* by A.E. Housman; to the editors of *Music and Letters* for the extracts from Sir Arnold Bax's obituary of Moeran; to Professor Aloys Fleischmann for the passages from his 1951 article *The Music of E.J. Moeran* in the Dublin review *Envoy*; to Stainer and Bell for the use of the preface to Moeran's arrangements of *Songs from County Kerry*; to Bryan Hesford for the extract from 'C.G.-F.' criticism in *Musical Opinion*; to William Heinemann for the short passage from the second volume of Michael Holroyd's *Augustus John*; to Triad Press for the quotation from Stephen Wild's *E.J. Moeran*; to Leonard Duck for the extracts from his *Musical Times* article, 'Inspiration: Fact and Theory'; to Professor David Greer for the quotation from *Hamilton Harty: His Life and Music* (Blackstaff Press).

I also express my gratitude to Walter Knott, Colin Scott-

Sutherland, Peter Todd, John Bishop, the Royal College of Music and Lewis Foreman for supplying most of the photographs used in the book.

I am indebted to the following music publishers for the use of short extracts from the various compositions for which they hold copyright: Exx. 1, 2, 3, 13, 14, 15 and 16 (Piano Trio, *In the Mountain Country, Seven Poems of James Joyce*) are used by permission of Oxford University Press; Ex. 4 (First Rhapsody) is reproduced by permission of Boosey and Hawkes; Exx. 5, 6, 10, 59, 63, 79 and 80 (Sonata in E minor for Violin and Piano, Second Rhapsody, Third Rhapsody and *Fantasy Quartet*) are reproduced by permission of the copyright holders J. and W. Chester/Edition Wilhelm Hansen, London; Exx. 7 and 8 (*Theme and Variations*, for piano) are reproduced by permission of Schott and Co. (copyright 1923). Novello and Co. deserve thanks for permission to reproduce: Exx. 11, 72, 73, 74, 75, 76, 77, 78 (Cello Concerto); 17, 18 and 19 (*Songs of Springtime*); 23 and 24 (*Nocturne*); 25 (Elgar: Symphony No. 2 in E flat); 25, 26, 27(a), 28, 30, 31, 32, 33, 34, 35, 36, 37, 38, 39, 40 and 54 (Symphony in G Minor); 41, 42, 43, 45, 48, 49, 50 and 52 (Violin Concerto); 55, 56, 57, 58, 61 and 62 (*Phyllida and Corydon*); 65, 66, 67, 68, 69 and 70 (*Sinfonietta*); 81, 83, 85, 86, 87, 88, 89, 90, 91, 92, 93 and 94 (Sonata for Cello and Piano); 95 (*Serenade*); 99 and 100 (String Quartet No. 2); 46 (Harty: Violin Concerto). Exx. 42 (Bax: Violin Concerto) and 44 (Bax: Symphony No. 3) are printed by permission of Chappell Music Ltd.; Exx. 60, 61 and 62 (*Overture for a Masque*), 64 (*Six Poems of Seumas O'Sullivan*), 20, 21 and 22 (Trio for Strings), 29 (*Six Folksongs from Norfolk*), and 96 (*Songs from County Kerry*) are the copyright of Stainer and Bell and are reprinted with permission. And, lastly, Exx. 97 and 98 (Symphony No. 2 (unfinished)) are reprinted by permission of Walter Knott.

Every effort has been made to secure necessary permissions, but in a few cases it has proved impossible to trace the copyright holder. I apologise for any apparent negligence.

Above all, every writer knows the family sacrifice made on the altar of a book, and I thank mine, and in particular my wife, for their patience and encouragement.

GEOFFREY SELF

I. EARLY LIFE, THE 1914–18 WAR AND FIRST PUBLICATIONS

Perhaps more than we would wish, our parentage determines what we are. Ernest John Smeed Moeran – known to family and friends as Jack – came of an Irish father and a Norfolk mother. The two strands of his heritage would dictate the course of both his life and his work.

Esther, his mother, had been born in Norfolk in 1866, and would survive as an octogenarian to grieve her son's death. His father, the Rev. J.W.W. Moeran, had been born in Dublin but was taken to England as a baby, never to return to Ireland. His paternal grandfather, the Rev. T.W. Moeran, was an Anglican priest, and for a while vicar of St Matthews, Toxteth Park, Liverpool. His son (Moeran's father) followed him into the priesthood. His student days at Cambridge were followed by curacies in Yorkshire and Upper Norwood in South London. In 1893 he was appointed vicar of Spring Grove, Isleworth, Middlesex, where on 31 December 1894 his son, the future composer, was born. An elder brother, Graham, followed his father and grandfather into the priesthood, but Ernest John, despite a number of respectable contributions to the music of the church, was no believer.

The place of birth – Heston – is of little significance, for the family were to move shortly to Bacton in Norfolk where the Reverend J.W.W. Moeran had been appointed to the living. A very remote region of the Fen Country, isolated, empty and desolate, it is a region of 'Lonely Waters', reeds and scrubland. The place cast its spell on the impressionable boy, who retained all his life a love of the fens, their people and their music.

In 1904, Moeran was sent to Suffield Park Preparatory School in Cromer as a boarder. Here he had lessons in violin – the first steps towards the superb violin writing in the Violin Concerto. The only musical nourishments in the Moeran home had been *Hymns Ancient and Modern* and the *Cathedral Psalter* –

but these had been sufficient for the boy haltingly to teach himself to read music and make a beginning at the piano. At this stage, there seemed to be little evidence of a budding composer; indeed, it was hoped the boy would become an engineer. Certainly, a love of things mechanical – motorcycles and fast cars – was a feature of his later years.

At the age of fourteen, he was sent to Uppingham School. In this he was undoubtedly fortunate, since Uppingham in those days was musically forward-looking. His teacher then was Robert Sterndale Bennett (grandson of Sir William Sterndale Bennett, the composer and friend of Mendelssohn), who commented: 'I doubt if any boy has grasped with more discernment and avidity or made better use of the opportunity which school music has to offer'.[1] He developed into a fine pianist and a useful violinist, taking part in the accompaniment of choral works, and in his last year forming a string quartet. His first efforts at composition date from his time at Uppingham. They included three string quartets and a sonata for cello and piano which took nearly an hour to perform.[2] According to his widow,[3] all were destroyed, for his self-criticism was strict. Professor Aloys Fleischmann suggests[4] that Moeran's interest in folk music went back to his days at Uppingham and that his collecting may have begun there.

He always retained an affection for his old school and had a deep admiration for Sterndale Bennett, who was himself a fine pianist. As late as 1944, Moeran could suggest his old teacher as a solo pianist for a performance of the exacting Third Rhapsody.[5]

In 1913 he enrolled as a student at the Royal College of Music. It was not an auspicious time to be starting a course, but there were to be musical experiences which would profoundly

---

[1] 'Obituary for Ernest John Moeran', *Uppingham School Magazine*, No. 631, March 1951.

[2] *ibid.*

[3] Peers Coetmore, quoted in Stephen Wild, *E.J. Moeran: An Assessment*, unpublished M.A. thesis presented to the University of Western Australia, 1966.

[4] 'The Music of E.J. Moeran', *Envoy*, Vol. 4, No. 16, p.61.

[5] In a letter to Douglas Gibson dated 1 January 1944. Gibson was the proprietor of J. and W. Chester, the publishers of the Third Rhapsody. Hunter Skinner was a boy at Uppingham at that time and remembers playing the orchestral part on a second piano while Sterndale Bennett played the solo part.

affect the course of his work. For the first time he heard the music of Elgar, and at a Balfour Gardiner concert he first met the work of Delius – not a mature, characteristic work, but the somewhat unrepresentative Piano Concerto. Nevertheless, the drug entered his system.

The college course came to an abrupt end. Moeran never returned in the Autumn of 1914, but instead enlisted on 30 September – into the Sixth (cyclist) Battalion of the Norfolk Regiment as a motor-cycle despatch rider. Within two months, he was promoted to Lance Corporal, and in June of the following year he was commissioned as a Second Lieutenant. Posted to the Western Front, he was attached to the West Yorkshire Regiment in 1917.

On 3 May of that year, at Bullecourt in France, he was severely wounded in the head, with shell particles too near the brain to be removed. Two months later, he was promoted to Lieutenant. With the ending of the War, he attended the School of Aeronautics (Royal Air Force) for two months but was finally released from military service in January 1919. After many Medical Boards he was awarded a disability pension assessed (according to Michael Bowles[6]) at 80–90 per cent. These are the bald facts. The physical injury was appalling enough; one cannot begin to imagine the mental scars.

The treatment for his injury involved the fitting of a plate into the skull and it is probable that this injury permanently affected his physical health and may ultimately have contributed to his death. For the rest of his life Moeran appeared to be accident-prone: his correspondence frequently refers to injury of some degree or other from falling over or colliding with things. Furthermore, his drunkenness – whether real or apparent – became a source of some embarrassment to his wife, his friends and his fellow artists. Modern medical authorities would recognise both these behavioural traits as characteristic of head injury, the treatment of which in 1917 was, to say the least, rudimentary. One authority offers the following comment:[7]

---

[6] In a letter to the author dated 26 January 1981.
[7] Dr E.H. Williams, in a letter to the author.

All patients who have had head wounds – especially those who have plates in the skull – are warned of the dangers of drinking alcohol. Even a small amount of alcohol may affect a patient out of all proportion to the amount consumed.

People who have plates in the skull may be subject to severe headaches and irrational behaviour, irritability, violence and lack of co-ordination (giddiness or falling about) which might be mistaken for a drunken state.

A head injury may possibly lead a man to drink (perhaps to deal with pain) who had previously been teetotal or at the least a modest drinker. Before and during the First World War, there were many doctors who did not appreciate (because they had no experience of shrapnel wounds) the far-reaching effects of this type of wound.

After his discharge, Moeran for the first time encountered Ireland and Irish society. Michael Bowles writes:

> While he was convalescent after the hospital, he was seconded for nominal duty to . . . I think . . . the Bedfordshire Regiment stationed at Boyle, Co. Roscommon. Boyle was a garrison town, the barracks being some sort of headquarters or depot . . . . The social and political division in garrison areas like Boyle were not, of course, as bitter as they are now in the North of Ireland, but they were nonetheless clear-cut. Jack with very light duties and, above all, competent skill in music, was very much in demand in Boyle society.[8]

The experience of the War, however, indelibly marked the outlook of artists who took part in it. In the 'twenties the memory of that experience would be reflected in their work. Moeran was no exception, and in addition he felt bitterly the loss of those who fell in the fighting. One telling piece of evidence of Moeran's strength of feeling concerning the waste of artists in wartime surfaced much later in a controversy in the musical press about the absence of Benjamin Britten in America at the outset of the 1939–45 War. Moeran wrote to *The Musical Times*:

> Provided that he keeps valid his artistic integrity, I consider that he is doing his duty by remaining where he is . . . .
> The death of Butterworth in 1915 was a tragedy, the nature of

[8] In a letter to the author dated 26 January 1981.

which no country with any pretensions to the preservation of culture and a respect for art can afford a recurrence.[9]

An interesting example, this, of Moeran's own civilised integrity – he didn't like much of Britten's music.

The earliest manuscripts of Moeran's work are preserved in the archive of the Victorian College of Arts, Melbourne, Australia. They include two pieces for piano (*Dance* and *Fields at Harvest*) dating from 1913, the year of his enrolment at the Royal College of Music, and a set of four songs from *A Shropshire Lad* (Housman) of mid-Summer, 1916. According to Rhoderick McNeill,[10] the Housman songs are 'entirely separate' from the *Ludlow Town* set of 1920, discussed in Chapter II. McNeill points out, however, that the melody of the fourth song of the 1916 set was to appear, with modifications, in the 1925 Housman setting, *Far in a Western Brookland*.

Three Pieces for Piano

One of the most characteristic moods in Moeran's music – a certain introspective, bleak quality – may be traced back to the trauma of those years in the 1914–18 War. But there is no evidence of this in the *Three Pieces for Piano* he wrote in 1919. These pieces – 'The Lake Island', 'Autumn Woods' and 'At the Horse Fair' – were his first publications (Schott, 1921). 'The Lake Island' is a piece of gentle impressionism immaculately laid out for the piano but heavily influenced by John Ireland, although (surprisingly) not specifically by that composer's *Island Spell* published a few years before. The pentatonic (black-note) ostinato saves the piece from the more extravagant Ireland-isms, and also disciplines the structure. It has a rapt serenity and stillness, and it is easy to see why, of all his early piano works, Moeran retained an affection for this one. 'Autumn Woods' is less satisfactory; Bax had written *November Woods* (for orchestra) in 1917 – a masterpiece of evocative and

[9] In a letter, published in the issue of October 1941. The editor, Harvey Grace, had attacked Britten's being domiciled in the USA during the War. Moeran and Gerald Cockshott came to Britten's defence. The mention of Butterworth here is significant, in that some Butterworth influence on Moeran can be detected. The point is discussed in Chapter II in connection with the First Rhapsody for orchestra.
[10] In a letter to the author dated 17 September 1983.

eerie atmosphere. By comparison, Moeran's piece is innocuous, drowned in Ireland harmony and showing little distinction of idea. 'At the Horse Fair' is a scherzo of a type Moeran was to make peculiarly his own. It is perhaps overly pentatonic, but is clean in texture and sparkling in rhythmic verve. From time to time the piano style and layout is Schumann-like – a characteristic to be met with again shortly in the Piano Trio.

The *Three Pieces* are uneven, with 'The Lake Island' showing more potential than its two successors. Even so Moeran would have had every reason for modest satisfaction with his first publications.

II. STUDENT DAYS

After his discharge in 1919 Moeran went back to Uppingham for a short while as assistant music teacher, before resuming his Royal College of Music course in 1920. He remained at the RCM until 1923, studying composition with John Ireland, but the incidence of the War had made him a somewhat mature student – he would be nearly twenty-nine when his student days finally ended. We may piece together a picture of him at this time as a shy but fun-loving young man, falling hopelessly in love from time to time[1] and obsessed with speed and motorcycles. He won the Gold Medal of the Motor Cycling Club in the 1922 London–Land's End speed trials. Of this obsession, Cecil Gray was later to write that Moeran's driving had a 'Nietzschean life-desiring effect on the passenger'.[2] This period nevertheless saw (in 1921) Moeran's first publications (the *Three Pieces for Piano* discussed above) and also a first orchestral performance – of the First Rhapsody at an RCM Patrons' Fund concert. It made some impression, for it was repeated at Bournemouth by Dan Godfrey in 1922, by Henry Wood at a Queen's Hall Promenade Concert and by Hamilton Harty and the Hallé Orchestra. Harty had become a powerful friend and Moeran was properly grateful for his advocacy: 'I am quite sure it will be a long time before I shall hear another performance to equal it', he wrote to Harty, in a letter which conveys something of his admiration for the great Irish conductor.[3] Moeran's first attempts at orchestral composition owed much to Harty's encouragement – a fact the more remarkable when it is remembered that Harty felt little sym-

---

[1] EJM in a letter to Peers Coetmore dated 26 December 1943. He discusses photographs of Peers taken when she was seventeen: 'That must have been in 1921. I was a student then and it was the following winter I met that cold hearted girl I told you about who I fell for in those days, and followed around for some three or four useless years'.

[2] *Musical Chairs*, Home & van Thal, London, 1948, p.61.

[3] Dated 28 January 1924.

pathy for much contemporary music. But Moeran's music had some appeal for him – perhaps even then he felt its latent Celticism.

The period was important, too, for the artists and musicians Moeran met who would influence and play his music and whose friendship would be lasting. John Ireland and Harriet Cohen were two of these. Harriet Cohen was a fine pianist who specialised in contemporary music, and her establishment became a meeting-place for artists. Other friends included Arnold Bax and Philip Heseltine (better known as Peter Warlock), and Bax subsequently remembered 'an evening party somewhere in Kensington or Chelsea' in the summer of 1919 at which he drifted into conversation with 'as charming and as good looking a young officer as one could hope to meet'.[4]

Clearly intending to announce his presence on the London concert scene, Moeran booked the Wigmore Hall in 1923 for a concert of his own music, apart from one work, Ravel's String Quartet in F – an exception which tells us something of Moeran's musical tastes at the time. The performers included Désiré Defauw, the Allied String Quartet and Harriet Cohen. By this time, Moeran had completed a number of major works, as well as many songs and piano pieces. Among the former were the Piano Trio (1920, revised 1925), the 'Symphonic Impression' *In the Mountain Country* (1921), the String Quartet in A minor and the Sonata in E minor for violin and piano. The last two works, together with some piano pieces for Harriet Cohen, were the major Moeran contributions to his Wigmore Hall concert. *The Musical Times* reviewer[5] noted the pentatonic basis of much of the music, commenting: 'The flavour is good, but we cannot entirely overlook the circumstance that with the pentatonic scale it is next to impossible to go wrong'.

The last quarter of the 19th century had seen an increasing domination of British music by the mainstream Austro-German composers. This domination continued into the early 20th century and can be plainly seen in the work of Parry,

[4] 'E.J. Moeran, 1894–1950', *Music and Letters*, Vol. XXXII, No. 2, 1951, pp.125–127.
[5] 'E.E.' (most probably Edwin Evans), *The Musical Times*, February 1923.

Moeran around 1922.

Stanford, Elgar and Delius. As Donald Tovey has shown,[6] the noble paragraphs of Parry derive from Schumann, while the pedigree of Elgar, too, will be found to embrace both Schumann and Brahms, although he strove also for the virtuosity of Wagnerian and Straussian instrumental polyphony. Stanford's debt to Brahms, despite nods in the direction of Irish folklore and melody, is obvious for all to hear, while the Sali and Vrenchen of Delius's *A Village Romeo and Juliet* are recognisably modelled on Tristan and Isolde, although on a less heroic scale. Even a figure as original as Holst had to struggle to expunge the influence of Wagner, as can be heard in works like *The Mystic Trumpeter*, or the opera *Sita*, which Holst himself described as 'good old Wagnerian bawling'.

Before the First World War the growing tension between Britain and Germany was inevitably reflected in the arts. The patriotisms it engendered were potentially disastrous for Delius whose early success was almost entirely in Germany; Parry and Stanford disappeared without trace after the War, and even Elgar suffered eclipse for a decade or so, despite (or perhaps because of) the stream of war-inspired music – *Polonia, Le Drapeau Belge* and *The Spirit of England*, for example – he had poured out during the conflict. To many, the opulence and lushness of Elgar and Delius seemed irrelevant in the cold post-War dawn.

The generation of British composers coming to maturity during and after the War sought a new basis for their art. To follow Vaughan Williams into folk music provided one such basis while another was sought in the emerging composers of France. Today Debussy may be seen to have been the revolutionary against the basic concepts of Teutonic music but the stronger influence on British composers at the time, with the exception of such a figure as Cyril Scott, was that of Maurice Ravel. Ravel's music made slow but inevitable progress here from about 1904, the year in which his String Quartet appeared. Vaughan Williams contracted his 'French Fever' about that time and he, of course, took lessons from Ravel in 1908. Ravel's influence is apparent in much of his earlier music, particularly in the *London* Symphony (1911–14) and in songs

[6] *Essays in Musical Analysis*, Vol. II, *Symphonies 2*, O.U.P., London, 1935, p.53.

like the *Songs of Travel* (1904) or *On Wenlock Edge* (1908–09). At the invitation of Sir Henry Wood, Ravel visited England in 1913 to conduct at the Proms.[7] By that time such works as the *Introduction and Allegro* for flute, clarinet, harp and string quartet, the *Rapsodie Espagnole*, and the *Pavane pour une Infante Défunte* were known in Britain, as was much of the early piano music. In 1917, the London String Quartet (its first violin was Albert ~~Ravel~~ Sammons) recorded three movements of the Quartet.[8] While Ravel's music may not have registered with the general public at that time, it was becoming increasingly familiar to musicians. The music of John Ireland shows much of Ravel's influence, and from 1921 or so onwards, so does that of his pupil, Moeran.

As Moeran's teacher at the RCM, Ireland seems to have been the catalyst not only of the Ravel influence but of that of Brahms as well. Ireland had been a pupil of Stanford, and the Schumann-Brahms tradition was fostered at the RCM by Stanford during his time as Professor of Composition there. Ralph Hill was later to write about the influence of Brahms on Ireland: 'So strong was the influence of that great German master upon Ireland's early compositions that he destroyed or withheld practically all the works he had written up to the year 1906'.[9]

Piano Trio

The first major work completed by Moeran as an Ireland student was the Piano Trio. Dedicated to André Mangeot, it was published in 1925 by Oxford University Press. It had been written in 1920 and received a performance by the Harmonic Trio at their Wigmore Hall recital in November 1921. By the time it was again performed there on 13 June 1925 (the concert was one of three organised by Moeran himself to promote his own music and that of his friends – among them Warlock, van

[7] Henry J. Wood, *My Life of Music*, Gollancz, London, 1938, pp.97–98. Ravel conducted the Suite *Ma Mère L'Oye*.

[8] Roger Nichols in a letter to the author. The record was Columbia (GB) L1038 and L1163, and the scherzo was omitted.

[9] Ralph Hill, 'John Ireland' in A.L. Bacharach (ed.), *British Music of our Time*, Pelican, London, 1951, pp.175–184.

Dieren, Arthur Benjamin, Arnold Bax and John Ireland), it had (according to Stephen Wild)[10] been largely re-written. *The Musical Times* critic thought it 'was not good Trio writing. Approach to its music was barred by chords that ever grew rankly upon the pianoforte score.'[11]

The Piano Trio is a work of imposing proportions and real energy. Certainly it may be criticised for the derivative nature of its styles, but it has such exuberance and uninhibited lyricism that it is easy to see why, at the time of its appearance, Moeran did seem to informed critics to be one of the most promising new talents, despite the reservations of *The Musical Times*. Furthermore, it is in the sturdy, muscular frame of the Trio that we are most aware of an emerging 'big' composer – a composer able to fill a large canvas – and it is this that makes the subsequent retreat into inconsequential songs in the ensuing years the more striking and disappointing.

Derivativeness is one of the major artistic heresies of the 20th century, liable to attract far more blame than would have been the case in earlier times – and Moeran had a sponge-like capacity to absorb the essentials of musical styles he admired, although the processing of these styles, to re-emerge in his own work, may well have been unconscious in his early years. The predominant stylistic influence in the Trio is, as we might expect, that of John Ireland, but in addition, there can be traced in it those composers – Brahms and Ravel – on whom Ireland founded his own style.

The aspects of Brahms bequeathed to Moeran by Ireland were mainly concerned with piano style and overall structural conception. Ex. 1 shows a sample of a piano style strongly reminiscent of Brahms in the wide spread of the chords and the general massiveness of the writing – not that it ever sounds like Brahms, for the harmonic style is not Brahmsian. Certain aspects of the piano style reach back even further than Brahms to that master's own mentor, Schumann, for whose music Moeran, on more than one occasion, expressed distaste.

Structurally, each movement appears seamless and the ideas melt into one another. Thus the principal sections of each

[10] *op. cit.*

[11] *The Musical Times*, July 1925.

Ex. 1

movement are unheralded and the possibilities of the themes unfold inevitably, as Holst once said of the music of Haydn.[12] Examined in detail, most of the principal ideas of each movement are seen to be linked by the use of a ʃparent cellʅ (Ex. 2).

Ex. 2

(a) Parent cell

(b) First movement

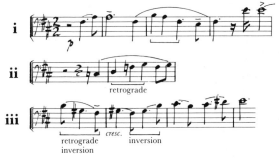

Thus a fundamental Moeran technique makes its first appearance, and in this study increasing recourse to the term will be necessary. It is a technique used by both Schumann and Brahms, and with the latter, for example, can be seen at its most impressive in the Second Symphony or the Clarinet Quintet.

Although John Ireland was primarily responsible for the Schumann-Brahms influence, Moeran had been in his youth an avid performer of chamber music, and it is likely therefore that he

---

[12] Imogen Holst, *Gustav Holst: A Biography*, O.U.P., London, 1969, p.97.

would have known their chamber music 'from the inside'. There is also musical evidence of at least a passing acquaintance with one other composer of chamber music – Fauré. Moeran's Trio has the dotted rhythms, the undulating melody and the tonal ambiguity characteristic of that composer.

Fauré

Fauré is indeed an unexpected influence, for although Moeran, along with Vaughan Williams and Ireland, came under the French spell, the principal spellbinder for all three composers was Maurice Ravel. In the Trio this influence can be heard principally in the harmony. Thus there are Brahmsian piano textures allied to seventh, ninth and other diatonic discords characteristic of the work of Ravel. The French master would on occasion use orientalisms and the pentatonic scale, and the third movement of Moeran's Trio, with its harmony in fourths, has absorbed some of these elements. A few months later, this general Ravel influence was to reflect, in Moeran's First String Quartet, a specific admiration for one Ravel work in particular.

Moeran's harmony in the Trio, however, is not solely the product of his infatuation with the music of Ravel. The influence of early Vaughan Williams is also present (which, admittedly, itself resulted from Vaughan Williams' own apprenticeship with Ravel), and above all there is the harmonic influence of John Ireland, revealed in the ubiquitous use of the added-sixth chord and in the increasing use of note-cluster chords.

Delius

Moeran's love of Delius is detectable in the Trio, but there is as yet little of that overall Delian harmonic saturation which was to become so marked a few years later, when it would be refined and channelled through the work of Peter Warlock. Rather is it at this stage a love for one specific Delius work, the 'English Rhapsody' *Brigg Fair* – a love betrayed by certain melodic characteristics in the slow movement. Additionally, more than one harmonic sequence suggests that Moeran may also have known that version of the Lincolnshire tune arranged for chorus and soloist by Percy Grainger.

Without doubt, the Trio is a compendium of influences which at that stage of his development Moeran made little attempt to assimilate or disguise. The work has been ignominiously forgotten – even the publisher retains no copy. Yet it has one priceless quality – a lyrical exuberance, a sheer outpouring of music on a protean scale reminiscent of Schumann in his prime, and for this reason, if for no other, it would merit occasional revival.

Hubert Foss mentions[13] a second piano trio, but all efforts to trace the work (if, indeed, it ever existed – no reference to it has been found in any other authority) have proved fruitless. It is possible that Foss took the view that the rewriting of the Trio discussed above was so extensive as to constitute a new work.

String Quartet No. 1

The String Quartet No. 1 dates from 1921, and was published by Chester in 1923. Moeran was active in collecting folksongs in Norfolk at the time and the melodic ideas of the Quartet do owe something to Norfolk song. While the harmonic style also derives partly from that suggested naturally by these folk-style melodies, it is influenced mainly by that of Ravel. At this stage of Moeran's studentship some considerable influence of John Ireland on the harmony might have been expected, but it is not marked. The reason may be that quartet composition is a strong discipline and there is not the scope for added-note chords and tone-cluster effects which came so easily when Ireland, or indeed his pupil, was writing for the piano.

The one work in particular which must be singled out as having more striking an influence on Moeran's Quartet than any other was the Ravel String Quartet in F. It would have pointed an alternative path to the dominant school (as far as the Royal College of Music was concerned) of Brahms, and significantly, but surprisingly, Moeran included the work in the concert he organised at the Wigmore Hall in 1923, where it was the only non-Moeran work in the programme – surprisingly, because the textural similarities with the Ravel Quartet are in places really quite striking and it seems naive of Moeran to have pointed the similarities by including both works in the same programme. The most notable parallels occur in the respective third movements which share the same key (A minor), cross-rhythms ($\frac{6}{8}$ alternating with $\frac{3}{4}$), *pizzicato* manner

[13] *Compositions of E.J. Moeran*, Novello, 1948.

and harmonic characteristics. The final movements also bear comparison, for the language of each includes a punched chord sequence set against busy passage work.

Despite such indebtedness, the Quartet marked a stage in Moeran's advance to technical mastery. It may not have the sheer lyrical flood of the Piano Trio, but there is, in compensation, an expertise in post-Ravel string-quartet textures – string writing of a skill to be found only in a composer who had played regularly in chamber music ensembles – and the growth we would expect in mastery of large-scale forms.

In the Mountain Country

So far as is known, Moeran's first orchestral work was the tone poem *In the Mountain Country*, dating from 1921. This first attempt at an orchestral piece is dedicated to the conductor Sir Hamilton Harty, and it marks the beginning of an association with the great Irish musician which would ultimately lead to the Symphony in G minor. *In the Mountain Country* reflects that nature-worship characteristic of other music of the period; Vaughan Williams' *Pastoral* Symphony is a near contemporary, and perhaps there is even in the title an unconscious echo of Vaughan Williams' *In the Fen Country* (1904). One melodic shape in the work is telling because it reveals again a composer vaguely present in Moeran's thought – and more especially as he contemplates a mountain piece: the rampant, leaping phrase (Ex. 3) that appears at letter E in the trumpet is familiar

Ex. 3

from the music of Delius. Delius had completed his *Song of the High Hills* in 1911, but it did not receive its first performance until 1920, one year before Moeran completed his work. The two English 'Naturalists', Vaughan Williams and Delius, may well have provided the inspirational spark for Moeran. But there any relationship ends, especially with the Delius work, for the crippling handicap of the Moeran is the dullness of its principal ideas. Dullness, of course, may well be a feature of landscape – Hardy extolled the 'swarthy monotony' of Egdon Heath, and Vaughan Williams' *Pastoral* Symphony achieves a quasi-philosophical rumination over Hardy-like wastes (the musical equivalent of 'a cow looking over a gate', said the nonetheless respectful Philip Heseltine[14]). But Moeran aspires to mountain music and his earth-bound and wooden little tune does not have within it the potential for ecstasy inherent in the *Song of the High Hills* and thus can never soar to reach that rapt contemplation of nature in solitary splendour which we would reasonably expect from the title. It may be doubted whether Moeran's genius lay in the direction of Romantic Impressionism. Indeed, it is remarkable how little the Impressionist movement in music affected him, when it is considered that so many of his compatriot contemporaries dabbled in it to some extent or other.

Moeran's harmony has been described as 'homespun'. While this seems generally insupportable, it may have some justification in this work. As yet, the harmonic enrichment he would learn from John Ireland is not apparent; some use of diatonic discord in the manner of early Ravel is there, but the principal harmonic influence seems to be that of Vaughan Williams – the Vaughan Williams, that is, of the *Tallis Fantasia* and, perhaps, the *London* Symphony. Texturally, the middle section claims attention as by far the most original part of the work. So far as I am aware, there is no model in earlier English music for its scurrying woodwind triplets, unless it be the scherzo of the *London* Symphony. It is possible that the idea came from Ravel and in particular from the first movement of *Le Tombeau de Couperin*.

It is in the orchestration that the work is most striking. Viewed as a student work, its orchestral assurance is astonishing, showing itself in an adventurousness, a willingness to use open, spare textures, with little 'fail-safe' doubling. In Elgar or Vaughan Williams, in compliance with European tradition, the strings are the basis of the orchestral sound. Here in this student work, this is by no means the case, for already the winds have a Sibelian independence which colours the whole sound. (There is an intriguing postscript to these com-

[14] Quoted in Cecil Gray, *Peter Warlock*, Jonathan Cape, London, 1934, pp. 78–79.

John Ireland, Moeran's teacher from 1919 to 1922, in a photograph from around 1920 by Herbert Lambert.

ments on *In the Mountain Country*. When everyone else, probably including the composer, had forgotten this early work, an unlikely performance took place: in early 1949 Stokowski conducted the New York Philharmonic Orchestra in it.)

First Rhapsody

The First Rhapsody for orchestra also dates from the composer's student days. It is dedicated to John Ireland and was written in 1922. This very accomplished work is a considerable advance on *In the Mountain Country* and, indeed, seems more coherent than the Second Rhapsody which followed it. Butterworth's Rhapsody *A Shropshire Lad* and the Delius *First Dance Rhapsody* would have prompted possible lines of approach; but the spell of *Brigg Fair* was still potent and it was this work which must have suggested the broad plan of introduction, theme and variations.

While at this stage Moeran still avoided the most obvious characteristic of Delius – the harmonic chromaticism – he had absorbed a much less obvious feature. Delius, although much influenced by German music, soon rejected German methods of construction which would have resulted in symphonies or symphonic poems. Instinctively he turned instead to the varia- *Delius* tion principle, characteristic of an English tradition reaching back to the 16th century. Lyrical inspiration may well find more apt expression in variation rather than symphonic technique. This proved true for Delius and, at this stage in his development, for Moeran too. He did acquire a fine symphonic technique in due course, but it was, nevertheless, founded on variation technique.

Certain quite specific points of Delian influence can be identified. A minor example is the manner in which the brooding mood of the introduction is shattered by a sudden loud chord at much the same point as Delius does the same thing in his *First Dance Rhapsody*. A major example can be seen in the central interlude of Moeran's Rhapsody (Ex. 4), clearly

Ex. 4

indebted to the corresponding langorous interlude in *Brigg Fair*. Further, there is in the Moeran a flute figure which acts as a kind of ritornello, with the function of separating and defining sections. Similarly, a flute figure is heard at the outset of *Brigg Fair*, and this, too, makes occasional later appearances. The Butterworth influence is apparent in the work's opening. The music starts in dreamy fashion with clarinet phrases supported by tonic minor/subdominant major harmonies in the *tremolando* lower strings. Both the basic concept and the harmony are reminiscent of the opening of Butterworth's *A Shropshire Lad* Rhapsody. These clarinet phrases have the whole tone/third structure of much Norfolk song, and, indeed, of much early Moeran. It is these intervals which form the parent cell, which is at the root of every idea in the Rhapsody – another early example of what became his normal method of invention.

The Musical Times reviewer, after calling it 'an attractive-looking work',[15] stated that it was based on folk tunes. He might have been forgiven for thinking so, but no folk tunes have been identified in the piece. The reviewer was kind, and ignored the very obvious stylistic sources. But despite such derivations, the First Rhapsody is a worthwhile work and, like *In The Mountain Country*, is notable for its clean, transparent orchestration. The climaxes have considerable power; for English music of its genre they are, perhaps, overheated and tend to be climaxes of volume only, for that climax created from the logical interplay of opposing parts would not be within Moeran's grasp until he came to the first movement of the Symphony in G minor.

Violin Sonata in E minor

It is in the Sonata in E minor for violin and piano (1923) that Moeran's debt to John Ireland is most apparent. But the work far exceeds in power, energy and scope anything similar by the older composer. There is here a thrusting passion, expressed in music much aware of contemporary trends. It is a work that points in the direction Moeran would, in all probability, have gone – the direction of music of some scale – if he had not, in the next few years, come under the influence of Warlock.

[15] *The Musical Times*, August 1925.

3 - note cells

The technique of the parent cell is taken to the farthest limits met with so far; we have to wait until the G minor Symphony before the technique is again so extensively used. As so often with Moeran, the cell itself consists of three notes only; here the descending pattern of tone plus a third, heard at the beginning of the first movement as A – G – E. All the primary and secondary material throughout the three movements of the Sonata enshrine this cell. Thus is structural unity promoted.

Sonata form

The early Piano Trio had used a four-movement form; the String Quartet had three, and this Sonata follows its example. The first movement is in sonata form, but this is not a form that Moeran follows without question. Rather, his approach appears to feel instinctively where structural weakness might occur. The principal idea, for instance, does not appear at the start of the recapitulation as the stereotype would require, but is reserved to form the climax after all other material has been repeated. A refusal ever to take a formal type for granted, and a capacity to modify according to the dictates of the material have already, at this early stage, become features of Moeran's work.

form X

The slow movement (a very slow *Lento*) has an overall A–B–A–B shape and seems, despite its considerable climaxes, to include the styles both of lullaby and of threnody.

The third movement is a complex and energetic rondo, based on one of Moeran's most powerful ideas (Ex. 5). He regarded

Ex. 5

Rondo

the rondo not so much as a set form but rather as a style, based on contrast. Thus each rondo that he wrote is to some extent formally different from its fellows. One recurring feature makes a first appearance in this last movement; this is a kind of processional, at once despairing and relentless. We shall meet its imagery again in the Symphony in G minor and in the Cello Sonata, and may well speculate on the origins of such passages;

style

possibly the source is Stravinsky's *The Rite of Spring*. The ballet had been produced in London in 1913, and the work was beginning to receive concert performances in the capital after the 1914–18 War. The section of the work which may have suggested all three passages is the 'Ritual of the Ancients'. There are certainly striking similarities to it of style, mood and idea in the last movement of the Sonata.

Not only are the movements bound by their common parent cell; further unifying strength is provided by a harmonic concept common to all movements. Appearing first in the development of the first movement, it is hinted at in the second movement, used extensively in the third and provides in due course the triumphant peroration of the work (Ex. 6).

Ex. 6

Many of the harmonies have a harshness and bite met with hardly anywhere else in Moeran – possibly not until the late Cello Sonata, and then only in a few passages. It was all too much for the *Musical Times* reviewer: 'must we really have ninths and ninths all the way . . . ?'[16] Certainly, the piano figurations which accompany the principal idea of the third movement suggest more than a passing knowledge of the piano music of Bartók. More remarkable, perhaps, is what is missing from this music. There is here no trace of that pastoral dream, that vision of nature, which forms the inspiration of so much of Moeran's work. The environment in which he worked was all-important to him, and, conceivably, the enforced stay in London for study left its mark. (Oddly enough, one theme from the first movement does sound not too far removed from a well-known London street cry, 'Won't you buy my sweet

[16] 'B.V.' *The Musical Times*, February 1924.

lavender?', which Vaughan Williams used in *A London Symphony*.)

The entire composition is bathed in the light of Ireland's textures and harmonic styles. There are the splashy arpeggii creating washes of harmonic colour, and Ireland's love of progressions of unrelated chords. No purpose is really served by pursuing further a detailed examination of the Ireland influence, since it is so pervasive as to constitute a language thoroughly mastered within which Moeran worked freely to produce his first real masterpiece.

One other influence makes an appearance here – fleeting, but identifiable. Moeran had met Arnold Bax in 1919 and their friendship lasted until Moeran's death. By the time of their meeting Bax had written such tone poems as *The Garden of Fand* (1916) and *November Woods* (1917). A prevalent mood in Bax is one of intense brooding – heavy and oppressive. It is a particular feature of his Second Piano Sonata, on which he would have been engaged at the beginning of the decade, and the opening of the slow movement of Moeran's Violin Sonata has something of this characteristic Bax mood.

Despite the stylistic derivations, the abiding impression made by the E minor Sonata is not that this or that passage could have been written by this or that composer. Rather the impression is of bigness, of a big work built from ideas of distinction, energy and passion.

In addition to these large-scale works Moeran wrote a number of piano works in this period which, despite his later expressed contempt for them, are of more than passing interest.

Theme and Variations

Most important of these is the *Theme and Variations*, written in 1920. This, the most extended of all Moeran's piano works, consists of a theme, six variations and a finale and is fairly demanding in piano technique. A set of variations will be as good or as bad as the theme allows it to be. Moeran's theme could pass muster as one of the Norfolk tunes he was shortly to collect and arrange but, apart from hints of Ireland's *Holy Boy*, it is original (Ex. 7). Unfortunately, while of haunting beauty,

Ex. 7

it does not offer too many opportunities for variation, and they
tend to be uneven in quality. The third variation (*alla marcia*) is
uncouth in texture, and the $\frac{7}{8}$ Finale is not entirely successful.
But it is the subtle fifth variation that sparks interest. Here in
the contrast between the violent declamatory octaves and the
pp una corda withdrawn chordal passages is a fleeting glimpse of
Moeran's deeper self, and indeed of his latent power (Ex. 8).

Ex. 8

On a May Morning

On a May Morning is typical of any number of similar pieces and
well within the capacity of amateur rather than professional
pianists. It is more saturated in Ireland than almost any other
Moeran piece – typical are the modulation to the submediant in
the eight bar, and the sequences of added-sixth inversions. Yet
there is also another hint of Moeran's latent structural ingen-
uity in the manner in which his languid opening quite naturally
becomes a gentle $\frac{6}{8}$ dance.

Toccata

Also dating from 1921 are the Toccata and the impressionistic
Stalham River. The Toccata is pianists' music (as opposed to

piano music), brilliant in its effectiveness. The structure is very simple – a ternary shape with a characteristic song-like centre, marred perhaps by the too-easy recourse to semitonal sliding in the harmonies. It served for a while as a test piece for College diploma students, and this is the measure of its success.

Stalham River

Stalham River is a miniature tone-poem descriptive of that timeless Norfolk landscape Moeran knew so well. The Ireland influence has penetrated deeply and is evident in the harmonic intensity. There is something, too, of Ireland's cosiness – the scene is observed from behind closed windows and that isolated landscape which 'in winter is completely lifeless and in summer sports wild flowers, birds, insects and reeds'[17] is hardly suggested. For that, we would have to wait a little while for *Lonely Waters*.

Fancies

In the following year, Moeran wrote the three piano pieces published under the title *Fancies*. These bear the titles of 'Windmills', 'Elegy' and 'Burlesque'. 'Windmills' is a *moto perpetuo* owing something to the first movement of Ravel's *Tombeau de Couperin*. As in 'The Lake Island', Moeran uses ostinato; this device, and the fact that the concluding 'Burlesque' taps the same stream as had provided 'At a Horse Fair' over two years before, makes for some similarities of approach between the two sets of pieces. 'Burlesque' has a contrasting idea of a style already familiar in Ireland, but to be borrowed back again by him a few years later in the E flat Piano Concerto.

These movements are pianistic and attractive, but it is the middle movement – an 'Elegy' – which probes altogether deeper levels of experience. For anyone with ears to hear back in 1922, this movement, amid all the pastoral dreaming and insouciant note-spinning of so much of Moeran's music at the time, should have been a warning and a pointer of paths he might follow, and of the hidden preoccupations never far below the surface, which were to reappear with increasing frequency.

[17] Christopher Palmer, *Delius: Portrait of a Cosmopolitan*, Duckworth, London, 1976, p.167.

Ludlow Town

The songs of the period are not as compulsive as the large-scale work. Typical is *Spring Goeth all in White* of 1920 (Robert Bridges), a flaccid work lacking personality. Much more promise is heard in the four Housman settings, collectively named *Ludlow Town*. The *Shropshire Lad* poems (1896) are studies in concentrated melancholia that had much appeal for the generation of musicians which had fought in and survived the 1914–18 War. Moeran's settings, dating from 1920, match the wan poetry appropriately, yet leave little feeling that it could have been set in no other way. Once more, both harmony and piano style are heavily indebted to John Ireland.

But the last song ('The Lads in their Hundreds') is interesting in that it is a prototype for a number of Moeran jigs. Significantly, the words are about Ludlow Fair. Moeran loved fair-days, which at various stages throughout his life proved a fertile source of inspiration.

Even though these piano pieces and songs, despite their many attractions, are not of the highest quality, to have written the group of major works discussed above at an age of under thirty is no mean achievement. It must have seemed to the composer, as it did seem to some critics, that he was on the threshold of a brilliant career.

1924- 1st sketches for gym

III. FOLK MUSIC AND FIRST SUCCESS

In the early years of the 1920s, Moeran threw himself into the musical cauldron in a way never to recur. He appears, for example, on the list of composer-conductors for the Bournemouth Festival of 1924; he acted as music critic for the *Weekly Westminster Gazette*; most bizarre of all, there was a non-musical role for him in what must have been a hilarious performance of Strauss' *Alpine Symphony*:

> At the back of the stage, Mr Moeran diligently exhibited numbers corresponding to the explanations in the programme, so that no one should mistake the glacier for the Thermos flask . . . . It goes without saying that Mr Moeran's scoring board would not have concerned anyone if Strauss's stuff in itself had started living its own life.[1]

The major composition project of 1924 was nothing less than a symphony. It should have received its first performance in that year by the Hallé Orchestra under Sir Hamilton Harty but was withdrawn. Moeran wrote to Harty:

> The work was practically in a state of completion when I came to the conclusion that I was (and still am) discontented about its structure. I have decided to rewrite a large portion of it.[2]

The relinquishment of a major performance opportunity under a great conductor such as Harty is strong evidence of Moeran's ruthless self-criticism. It would be twelve years before the rewritten Symphony appeared.

When we look at the list of compositions for the years 1923 to 1925, it is not difficult to see that Moeran must have worked at intense pressure at this time. There was an outpouring of songs and piano pieces, and the rewriting of the Piano Trio, all at a time when major work on the Symphony was in progress. One

---

[1] 'C.', *The Musical Times*, December 1923.

[2] Rhoderick McNeill, 'Moeran's Unfinished Symphony', *The Musical Times*, December 1980. He quotes a source in *Musical Opinion*, 1926.

reviewer, discussing a batch of newly published songs, went so far as to pronounce them 'among the best things I have seen since Peter Warlock burst upon us'.[3] The impact of this outpouring prompted Warlock himself to write that there were 'those who consider him one of the most promising personalities in the musical world of today'.[4] The publication in 1926 of the booklet in which Warlock wrote that statement seems to underline that apparent promise.

In a letter to Bernard van Dieren (7 September 1923) Warlock wrote:

> I shall be returning to Essex tomorrow or Saturday for about ten days and am going on a folksong hunt with Moeran and a phonograph in the eastern counties.

As a countryman, Moeran had little difficulty in encouraging those who knew the old songs to perform for him. He was to collect songs in various parts of the country, and to contribute on occasion to *The Journal of the English Folk Dance and Song Society.* As Julian Herbage wrote:

> Essentially, he was a very lonely man, needing friendship and understanding but not knowing how to get either. If you had ever met Jack Moeran in a Norfolk Broads pub taking down folksongs you would have got a clue to all his inhibitions.[5]

Folk music was to play such a dominant role in Moeran's work that it may be helpful briefly to review the early folk-music collecting movement. On the walls of the Vicarage (more correctly, Perpetual Curacy) of Hambridge in the county of Somerset there is a plaque, placed there by the English Folk Dance and Song Society. It commemorates the work of one of the founders of the folksong collection movement in this country, Cecil Sharp (1859–1924). He was staying in Somerset, and while sitting one day in the garden of the Vicarage he heard the vicar's gardener singing. The song he heard was *The Seeds of*

---

[3] 'H.G.', *The Musical Times*, December 1925.

[4] Anonymous (but in fact by Philip Heseltine), *E.J. Moeran: Miniature Essays*, J. & W. Chester, London, 1926. The pseudonym Peter Warlock was adopted by Philip Heseltine for his work as a composer while he used his own name for other activity. I shall use both names here, the choice depending on the context of the reference.

[5] In a letter to Arthur Hutchings – undated, but thought to be 1970.

Love. When pressed, the gardener was forthcoming with other songs, many of them now forming the staple diet of the national song repertoire. Sharp was at that time principal of a conservatory of music in Hampstead; from then onwards, however, he travelled the country noting down songs and cataloguing them. Subsequently he did the same for the Eastern seaboard of the United States of America.

Cecil Sharp was not the first collector of English folksongs; a number of anthologies of national songs had appeared before his time. But he was the first systematic worker in the field, soon to be joined by others – Vaughan Williams, Maud Karpeles and Percy Grainger, to name but a few. And E.J. Moeran.

There never was a nationalist music movement in the United Kingdom comparable, say, to that of Bohemia or Russia, for the insular nature of Britain, which had suffered no real threat of invasion for close on a thousand years would have rendered such a movement unnatural and unnecessary. The jingoism of the turn of the century was quite another thing from the exploration of national consciousness such as we find, for example, in the work of Smetana or the Five. What Sharp, as a middle-class urban dweller, had found were the last traces of a rapidly disappearing rural utterance. The growing industrial society had virtually ensured its disappearance, without creating a corpus of industrial song comparable in quality. Even at the turn of the century, there was no real comparison between the self-conscious, isolated singing of the all-too-rare English farm worker, and the vigorous social music of some continental peasantries – except, perhaps, in Norfolk.

This is how Moeran, writing in 1948, described his fellow countryman:

> The Norfolk man is naturally gregarious. Moreover, he regards his songs as a part of his weekly outing when he gets his pay, just as much as his pipe and his pint of beer. There have been, of course, exceptions, but it is difficult to get the individual singer going. Norfolk men like an audience; also, they still like singing against one another to see who can sing the better song.[6]

[6] 'Some Folk Singing of Today', *Journal of the English Folk Dance and Song Society*, Vol. V, No. 3, 1948, pp.152–154.

According to Aloys Fleischmann,[7] Moeran's interest in folk-song dated from his school days at Uppingham, and his first songs were collected then. Moeran himself dated his first experience of the meaning of folk music to a specific perform-ance of some music by Vaughan Williams:

> It was on a wet evening in the early spring that I attended St Paul's Cathedral to hear a Bach Passion and, finding the building packed out, rather than spend a blank evening and with decidedly lukewarm enthusiasm, I made for the Queen's Hall and paid a somewhat grudging shilling to sit through one of those concerts of modern British music. There was a rhap-sody of Vaughan Williams based on folksongs recently collected in Norfolk by the composer. This, and other works which I heard that night, though not all directly inspired by actual folk music, seemed to me to breathe the very spirit of the English countryside as it then was.[8]

Vaughan Williams had been collecting songs in Norfolk since 1904. It is easy to see that a city-based collector, possibly an upper-middle-class academic or professional, making a foray into the countryside for folksongs would at best meet that clamping-down known by all foreigners on entry to a country pub, and at worst would be treated with ridicule. Julian Herbage came near to understanding why Moeran devoted so much time to collecting; Warlock shows why he was so success-ful at it:

> His familiarity with the neighbourhood gave him facilities which are often denied to the stranger . . . . He collects these songs from no antiquarian, historical or psychological motives, but because he loves them and the people who sing them. It is of no more interest to him whether a tune be referable to this, that or other mode, or whether a variant of its words is to be found on some old broadside, than it is to the singers themselves. For him, as for them, the song itself is the thing – a thing lived, a piece of communal life of the country . . . It is no good appearing suddenly at a cottage door, notebook in hand, as though you might be the bum-bailey or the sanitary inspector . . . nor should you spoil the ground for other collectors by forgetting that old throats grow dry after an hour's singing . . . . Perhaps

[7] 'The Music of E.J. Moeran', *Envoy*, Vol. IV, No. 16, pp.60–66.
[8] Christopher Palmer, *op. cit.*, p.166.

> the finest tribute that could be paid to Moeran's personal
> popularity in the district was the remark of an old man at Sutton
> [in Norfolk] after a sing song to which Moeran had brought a
> visitor from London: 'We were a bit nervous of him: with you,
> it's different, of course – you're one of us but he was a regular
> gentleman, he was'.[9]

Moeran himself thought the village pub was the only place to
collect Norfolk songs:

> For the most part in East Anglia it seems difficult to collect folk
> songs privately in the seclusion of a cottage. I have tried it time
> and again, only to be met with a proposal to meet the following
> Saturday at an inn.[10]

A footnote shows that he found the practice different in Eire:

> I find the people there prefer to come up to the country house
> where I have my pied-à-terre and do it à deux.

A few years before this was written, Moeran had told his future
wife:

> O'Donnell . . . left me in a house, the lady of which turned out to
> be a veritable mine of folk music. I was only there for half an
> hour, but during that time, I was regaled with songs which she
> sang: she also produced a queer kind of keyed concertina on
> which she produced hornpipes and jigs at an amazing standard
> of technique, also a dance measure which she called the slide.[11]

Christopher Palmer has an interesting quotation from Moeran
which gives some of the flavour of his early collecting:

> The following Sunday I was at home at Bacton and, after
> church, I tackled the senior member of the choir on the subject
> of old songs. He immediately mentioned *The Dark Eyed Sailor*,
> but the day being Sunday, I had to curb my impatience to hear a
> real folk song, sung by a traditional singer, until the next day. I
> soon discovered that in Bacton and the immediate district there
> seemed to be very few songs left, and these I succeeded in noting
> down. The war soon came to put a stop to my activities for the

[9] Philip Heseltine, 'Introductions XVIII: E.J. Moeran', *Music Bulletin*, June, 1924,
pp.170–174.
[10] 'Some Folk Singing of Today'.
[11] In a letter to Peers Coetmore dated 25 October 1943.

time being. The only songs I had heard had been sung to me by elderly people who assured me that the old songs were fast dying out and the singers with them. By the time the war was over, I assumed there was no longer anything to be had, and I did not resume my attempts at collecting. However, in the last summer of 1921, I received an urgent message from the folksong enthusiast, Mr Arthur Batchelor, to come over to Sutton, near Stalham. It appeared he had accidentally overheard an old roadman singing softly to himself over his work. This turned out to be none other than the late Bob Miller, known for miles around, I never discovered why, as 'Jolt'. Bob admitted that he knew some 'old uns' but he was at pains to point out that he had not really been singing, but 'just a-tuning over to himself'. I soon fixed an appointment to spend the ensuing evening in his company at a local inn, and he gave me a splendid batch of songs, some of which were hitherto unpublished. Moreover, by his enthusiasm and personality, he opened the way to a series of convivial evenings at which I found that the art of folk-singing, given a little encouragement, had by no means died out.[12]

Moeran's collecting was extensive; as early as 1926, Heseltine claimed it numbered some 150 songs.[13] The Norfolk collection was made in these early years. The tunes and words were published, with annotations, in *The Folk Song Journal*,[14]

[12] Palmer, *op. cit.*, p.166.
[13] In *E.J. Moeran: Miniature Essays*, p.5.
[14] *Folk Song Journal*, No. 26, 1922. The following were selected:

Name	Singer	Place	Collected
The 'Bold Richard'	James Sutton	Winterton	July 1915
The New York Trader	Ted Goffin	Catfield	October 1921
The Captain's Apprentice	a) James Sutton	Winterton	July 1915
	b) Harry Cox	Potter Heigham	October 1921
The 'Royal Charter'	James Sutton	Winterton	July 1915
Polly on the Shore	W. Gales	Sutton	October 1921
In Burnham Town	Harry Cox	Potter Heigham	January 1922
The British Man O'War	Robert Miller	Sutton	October 1921
High Germany	Robert Miller	Sutton	October 1921
The Press Gang	James Sutton	Winterton	July 1915
The Farmer's Son	James Sutton	Winterton	July 1915
If There Be Danger	W. Gales	Sutton	October 1921
The Old Fat Buck	Ted Goffin	Catfield	October 1921
The Bold Poachers	Robert Miller	Sutton	October 1921
The Fowler (The Shooting of his Dear)	W. Gales	Sutton	October 1921
Down by the Riverside	Harry Cox	Potter Heigham	January 1922
Hanged I shall be	'Shepherd' Taylor	Hickling	October 1921
Banks of the Lee	W. Gales	Sutton	October 1921

and then in 1924 he published six of the finest with piano accompaniments. A Suffolk collection appeared in 1932 and then, as his last published work, there came in 1948 a collection of Kerry songs which had been gradually amassed over the period 1934 to 1948. Nor was his interest limited to the songs only. He had a discriminating appreciation of the singers themselves and was, in fact, instrumental in persuading the Gramophone Company to record Harry Cox,[15] one of the finest.

There was, in Moeran's mind, a fusion of song, singer and environment. The music and the folk, and the place in which they both originated, were to him aspects of the same entity, indissolubly linked, and all necessary as life-blood to his inspiration. Thus it was that he could not complete a work unless physically living in the place in which it was conceived. Norfolk people and the Norfolk scene in the early years of the century provided, as they had for Vaughan Williams a few years before him, an entirely sympathetic medium for the nurture of his creative spirit.

That part of Norfolk with which he was most at home was the district around the busy market town of Stalham – a countryside of sedge, reeds, wild flowers and water:

> So I'll go down to some lonely waters
> Go down where no-one they shall me find.
> Where the pretty small birds do change their voices
> And every moment blow blustering wild.[16]

Arthur Hutchings recalled a conversation with Moeran in a broadcast talk on him:

> Just after the first performance of the G minor Symphony, I spoke of Delius as an escapist; and he suddenly snapped: 'Good Lord, you can escape into a crowd of fools, roaring round in cars or going from silly party to silly party'.[17]

More than usually, Moeran had the urge of the creative artist to escape 'where no-one shall me find' for solitary communion with nature. The image of such artists is indelibly etched across

[15] Maud Karpeles, *Introduction to English Folk Song*, O.U.P., London, 1973, p.60.
[16] Norfolk folksong, 'Lonely Waters'.
[17] In a talk on *Music Magazine*, BBC Radio 3, 27 December 1970.

the face of English music of the period. Usually, the artist is
symbolised as one solitary voice (the human) rhapsodising over
the orchestral tapestry (nature). Examples range from Delius
(*Song of the High Hills*), through Vaughan Williams (*Pastoral
Symphony*), to Moeran himself in the orchestral tone poem
Lonely Waters, based on the folksong from which are taken the
words above. Such music as this, the piano piece *Stalham River*
or the slow movement of the G minor Symphony (which,
Moeran tells us, 'was conceived among the sand dunes and
marshes of East Norfolk') convince us that the Norfolk countryside and its people were, at that time, quite fundamental to his
artistic needs.

Folksong Settings

The Sailor and Young Nancy is justly one of Moeran's most
popular arrangements and is a good introduction to his folksong work. His noting down of the tune reveals the care he took
to preserve it exactly as he heard it sung; thus the extra beat –
perhaps the breath – that the singer put into the refrain is
carefully kept in the arrangements. The version for solo voice
and piano is somewhat more highly spiced harmonically than
the SATB version he made later (1948–49) for T.B. Lawrence
and his Fleet Street Choir.

Something similar happens with *The Jolly Carter* (Suffolk),
made into an arrangement for voice and piano in the early
1920s, and then reworked a quarter of a century later into an
SATB version of infinitely more subtlety and effectiveness. The
early versions for voice and piano simply reflected the language
of his concurrent salon and art songs. Two of the latter – *The
Beanflower* (Dorothy Sayers) and *Impromptu* (D.A.E. Wallace) –
were published together by Chester in 1924. They have the
subject of flowers in common and are linked musically by a
melodic idea also common to both. Some of the more superficial
aspects of early Ravel are in evidence (the chains of sevenths
and ninths, for example) but they are used with little subtlety.
Some of these elements are refined and absorbed more satisfactorily into the setting of *The Little Milkmaid* (Suffolk; O.U.P.,
1925) to provide a smooth – even bland – accompaniment in a
harmonic language of what used to be called diatonic discord.

This first dip into Suffolk would be a prelude to the set of Suffolk songs written a few years later. Generally in his folksong work, Moeran kept to the eastern seaboard and such an arrangement as the *Dorset Gaol Song* has therefore the interest of rarity. This rollicking version for voice and piano with *ad lib* chorus typifies a kind of song for social singing of which Moeran (and indeed Warlock) left some choice examples.

But it was Norfolk song which at this stage made the most profound impression on him. He told Arnold Dowbiggin[18] that he had an 'enormous collection' of them, and that he intended to arrange more of them than the six that had appeared in print. For these six – the *Six Folksongs from Norfolk* arranged in 1923 and published by Augener the following year – he chose a group from the tunes he had already published in *The Folk Song Journal*.[19] Two of the tunes were in due course to be the basis of orchestral works. 'Lonely Waters' and 'The Shooting of his Dear' are at the root, respectively, of the short orchestral piece *Lonely Waters* and the Symphony in G minor, both of which date in conception from 1924 – a mere year after the arrangement of the songs.

In his accompaniments, the influence of John Ireland is still apparent. It can be seen, for example, in the setting of the last verse of 'The Bold Richard' where Moeran devises a counter-subject in the manner of his mentor. In this song, although the basic harmony is triadic, fourths rather than thirds predominate in the treble harmony and the Ireland influence is pervasive right down to the keyboard layout. Moeran's folksong accompaniments are generally straightforward and unobstrusive, especially where, as in the case of 'Down by the Riverside', the melody is attractive in itself. Folksong arrangers sometimes submerge their tunes with over-elaborate accompaniment – Bax and Grainger, for example. Michael Bowles makes the comparison here of Bax and Moeran very neatly:

> Bax, I think, was too rich; like, I suppose, trying to make a simple summer frock for a girl from a rich brocade instead of a pretty cotton or linen.[20]

[18] In a letter dated 5 February 1931.
[19] *Folk Song Journal*, No. 26, 1922, pp.1–24.
[20] In a letter to the author dated 21 March 1981.

Harmonically, the *Six Norfolk Folksongs* offer portents of things to come. 'The Press Gang', for example, shows a preference for harmony in fourths and fifths which gives the music a characteristic bracing quality, and an occasional harshness of harmonic treatment reveals a facet of Moeran rarely seen in these early years, but to become more marked as time went by.

The chief interest of the set, however, is in those two songs mentioned above which were to generate subsequent works for orchestra. Ex. 9 quotes the superb melody of 'Lonely Waters' in full. While at the start its tonal centre seems to be a modal D minor, there is in its ending a suggestion that it could have been in F major. The effectiveness of Moeran's treatment is enhanced by the fact that it is centred in G minor, creating an almost impressionistic ambiguity of tonal commitment. A minimum of notes is used; like a fine diamond, this melody asks for and receives the lightest of settings.

Ex. 9

*Variant for last verse only

'The Shooting of his Dear' is a cautionary narrative song in the Dorian mode – a mode which invites easily the tonic minor/subdominant major harmony already characteristic in such works as the First String Quartet and the First Rhapsody. The few introductory bars give some very early instances of characteristic Moeran fingerprints; the use of the added-sixth chord, for example, and that tonal ambivalence between major and minor (see Ex. 29 on page 118).

The extent to which Moeran actually used folksongs in his own compositions is arguable. I am, of course, here excluding works like the exquisite piano miniature *The White Mountain* or the *Irish Lament* for cello and piano, since these are really straightforward settings of folksong. Certain authorities deny that Moeran was in the habit of using actual folksong for structural purposes. Michael Bowles says:

> He often told me, he did not generally intend to adapt any specific folk tune to thematic purposes; he had country songs in his ear and drew from this 'fund' in a general way . . . . I can easily agree, however, that he modelled his general style of melody on the general style of folksong.[21]

use of FS

Aloys Fleischmann is particularly penetrating on Moeran's response to folk song; he, too, doubts the use of actual melody:

> The idiom of Irish folksong may often be sensed . . . not through the superficial use of actual tunes, but as a subtle undercurrent, in inflections which suggest the voice of the Irish countryside, the mood of its landscapes, the spirit of its tales and romances[22]

Irish f.s.

Lonely Waters

An attempt will nevertheless be made in Chapter VII to show the origins in one specific folksong of the Symphony in G minor, and there can, of course, be no disputing the folksong origin of the short orchestral piece *Lonely Waters*.

Moeran prefaced his score of this work with the following note:

> This work is based on a fragment of song still frequently to be heard on Saturday nights at certain inns in the Broads district of East Norfolk. Whenever possible, it is preferable to perform the piece in the version with the voice part; but it should be understood that the singer need not be a professional one, in fact anybody with a clear and natural manner of singing may sing the verse. And in any case, the singer must be in an unobtrusive position, sitting at the back of the orchestra or out of sight altogether.

Hubert Foss considered this exquisite little tone-poem (one of *Two Pieces for Small Orchestra*; the other, *Whythorne's Shadow*, is discussed below) to have been written in 1930 and 1931.[23] In an

[21] In a letter to the author dated 26 January 1981.
[22] *loc. cit.*
[23] *op. cit.*

article published in June 1924, however, Philip Heseltine referred to '*Lonely Waters* which he has treated in a more extended manner in a very attractive little piece for small orchestra'.[24]

There is thus a problem of dating. In support of Heseltine, 1924 was the year in which Moeran nearly completed the first version of the Symphony in G minor, which I hope to show later to be based on another of the *Six Folksongs from Norfolk*. It would be neat and fitting if 1924 had seen the conception of two works from the same fertile source. But in support of Foss it must be said that *Lonely Waters* is a work of striking maturity, for its textures show something of the polyphonic resource which Moeran was striving to master during the early 1930s.

Perhaps Heseltine and Foss are both right. It seems likely that Moeran *had* written a first version of *Lonely Waters* in 1924; and just as the Symphony of that year was to be completely rewritten in the next decade, it is probable that the tone-poem also was subjected to a revision in 1930–31. It would naturally have been affected by the stylistic developments of the intervening years.

There is a further problem. As the piece stands in the Novello edition of the full score, alternative endings are given. One version has a solo human voice to sing the folksong while the other substitutes an equivalent passage for the cor anglais. But this passage is not a statement of the folksong, and one wonders why – the song would lie well within both the range and the character of the cor anglais. Moeran's prefatory note quoted above makes clear his preference for the vocal ending. The cor anglais version reflects more than a passing knowledge of Warlock's *The Curlew* which had been written over the period 1920–22 and which has similarities of mood in its desolation and loneliness with the Moeran work.

Lonely Waters is dedicated to Ralph Vaughan Williams and is indeed close in spirit and style to his *Pastoral* Symphony, which had first been performed on 26 January 1922. The Vaughan Williams work also featured an important part for solo human voice. Was one of Moeran's alternatives the original from the 1924 version, the other perhaps being written for the later one

[24] 'Introductions XVIII: E.J. Moeran'.

of 1930–31? If so, we cannot say at present which came first.

A further intriguing point concerns the choice of key for the work. In the song arrangement published in *Six Folksongs from Norfolk*, the music was set in a modal G minor with a key signature of one flat. The tone-poem, however, is set in six sharps, that is, a modal G sharp minor. While Moeran may have thought that the chosen key had a desired quality or individuality, it is difficult to see any practical advantage or necessity for it.

No feature of the song-setting is used in the tone-poem. This is readily understandable: what was needed in the setting was an unobtrusive support for a particularly fine melody. In the tone-poem, on the other hand, the orchestral textures attempt to probe to the core of the words – particularly those of the last verse. The *Lonely Waters* are a refuge 'where no one they shall me find'. These textures rely heavily on chains of second-inversion triads moving in quavers, over which the woodwind sing phrases rather like birdsong in character. The whole style of the opening may be seen as a further response to the VW *Pastoral Symphony,* which opens with similarly undulating chains of triads, although Vaughan Williams gives them to the woodwind where Moeran gives them initially to the strings. Moeran's undulation movement is upward where Vaughan Williams has a downward movement. Most of Moeran's material can be traced to the phrases of the folksong, which makes two complete appearances (three in the version with vocal ending) and one partial one. Thus the work has some of the characteristics of a very free set of variations in which the theme is at times repeated, a method again recalling that of Delius in *Appalachia* or *Brigg Fair*. The placing of the three statements of the song, separating episodes of related material, also gives the work some of the characteristics of a rondo. This was a favourite structural approach of Moeran, who brought to it almost infinite variety and resource. His resource is best heard in the episodes, crafted so skilfully from the folksong; one of the episodes is reminiscent in mood of the secondary idea of the first movement of the Symphony in G minor – underlining the possible linked conception in time of that work and the present one.

A portrait from the later 1920s.

Moeran writes naturally for his small orchestra to take advantage of its chamber-group sound. Thus the woodwind (and particularly the flute and oboe) sustain the principal melodic material and the horn, too, is used melodically rather than in its traditional orchestral role as harmonic 'glue'. Yet the music rises to a considerable climax, with a *fff* dynamic and one single cymbal stroke.

In some ways – structurally, for example – *Lonely Waters* is similar to the early Rhapsodies: it is, however, infinitely superior to them in the skill with which the composer organises the transitions from one section to another. This mark of technical assurance hardens my belief that the published version represents a considerable recasting of whatever original version was known by Heseltine. As we have it, *Lonely Waters* is a near-perfect miniature.

Rhapsody No. 2

The Rhapsody No. 2 for orchestra was originally composed for the Norfolk and Norwich Centenary Festival in 1924. It is a flawed work. Its textures are on occasion crude, its transitions (as I have suggested) are unconvincing, and the attempts made at polyphony betray an uncertain apprentice hand. Yet Moeran, who was obsessively self-critical and who destroyed so much early work, thought sufficiently of it to produce in 1941 a revision for smaller orchestra. Admittedly, in that year he was being courted by the firm of J. & W. Chester for works they might publish, and he took this one away from its original publishers (Hawkes) to give it to them in its revised version.

In spite of its imperfections, it is an attractive enough piece and reveals in embryo a number of features which were to be developed in the mature composer. Indeed, it is one of his earliest attempts at a rondo – a form he was to treat in masterly fashion as a pliable shape to be moulded as the need arose. The work is one of the earliest to show Moeran's inexhaustible resource in melodic variation; melodic fragments are disguised rhythmically to generate what appear to be entirely new ideas. *Sibelius*

Apart from its intrinsic qualities, the Second Rhapsody is important as a work which stands at the crossroads of Moeran's output, for there are features not only of Norfolk melody, but also of those of Ireland. Exx. 10(a) and (b) bear this out: they

Ex. 10

seem to be Irish jigs in embryo. Further, the melodies of the Rhapsody No. 2 show characteristics which will recur again and again. One of these is the alternation of major and minor; and the preoccupation with the third in major and minor forms alternately lights and clouds Moeran's music until in one final masterpiece, the Cello Sonata, the obsession with the third crowds out all other factors. Another melodic characteristic is a cell of three steps followed by a leap. In this work the leap is a third; under press of stronger emotion it may become as wide as a sixth. This feature is more characteristic of Irish than of Norfolk traditional song.

This Rhapsody provides one of the earliest instances of a familiar Moeran phenomenon: a passage of warm lyricism will, with little warning, freeze, die or turn sour. There is also another fingerprint – the sudden erupting sunburst of sound. This is a Delian feature and it may be found in that master from lesser manifestations in, for example, *A Song before Sunrise* to orgiastic outpourings in the *Song of the High Hills*. But this Delian influence is more specifically that of the orchestral rhapsody *Brigg Fair* again. The model is appropriate: it, too, is East Anglian in the sense that a Lincoln tune is used, and its mixture of ternary, variation and rondo shapes has similarities with Moeran's Rhapsody. There the parallel ends – *Brigg Fair* is the work of a master; Moeran's rhapsody shows only the promise of mastery.

His absorption in folksong would lead in due course to the creation of imitation or pastiche folksong. His music furnishes quite a number of these, and it would be a mistake to dismiss them merely for their artificiality, in any case more apparent than real. Some are beautiful, and at least two are moving because of the folk associations they suggest (deliberately, I think) in the works in which they appear. There is one in the last movement of the Cello Concerto (Ex. 11) which has a

Ex. 11

'Scotch snap' phrase ending, and its phrases show the rhythms of both Norfolk and Irish song. This melody is by any standard a fine one. Similar examples can be found in the Air from the *Serenade* and in the second movement of the *Sinfonietta*. The pastiche folksong is clearly an integral part of Moeran's language with a specific emotional function. The example from the Cello Concerto in particular is similar in effect to that of the two interludes interpolated by Elgar into his Symphonic Study, *Falstaff*. A vision of a different world slips gently across our perception; for a moment, the music reaches back, just as it does in the Elgar, to its roots in nature. In Elgar's case it was back to the Severn and Worcestershire – 'something you hear down by the river';[25] and in Moeran, back to the Kerry hills or the Norfolk saltings. For it was there that gave birth to the folksongs themselves and it was there that provided Moeran with his primary source of inspiration. The pastiche folksong is thus a symbol of Moeran's imaginary Garden of Eden, his pure world of nature.

The *Sinfonietta*, according to Dr Dick Jobson,[26] was conceived while Moeran accompanied him on his daily rounds in Herefordshire; the middle movement of the Violin Concerto is

[25] William H. Reed, *Elgar as I Knew Him*, Gollancz, London, 1936, p.141.
[26] In a letter to Martin Apeldoorn dated 31 December 1974.

the music of the Kerry fairs – according to Hubert Foss, 'one important theme is a tune written in imitation of the effect of a tune he heard a young man playing on the melodeon at one of the Irish fairs'.[27] *Lonely Waters* makes the point best: although it is based on the song of that name, it is inspired over and above this not just by the song but by the landscape which nurtured the song.

Folk music permeated every aspect of Moeran's work. Foss believed it liberated his lyrical impulse, and worked through his textures so that the orchestral parts tend to be vocal in nature rather than instrumental. Certainly the influence persisted. Many British composers of the first half of this century dabbled in folk song, but most moved from it as their styles developed. Even Vaughan Williams, the founder of the folk nationalist movement, had eliminated many traces of it by the time of his Sixth and Seventh Symphonies. Moeran stayed with it. One work only eschews folk influence. This is the Cello Sonata – and even here the music is dominated by the interval of the minor third, which might be claimed to be the primeval interval of Norfolk (and Kerry) folk music. The Sonata is a very late work, and it is not possible to say whether or not the changes of style it shows would have been maintained if Moeran had lived to write more.

[27] *op. cit.*

Period of sterility

IV. WARLOCK AND DELIUS

Moeran and Warlock struck up a warm friendship, and in 1925 Moeran went to live with his friend in a house rented at Eynsford in Kent, where he joined a wild and eccentric camaraderie. From what is known of Moeran's need for solitude for his work, this open house could hardly have provided him with any kind of congenial working conditions, for life at Eynsford was, to say the least, anarchic. The permanent residents in the cottage were Warlock, Moeran and Warlock's manservant Hal Collins – himself an artist of no mean talent. This would be augmented from time to time and especially at weekends by a mixed and floating group of artists and musicians – John Goss, Cecil Gray, Bernard van Dieren, Hubert Foss, Constant Lambert and Nina Hamnett, to name some of the more prominent. There was also a tramp, 'Darkie' (so called on account of his complexion). Although Nina Hamnett's autobiographical notes are in some respects unreliable, she gives a vivid account of these weekends.[1] Clearly, heroic quantities of beer were consumed, both in the cottage and across the road in the garden of The Five Bells – although a cocktail of gin and Eno's Fruit Salts was favoured first thing in the morning.

She remembers and remarks on the intellectual brilliance of the company; Gonville Williams, a protégé of John Goss, also mentions this, but remembers that within it Moeran appeared 'raw, musically'.[2] He recalled him as a shadowy figure singing folksongs on the Friday nights. Nina Hamnett mentions him and Warlock playing piano duets – in particular a Victorian curiosity brought down by Lambert called *The Fairy Queen*, performances of which usually ended when one duettist pushed the other off the stool.

Next to the house was a chapel. It was the delight of the company to rival Sunday services in the chapel with its own

[1] *Is She a Lady?*, Allan Wingate, London, 1955.
[2] In conversation with the author, 23 November 1982.

Philip Heseltine/Peter Warlock.

ribald performances, sometimes including stentorian unexpur-
gated sea-songs. The congregation in its charity prayed for its
tormentors. One wonders how the villagers reacted. Certainly
the police were called on occasion.

Gonville Williams observed[3] that the company was on the
whole very 'upper crust' and sophisticated; within it Moeran
appeared gauche, clumsy and awkward of manner. One of the
group – Cecil Gray – eventually showed extreme right-wing
political tendencies, but generally, in what was a period of
intellectual ferment, the political trend was to the left.

For as long as the money held out, life went on in the
Eynsford menage in a carnival of wit, revelry and a haze of
drunken dissolution.[4] There was little effect discernible on the
musical output of Warlock, but that on Moeran is all too clear.
Where in the two or three years before joining Warlock, his

[3] *ibid.*

[4] Fred Tomlinson, Chairman of the Peter Warlock Society and author of *Warlock and
van Dieren* (Thames Publishing, London, 1978), in conversation with the author,
believes this picture to be somewhat exaggerated.

output and publication rate had been copious, in the period 1925 to 1928, his creative stream dried up. Moeran wrote later:

> I lost faith in myself round about 1926 and composed nothing for several years. I even nearly became a garage proprietor in partnership with Cockerill the ex-air ace . . . . I had an awfully lazy period in Eynsford. If you knock off for a long time, it is frightfully hard to get going.[5]

According to Ian Copley,[6] Warlock himself did in the end complain of 'artistic sterility'. From his personal observation of Warlock, Gonville Williams is of the opinion that he could neither escape from the image he had created nor grow further musically in it.[7] In due course, Moeran turned away from the group and in so doing probably saved his musical soul.

The sojourn in Eynsford ended in 1928 as funds gradually ran out. The years he spent there were the nearest Moeran came to a home of his own, and for the rest of his life he lodged either with his parents or with a variety of landladies. The chief musical casualty of Eynsford may well have been the completion of the Symphony promised to Harty, although there could be some truth in Foss' suggestion[8] that Moeran thought himself to be unready for such a major work at that time. But he had already shown his capacity for work on a large scale. My own view is that, thrown into close daily contact with a man of Warlock's intellectual power and brilliance of personality, the quieter, more gentle Moeran lapsed into creative impotence. The marvellous assurance of the early orchestral works and the capacity to think big, so evident in the early chamber music, evaporated. The sheer exuberance and youthful energy of such an outpouring as in the Piano Trio would never really return.

The unfortunate personal legacy of Eynsford was the growth of the chronic alcohol problem which dogged him for the rest of his life.

Warlock influenced Moeran not only directly but also through the love they shared for the music of Delius. Warlock first came under the influence of Delius while only sixteen, as a

[5] In a letter to Peers Coetmore. The date is illegible, but it appears to be in 1948.
[6] *The Music of Peter Warlock*, Dobson, London, 1979, p.17.
[7] In conversation with the author, 23 November 1982.
[8] *op. cit.*, p.6.

schoolboy at Eton. Moeran first experienced it at a Balfour
Gardiner concert in 1913, when he was nineteen. In Warlock's
case, the revelatory work was the partsong *On Craig Dhu*; for
Moeran it was the Piano Concerto.

Delius lived most of his working life in France, but his earliest
successes were in Germany, and he made only sporadic visits to
his home country. But Sir Thomas Beecham found an affinity
with his music, and under his evangelistic influence it made
steady progress here, to culminate in the first large-scale
festival of his work held in London in 1929. Warlock played a
considerable part in organising the festival. By that time, the
illness which was to kill Delius was already well advanced. Yet
somehow, the image of a blind, paralysed composer living a
hermit-like existence in distant parts increased his appeal, and
at a time when that of Elgar was waning. In essence, the secret
of the appeal of Delius was that he was that rare phenomenon in
an Englishman – a sensualist. As such, he was seen as an
antidote to what was felt to be the academicism of the Establishment – Parry, Stanford, and perhaps even Vaughan Williams and Holst. His art derived from three sources: Wagner,
negro spiritual improvisation, and Grieg, and perhaps there
was also, in early days, a little of Richard Strauss – the
symphonic poem *Don Juan* was one of the few scores by composers other than himself that Delius possessed.

Moeran knew the work of Delius intimately. According to
Pat Ryan, the Hallé's principal clarinettist, 'Moeran played
right through the *Mass of Life* after a night of drinking'.[9]
Further testimony to Moeran's love of Delius comes from Eric Fenby:

> I shall never forget his outburst during my playing of the Ravel
> transcription of the Margot piece. 'Marvellous! Marvellous! I'd
> have given anything to have written that passage!'[10]

And in letters to Lionel Hill[11] he instanced (apart from the *Mass*

---

[9] Stephen Wild, *op. cit.*, p.21.
[10] In a letter to the author dated 7 July 1983. Delius, with Fenby's help as
amanuensis, had turned music from his opera *Margot la Rouge* into the *Idyll: Once I passed
through a populous city*. Fenby met Moeran at the Winchelsea house of Robert Nichols,
where he had been sent by Delius in the early 1930s for Nichols to supply new words for
the *Margot* revision. Nichols offered a selection from Walt Whitman.
[11] 'Delius – Moeran – Sammons', *Delius Society Journal*, January 1983, pp.4–11.

Outside the 'Five Bells' at Eynsford. From left to right: Hal Collins, Moeran, Constant Lambert and Peter Warlock.

of Life) the *Songs of Sunset, Sea Drift, A Village Romeo and Juliet, First Dance Rhapsody,* 'Most of' *Brigg Fair, Appalachia* and the *Song of the High Hills* as masterpieces.

The direct influence of Delius on the work of Moeran has nevertheless, as Foss suggests,[12] been overrated. One might have expected to see it in a work he dedicated to Delius (the piano piece *Summer Valley*) – certainly Warlock's own tribute (the *Serenade* dedicated 'To Frederick Delius on his Sixtieth Birthday') is fulsome in its imitative flattery. The influence is indeed present in the work Moeran dedicated to the *memory* of Delius, his *Nocturne*, a setting of words by Nichols for chorus, baritone solo and orchestra. *Summer Valley* bears little trace of Delius and could as easily have come from the pen of John Ireland.

But it would be a mistake to look only at technique for evidence of influence. The Delius influence on Moeran is there, but it is nebulous and difficult to define; it is more a matter of

[12] *op. cit.*

artistic aim. Delius was, despite his Yorkshire hardness, the Romantic Artist *par excellence*. He was an aristocratic figure, proud in his isolation. His art attempts to capture in sound imagery a fleeting moment of emotion, sparked off, perhaps, by contemplation of natural phenomena (sunset, spring, etc.) or human experience (parting, ecstacy of love, etc.). Delius' range is narrow, but it is correspondingly intense, whereas Moeran's attempted range is somewhat wider. Within it, he has undoubtedly assimilated Delian concepts of the nature, power and function of music.

Philip Heseltine was born in 1894, the same year as Moeran. Even as a pupil at Eton, he impressed by his potential ability, and as a personality he must have been unnervingly forceful and brilliant. The late Lord (Kenneth) Clark, who knew him from boyhood, gives us this picture:

> As a boy he had been gentle and withdrawn; I always remember him on our yacht suffering tortures of sea sickness, but soldiering on through a score of Purcell . . . .But when he broke loose on the world he developed a strain of combative amorality which made him legendary in the life of the early twenties. He was the origin of Coleman in Aldous Huxley's *Antic Hay* . . . . From about 1915 onwards, Phil was held up to me as an awful example of what could happen to me if I became an artist . . . . With the last sweepings of the Heseltine fortune, he had purchased a dying periodical called *The Sackbut*, a Magazine for Organists, and transformed it into a stockpot for all the tastiest morsels in war-time Bloomsbury, a sort of house magazine of the Eiffel Tower restaurant. There were stories by Ronald Firbank, erotic drawings by Augustus John, 'very nude' nudes by Gaudier Breszka [*sic*] and pages of musical score by Bartók, van Dieren and Kaikhosru Sorabji. It also contained violent attacks by Phil and Gray on the accepted editing of English madrigals, done by a pillar of the musical establishment called Canon Fellowes with as many concessions to Edwardian taste as Tristram's copies of English mediaeval paintings. I like to imagine the feelings of the old readership of organists, when this spicy dish arrived on their tables . . . . Alas, the outrageous jokes of Aldous Huxley's Coleman evidently concealed a profound melancholy.[13]

[13] *Another Part of the Wood*, Murray, London, 1974, pp. 53–54.

And Aldous Huxley was not the only author to base a character on Heseltine. According to Ian Copley, Heseltine had the probably unique distinction of being introduced as a character into no less than five novels'.[14] His life had two distinct strands, which may have led his first biographer Cecil Gray so far as to see Heseltine/Warlock as a schizophrenic[15] – a diagnosis now much disputed. He was a scholar and under his own name published scholarly editions of sixteenth-century music, including music for the lute, while under the pseudonym Peter Warlock (one of a number) he published some of the finest songs by any English composer, together with some not inconsiderable piano pieces and short orchestral works.

Warlock came early under the Delius influence; in a sense, he was the son Delius never had. For the first years of his career, his worship at the Delian altar was total and unquestioning, and his judgements on Delius had an embarrassing extravagance. The *Mass of Life*, for example, is a masterpiece, but it is not, as Warlock would have it, to be compared only with the Mass in B minor. In his early days, the influence in particular of Delius' harmonic processes is potent. Later the influence moderated as he came under the sway of that multi-talented but austere genius, Bernard van Dieren. The intense chromaticism characteristic of Delius remained, but now it derived from a far more linear technique. This mature Warlock style can be best sampled in such a song as *Sleep* (a John Fletcher setting of 1924).

Dr Copley raises the interesting possibility that some such artistic interaction may have been present in Warlock and Moeran as occurred between Holst and Vaughan Williams.[16] That there was the occasional instance of artistic cooperation is revealed by Gerald Cockshott, who relates how the song *Malt-worms* was composed jointly between them:

[14] I.A. Copley. 'Warlock in Novels', *The Musical Times*, October 1964, pp.739–740. In this article, Dr Copley identifies Warlock as the basis of the following characters:
(a) D.H. Lawrence: Halliday in *Women in Love*
(b) Aldous Huxley: Coleman in *Antic Hay*
(c) Ralph Bates: Robert Durand in *Dead End of Sky*
(d) Robertson Davies: Giles Revelstock in *A Mixture of Frailties*
(e) Osbert Sitwell: Roy Hartle in *Those were the Days*.
[15] *Peter Warlock*, Jonathan Cape, London, 1934.
[16] *The Music of Peter Warlock*, p.45.

Moeran had the poem with him on a midday visit to a pub in Eynsford and had set the chorus when Warlock came in. Warlock suggested a tune for the first two lines of the verse, doing, as Moeran put it, 'the steps up' – a series of ascending thirds of which he was very fond. Moeran then continued with lines three and four . . . . When an accompaniment had been written to the verses, Moeran set to work harmonising the chorus, while Warlock scored the verses in the next room, writing out the parts in pencil. There was no full score. Moeran then re-copied the parts in ink, the composers caught the seven o'clock bus to Shoreham, and the work was rehearsed there and then. Unfortunately, the performance never took place . . . . All the band parts have since been lost; but it is said that 'Malt-worms' is still to be heard in the 'Crown' at Shoreham . . . .[17]

A further possible instance is Warlock's *Yarmouth Fair*, the tune of which was supplied by Moeran who had noted it down from a folk singer in Norfolk.[18] The essence of the Vaughan Williams/Holst interaction, however, was one of mutual critic-ism and there is, as yet, little evidence of this in the case of Moeran and Warlock.

Summer Valley

Warlock was a miniaturist; Moeran has been considered to be a miniaturist but I believe this to be a misjudgement. Yet it is undeniable that, for five years between 1925 and 1930 or thereabouts, his work tended to be mainly in the smaller forms – that is, when he worked at all. This might well be a direct and unfortunate response to Warlock. Typical are the piano pieces *Summer Valley* and *Bank Holiday*. *Summer Valley* is a gentle pastorale in $\frac{6}{8}$ time. This barcarolle rhythm was a favourite of Delius, who used it in his *A Song before Sunrise* and in *On Hearing the First Cuckoo in Spring*. English composers tended to fall back on this rhythm all too easily, and there are many examples in Warlock and Ireland of its use. Ireland's *Holy Boy* uses it and in certain passages *Summer Valley* has echoes of the Ireland piece.

[17] Gerald Cockshott, 'E.J. Moeran's Recollections of Peter Warlock', *The Musical Times*, March 1955, p.128.
[18] The tune was noted down by Moeran from the singing of Mr John Drinkwater at Clay in Norfolk (note in the score, published by O.U.P., 1925).

Warlock and Moeran, with members of the Shoreham (Kent) Dramatic Society, in 1928.

The work as a whole suffers from too little contrast and there is insufficient relief from that prevailing rhythm. Such faults might conceivably have been less apparent had the work been written for small orchestra with its wider range of colour to disguise monotony. It sounds well enough on the piano but is not really piano music. Possibly *A Song before Sunrise* was the model; in small-orchestra garb, *Summer Valley* might have made a fit companion for *Lonely Waters* and *Whythorne's Shadow*.

Bank Holiday

Bank Holiday is a boisterous encore piece. In style it may be compared with the first version of Warlock's *Mr Belloc's Fancy*. As Ian Copley has shown,[19] the wide-spreading left-hand chords are similar in both works, but Warlock simplified the second version of his song. While the style of the Moeran piece may derive from the Warlock, the splashy nature of the piano writing, especially in the closing bars, suggests that the Ireland influence was not yet eradicated.

[19] *The Music of Peter Warlock*, pp.85–86.

The work is cast in a simple ternary form, with a curious central section in which two bars are repeated thematically with varying subsidiary parts no less than twelve times – six at one pitch and six at another. The effect is something similar to a miniature passacaglia, but with the repeated phrase in the treble rather than the bass register. Obsessive episodes such as this occur elsewhere in Moeran – notably in the last movements of the Violin Sonata, the Symphony and the Cello Sonata. Moeran loved festive convivial occasions, and this piece celebrates a holiday effectively enough. The mood would return when the Kerry Puck Fair provided the inspiration for the central movement of the Violin Concerto. That movement is finely wrought, whereas there are in *Bank Holiday* signs of haste and slipshod craftsmanship – the tone-clusters and sliding chromatic chords, for example. We know that Warlock was not above writing potboilers for immediate cash; perhaps Moeran needed to do the same on occasion.

The White Mountain

More successful, because of its utter simplicity, is the piano setting of *The White Mountain*. Here the extremes of chromaticism are avoided, for they would be inappropriate to a simple folksong, which seems well suited to the diatonic sevenths with which Moeran adorns it.

In later years, he was wont to dismiss most of his early piano music as 'tripe'; he even had reservations about the later Rhapsody No. 3 in F sharp for piano and orchestra. Certainly, he was to write no more music for piano solo after the *Prelude and Berceuse* of 1933.

Songs, 1925–28

Sadly, the songs dating from this period (1925–28) are rarely impressive and do seem to bear out the composer's own poor view of his work at this time. The bulk of the original songs of this period mentioned here in fact date from 1925 – before Moeran went to live at Eynsford.

The Merry Month of May (Thomas Dekker) sports its folksong influence in pentatonic melody. Neither this song nor *A Dream of Death* (Yeats) show much individuality, but a hint of the

A lithograph of Delius by Augustus John, with whom Moeran shared a mistress in the 1920s (see p. 231; picture courtesy of the Royal College of Music).

authentic Moeran voice emerges, albeit fleetingly, in *Come Away, Death*. *In Youth is Pleasure* (R. Wever: 'Lusty Juventus') may detain us a little longer. The setting is a choice piece of irony in which the words are matched to a diatonic melody while the accompaniment proceeds in intense Ravelian harmony. These harmonies perhaps accompany an unwritten text concerned not with youth but with the dregs that remain when youth has gone. The agonised chords which adorn the word 'Pleasure' make their point. The song is an early example of Moeran's tonal ambiguity: major is cancelled out closely after by minor, and in the last bars, simultaneous major and minor symbolise effectively the transience of pleasure.

'*Tis Time, I think, by Wenlock Town* and *Far in a Western Brookland* testify to Moeran's continuing interest in Housman. As poetry, *Wenlock Town* has an obvious kinship with Rupert Brooke's *Spring Sorrow* — in form, word and thought. In both poems, the thought is of a spring never to be experienced by the poet. John Ireland set the Brooke in 1918, and Moeran the

Housman in 1925–26, and the two settings show some interesting phrase parallels. In Moeran's song, the influence of Warlock is, as we might expect, beginning to bite, and there is a
Delian harmonic colour to heighten moments of anguish of
what is distinctly Delian poetic thought.

Far in a Western Brookland has not stimulated Moeran to the
same extent; in style it is a throwback, at a time when he was
fast developing, to the Norfolk settings of the previous two
years. *Troll the Bowl* is a big, splashy song, written for John Goss
who seems to have been the unofficial singer to the court of
Warlock and his friends. It is a fine drinking song, and an
unashamed applause-raiser to end a recital.

Despite occasional flashes of interest, this handful of piano
pieces and songs seems a poor harvest for three years in the life
of a young composer who then should have been at the height of
his powers. He would find his path again, but this was not to
happen until he ceased his day-to-day contact with Warlock.

V. STYLISTIC RE-APPRAISAL

Although no longer living with him, Moeran kept up contact with Peter Warlock, lending him his piano in October 1930,[1] and a month later seeking his help and advice on writing for brass bands.[2]

In the early part of 1929, Moeran was one of a party of Warlock's friends who went on an expedition to visit Delius at Grez. Delius, not unreasonably, was annoyed at the unexpected disturbance caused by this unruly group; indeed, according to Eric Fenby,[3] Moeran was mislaid on the way. When he did turn up, the others had left to see Warlock's uncle, who lived nearby. Moeran was unceremoniously dispatched in the same direction. Dr Fenby is doubtful whether Moeran ever did meet the composer he venerated perhaps above any other.[4]

Serious work had begun again from about 1929 onwards, with two important compositions dating from that year. One was the *Seven Poems of James Joyce*. The other, very much in the Warlock/Delius idiom, remains one of the works by which the composer is best known. This is the *Songs of Springtime* written in the vicinity of Acle, Norwich, where Moeran was recovering from illness.

He seems, indeed, to have been ill over a long period of eighteen months from September 1929 right through to the Spring of 1931, and speaks of being 'bedridden at Ipswich with a damaged knee'.[5] There were many letters of concern from his friends – among them Augustus John, Hamilton Harty, James Joyce and Robert Nichols. With the death of Warlock on 17 December 1930, apparently by his own hand, it must have seemed the end of an era for Moeran. His bitterness at what he

---

[1] Warlock, in a letter to Moeran dated 6 October 1930.

[2] Moeran to Warlock; letter dated 23 November 1930.

[3] *Delius as I Knew Him*, G. Belland & Sons, London, 1936, pp. 59 and 63.

[4] Letter to the author dated 7 July 1983.

[5] In a letter to Gerald Cockshott dated 15 September 1941: 'I was too ill to see [Heseltine] except for very short talks.'

saw as a contributory cause of his friend's death – the neglect of Warlock's music – found expression in a letter to Arnold Dowbiggin:

> The lamentable neglect towards Warlock's magnificent output, many of them masterpieces, has embittered me against singers in general. The majority of his songs he never even heard sung. I cannot help feeling that he might have been still with us had he been given some of the recognition he deserved. The musical profession as a whole is to be blamed for allowing a man of his genius to exist very nearly in penury.[6]

There is evidence of much re-appraisal on his part, for he, too, was suffering from a slump in performances (and therefore income) brought about by his prolonged illness:

> Singers have shown complete lack of interest in my work, so much so that I feel myself more and more impelled to write music to play among congenial companions with whom I have musical tastes in common, so I am back again at chamber music and during the past year have occupied my unlimited leisure through being laid up in finishing a Sonata for Two Violins, and a Trio for Strings.[7]

But the re-appraisal was to be more far-reaching than just a change in the *type* of work; style and technique were also being reviewed:

> I have started a String Trio and if I can keep it up I hope the purgative effect of this kind of writing may prove permanently salutary.[8]

So it was to prove.

[6] Dated 18 February 1931. Anne Macnaghten (in a letter to the author, dated 27 June 1983) confirms Warlock's chronic poverty at this time. Moeran had completed his Sonata for Two Violins towards the end of 1930, and Miss Macnaghten and André Mangeot played it over to him. Moeran employed Warlock as copyist to make a further copy of the work
> in his beautiful writing – For this Moeran paid him £2.2.0 and I had to take the cheque round to the basement flat in Tite Street (Chelsea) where Heseltine lived. I saw him in his big, camel-hair coat, walking towards me on his way to the pub; he was very pleased to have the two guineas but when I asked him what he would do with it he only laughed and said 'drink it' and brushed aside my protest. It was very soon after this that he killed himself.

[7] EJM, in a letter to Philip Heseltine dated 23 November 1930, just over three weeks before the latter's death.

[8] *ibid.*

He was endeavouring to make some kind of mark on the wider international scene at this time. There had been some success for him at a Festival of English Music in Homburg in 1930, but he realised that his somewhat insular nationalism would meet the traditional European opposition to music which did not flow in the mainstream.

In 1931, the *Two Pieces for Small Orchestra* (*Lonely Waters* and *Whythorne's Shadow*) received their first performance, given by the London Chamber Orchestra conducted by Anthony Bernard. The scores were given to Hamilton Harty, who never lost faith in Moeran all the years he had to wait for his Symphony:

> I am glad to possess some autograph music of yours, and will place the score with the few pieces which I keep in a special place, and regard as particularly my own.[9]

Throughout this period Moeran appears as a shadowy figure, leading a nomadic existence, and his movements are difficult, if not impossible, to trace. There are glimpses of him sunbathing with the young Benjamin Britten on the beach at Lowestoft in the summer of 1934,[10] and turning up in France at Martigues to stay with Augustus John:

> He came to collect folk songs but, as far as I could see, only succeeded in getting hold of a defective piano on which to record them.[11]

Perhaps he collected at least one folksong – an *Alsatian Carol* was arranged in 1932.

The rate of publication increased somewhat over the period 1928 to 1935. The year 1931 saw Moeran's attempts at religious music, which he must have seen as a lucrative market – and he was short of funds at the time. Although there is evidence that he had little or no religious belief, he published in this year a *Magnificat and Nunc Dimittis* ('into which I cannot resist inserting some luscious Stainerisms') a *Te Deum* and *Jubilate* ('fairly easy'[12]) and an anthem *Praise the Lord O Jerusalem*. Despite Moeran's poor opinion of his church music, the service settings

---

[9] In a letter dated 19 April 1935.
[10] Michael Kennedy, *Britten*, J.M. Dent, London, 1981, p.13.
[11] Augustus John, *Chiaroscuro*, Vol. I, Jonathan Cape, London, 1952, pp.114–115.
[12] EJM, in a letter to Peter Warlock dated 5 November 1930.

have an honoured place and are widely loved — and as
Meredith Davies recalls,[13] he liked to hear his canticles, and
would go into Hereford Cathedral whenever they were down
for performance. Other works published in the period include
the String Trio (Augener, 1936), *Songs of Springtime* (Novello,
1933), the *Two Pieces for Small Orchestra* (Novello, 1935), and the
Nocturne for baritone, chorus and orchestra (Novello, 1935),
written to the memory of Delius, who had died the previous
year. Moeran's interest in solo song continued throughout the
1930s, but he wrote no more music for piano solo after the
Prelude and Berceuse written in 1933 and published in 1935.

It is difficult to escape the conclusion that Moeran's fallow
period had coincided pretty well with the time he spent at
Eynsford and with his close association with Peter Warlock, for
only with his friend's death was his own creativity released
again. Yet it is at this point that Warlock's influence becomes
most marked. (Lest this seems an indefensible paradox, one has
only to think of a parallel in poetry: that of the poet/novelist
Thomas Hardy, whose first wife – an inhibiting factor while
alive – prompted in death a flood of necrophiliac love poems.)

Seven Poems of James Joyce

The return to creativity was fertilised by his love of the poetry of
James Joyce. The year 1929 saw the setting of a number of
Joyce texts, and, according to Peter Dickinson,[14] Joyce, no
mean singer and musician himself, much admired Moeran's
settings of his words.[15] The songs were *Rosefrail*, *Tilly* (from
Pomes Pennyeach of 1927), and the *Seven Poems of James Joyce* which
comprised the following texts from *Chamber Music*: 'Strings in
the Earth and Air', 'The Merry Greenwood', 'Bright Cap',
'The Pleasant Valley', 'Donnycarney', 'Rain has fallen', 'Now,
O Now, in this Brown Land'.

By now, the exposure to the music of Warlock had much
enriched Moeran's harmonic language, while it had also

[13] In conversation with the author.

[14] In a BBC (Radio 3) broadcast on 2 November 1982, on Herbert Hughes' *Joyce
Book*.

[15] In his autobiography (*As I Remember*, Faber & Faber, London, 1970, pp.100–101)
Arthur Bliss remarks that Joyce told him he liked *his* setting in the *Joyce Book* best of all –
but Bliss suspected Joyce said that to all the composers.

clouded his outlook, so that the blithe optimistic quality of much of the early music appeared less often. In particular, the deep melancholy of Warlock's masterly Yeats cycle *The Curlew* had left its mark on him. Freed from the inhibiting presence of Heseltine, yet steeped in the style of Warlock, in these seven songs Moeran produced some of his finest work for voice and piano. His latent consciousness of his Celtic inheritance, rising to the surface over recent years, here burst forth. The work is thus very personal, for on the one hand it quotes from the composer's earlier work while on the other it is itself quoted in later pieces.

In his chamber and symphonic works as I have said, unity is achieved through the 'parent cell' technique. In the Joyce song-cycle, the poems themselves have a kind of unity since all treat love against a background of nature seen in its changing seasons. Musically, unity is promoted by the use, in three songs, of a single chord and sequences based upon it (Ex. 12).

Ex. 12

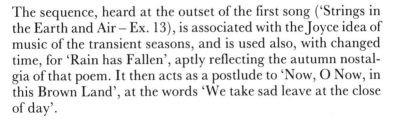

The sequence, heard at the outset of the first song ('Strings in the Earth and Air – Ex. 13), is associated with the Joyce idea of music of the transient seasons, and is used also, with changed time, for 'Rain has Fallen', aptly reflecting the autumn nostalgia of that poem. It then acts as a postlude to 'Now, O Now, in this Brown Land', at the words 'We take sad leave at the close of day'.

Ex. 13

Moeran remembered this sequence two years later when he came to set Housman's *Loveliest of Trees* and again, perhaps to

bitterness, some ten years later for *Where the Bee Sucks*
(Shakespeare). By then, it had all the loaded associations of
Joyce, and perhaps of Housman; to use it to set the words
'Merrily shall I live now' shows a nice irony but gives a
worrying insight into Moeran's mind.

The fourth song, 'The Cool Valley', looks back to the piano
piece *Summer Valley* of 1925. There, the principal idea was
expressed in barcarolle rhythm – a favourite of both Warlock
and Moeran. In the song, the idea is re-worked in $\frac{5}{8}$ time to
form an instrumental prelude. Was the reminiscence conscious? It was certainly prompted by the identity of idea,
whether conscious or unconscious:

> O cool is the valley now
> And there, love, we will go
> For many a choir is singing now
> Where love did sometime go.

Or perhaps he had this poem in mind when writing *Summer
Valley*.

The Moeran fingerprints we would expect are present, and
none is more apt than the three-steps-and-a-leap melodic shape
(Ex. 14) in 'Strings in the Earth and Air' – used so often, but
here used to adorn the words which embrace his very calling
and profession.

Ex. 14

And fin-gers stray-ing up-on- an in-stru-ment.

'The Merry Greenwood', with its dew-fresh images of spring,
readily prompts Moeran to a piano part reminiscent of John
Ireland in sunlit mood. The melody, however, is that joint
Warlock/Moeran property – 'steps up'. In a little while,
Moeran would set 'Good Wine' for the *Songs of Springtime*. The
same 'steps up' melodic formula would be used and – even
more striking – the phrase endings would be identical. On the
surface there appears to be no parallel between the poems, and
so for justification of this identity we have to look for the

parallels between the works in their entirety, when it becomes readily apparent that the theme common to both is transience.

The last song, 'Now, O Now in this Brown Land', is perhaps the most interesting, not only for itself, but also because of its significance for Moeran's later work. 'This Brown Land': Ireland is presumably implied. The introductory bars for the piano (Ex. 15) are astonishingly prophetic of the opening of the later Violin Concerto – the work most closely associated with Ireland and all things Irish.

Ex. 15

Slow and very smooth

'Tilly'

Of the two other Joyce poems set at this time, one – 'Tilly' – has an interesting history.[16] Joyce published his *Pomes Pennyeach* in 1927, and there were a baker's dozen of them. Herbert Hughes and Arthur Bliss planned to invite a number of composers to set these poems to appear in a book as a tribute to Joyce – *The Joyce Book*.

The composers who contributed included George Antheil, Arnold Bax, Albert Roussel, Herbert Hughes, Eugene Goossens, Arthur Bliss, Herbert Howells, John Ireland, Bernard van Dieren and Roger Sessions. Gustav Holst, Constant Lambert, William Walton and Peter Warlock were approached but did not in the end produce a song, while Darius Milhaud declined as he was not to be paid. Moeran's contribution was the first – the extra one of the baker's dozen. It was called 'Tilly'. In Dublin, when the milkman delivered milk in a jug, he added extra measure, called the Tilly. Joyce loved the book (a de luxe edition limited to 500), but apparently complained that there were no net proceeds for him.

[16] This information on 'Tilly' is based on Peter Dickinson's broadcast of 2 November 1982.

The poem (originally called 'Ruminants') superficially concerns cattle driven along 'a cold red road', but is thought to reflect Joyce's feeling for his family after the death of his mother. Moeran's setting is an astonishing advance on his previous songs – even on the *Seven Poems of Joyce*. There is no facile tune-making, and the wavering chords of the first page anticipate the later Vaughan Williams. The voice part moves in recitative of considerable sensitivity and freedom. The song takes its place as an important facet of the re-appraisal.

Six Suffolk Folksongs
In February 1931, writing to Arnold Dowbiggin, Moeran mentioned that he was on the point of finishing a set of six Suffolk folksong arrangements. In the same letter, he expressed the hope that Augener might publish them 'as a companion vol. to my Norfolk book'; in the event they were brought out in 1932 by Curwen. A prefatory note states that the songs were noted down from the singing of George Hill of Earl Stonham and Oliver Waspe of Coddenham. They were worked on at Ipswich and are thus another product of his prolonged convalescence there. The songs are: 'Nutting Time', 'Blackberry Fold', 'Cupid's Garden', 'Father and Daughter', 'The Isle of Cloy', and 'A Seaman's Life'.

These arrangements are rather more sophisticated than the companion Norfolk set, with much freer use of independent accompaniment figures. But the Norfolk set contained at least three melodies of exceptional beauty; generally, while the settings are of a high order, the Suffolk songs themselves lack distinction.

Alsatian Carol & Ivy and Holly
The two songs for solo, male voices and piano – *Alsatian Carol* and *Ivy and Holly*, written in 1932, are traditional tunes to which other words have been fitted. The *Alsatian Carol* (published in *Cantiques de Strasbourg* in 1697) is a reasonable fit to the words of Isaac Watts' *Cradle Hymn*. Moeran spent some time with his friend Augustus John in France, hoping to collect some French folk tunes. According to John, the visit was of dubious success,

but it seems likely that this tune at least was collected.[17] *Ivy and Holly* marries an adaptation of words by John Keegan (1809–1849) to the Irish tune 'O'Carolan's Lament'. Although the words do not altogether happily agree with the tune, the arrangement is rather more successful because the chorus part is more substantial and through-composed.

Magnificat and Nunc Dimittis

Moeran may well have been contemptuous of his religious music ('this tripe for the church'), but with the *Magnificat and Nunc Dimittis* in D at least, it is difficult to endorse his opinion. It is no mean achievement to write a tune so strong, memorable and singable as the opening statement (Ex. 16). The *Nunc Dimittis* is similarly apt and masterly in its effortless art. As for the 'Stainerisms', they are hardly apparent – for Moeran was not capable of tastelessness in his work.

Ex. 16

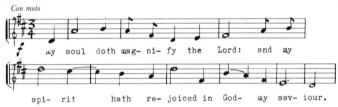

Prelude and Berceuse

There was very little piano music in this period, and the *Prelude and Berceuse*, dating from 1933, were the last of his solo pieces for the instrument. They were dedicated to the pianist and composer Freda Swain, who frequently included Moeran's work in her programmes. The 'mush of Delius-like chords'[18] may have been expunged from the chamber works, but is luxuriantly indulged here. The *Prelude*, curiously forlorn, subjects an obsessive little phrase in G minor to chains of poignant harmony. The phrase is not unlike that in the middle of *Bank Holiday*, similarly obsessive and treated similarly – and coincidentally

[17] *op. cit.*
[18] EJM, in a letter to Peter Warlock dated November 1930.

also in G minor. The contrasting idea, with an unnerving resemblance to 'Tom, Tom, the Piper's Son', turns out itself to be suggested by the G minor phrase; and then it becomes apparent that this same germ, returning like a loop within the minor third, except when the last note escapes to the upper octave (when it can be recognised as three-steps-and-a-leap), is being toyed with and worried at in work after work. Even its 'Tom, Tom, the Piper's Son' development will return – most notably in the Violin Concerto.

There are slender but subtle links between *Prelude* and the succeeding *Berceuse*, although the latter is less immediately striking. Moeran here experiments with a harmony in which the left hand moves throughout almost exclusively in second inversion chords.

These two pieces are not difficult, and are well worth the attention of the more adventurous pianist. Possibly these, too, are valedictory to Warlock, whose shade haunts the *Prelude* and whose eternal rest may be rocked in the *Berceuse*.

Loveliest of Trees & Blue Eyed Spring

Again, Warlock is not too far away in the two songs *Loveliest of Trees* (setting of Housman; Curwen, 1932) and *Blue Eyed Spring* (setting of Nichols; Curwen, 1934). In the Housman setting, it is the harmony which reflects his influence, particularly in the semitonal shifts from E major harmony to E flat and back again. *In Blue Eyed Spring*, however, it is the rhythm which is indebted to Warlock: the idiosyncratic division of $\frac{6}{8}$ time clearly derives from Warlock's *Jillian of Berry*.

In the Moeran song, by some inexplicable magic, the complete disregard in the melody of the natural word-accents does work in its uproarious evocation of the eruption of spring.

With regard to the fine setting of *Loveliest of Trees*, it would have been the poignant realisation by the poet of the passage of time – of transience – which fired the composer:

Now of my three-score years and ten
Twenty will not come again.

This thought would naturally cloud the hope of a man no longer in the first flush of youth. Musically, the passage in

question is distanced from the rest of the song by the characteristic appoggiatura chord sequence already familiar from its use
in the Joyce songs ('Strings in Earth and Air'). It would be used
again in *Whythorne's Shadow* and yet again in 'Where the Bee
Sucks' (the second of the 1940 Shakespeare songs). All, in
different and sometimes obscure ways, are concerned with
transience, and the chord sequence thus seems for the composer a potent musical symbol.

Songs of Springtime

Transience is, of course, a principal motivating force in the art
of Delius, and in this Delian period of Moeran's activity, it is a
major preoccupation. The *Songs of Springtime*, written in 1929,
are the distilled essence of this pre-occupation. They received
their first performance in 1933 by the Oriana Madrigal Society
under Charles Kennedy Scott. Moeran himself conducted but
rarely – but he did subsequently give at least one performance
of these songs, some years later with the Huddersfield Choral
Society. One imagines that such a society would have been too
unwieldy for them, since they are designed for a small choir. In
them is heard the most direct influence of Warlock, whose
enthusiasm for 16th-century vocal music is also reflected.

There are seven songs in all: 'Under the Greenwood Tree'
(Shakespeare), 'The River God's Song' (John Fletcher), 'Love
is a Sickness' (Samuel Daniel), 'Sigh no more, Ladies'
(Shakespeare), 'Spring, the Sweet Spring' (Thomas Nashe),
'Good Wine' (William Browne), and 'To Daffodils' (Herrick).

Few other poems are so apt as 'Under the Greenwood Tree'
to commence a cycle about Spring, but Moeran is hardly
daunted by the need to produce yet another version of these
frequently set lines. The two verses are treated similarly, but
there is a departure into chromaticism at the words:

> And loves to live i' the sun,
> Seeking the food he eats,
> And pleased with what he gets.

Nevertheless, the effect does not mirror the blithe innocence of
the words (Ex. 17). Rather there is a feeling of irony; it is

another example of the clouding of lyricism which is such a
Moeran fingerprint.

Ex. 17

'The River God's Song' is problematical. For half its length it
is a finely proportioned and phrased setting, Dowland-like in
its pavane movement, dignified in its grave F minor harmonies,
moving like lute-song to the relative major key of A flat. The
problem comes at the words: 'but ever live with me, and not a
wave shall trouble thee'. Clearly feeling that some emotional
lift is needed here, Moeran attempts an abrupt modulation to C
major. This is not a distant modulation, but in performance it is
always jarring in effect, and is difficult to keep in tune. Thereafter, the setting recovers neither its balance nor the composure
of its opening.

One of the most intense partsongs in English music, 'Love is
a Sickness' is a fine setting of words by Samuel Daniel (1562–
1619) which is related in spirit to some of the more melancholy
work of Dowland. We do not know how much Dowland
Moeran knew, and we must assume that his contact with this
music would have been filtered through Heseltine, who
assuredly did know it well. The key of G minor is used by
Moeran for his most personal utterance (the Symphony, for
example), and is coincidentally shared by Warlock's song *Sleep*,
to which the song bears more than a passing resemblance. It is
also worth remarking that G minor or G is the tonality of

fourteen of the twenty-one numbers in Dowland's *First Book of Ayres* (1597–1613). Both Warlock's song and that of Moeran move gently to the relative major to conclude their second lines; so do many of the Dowland songs. One of them ('Unquiet Thoughts') even suggests its ancestry of the Warlock with an identity of phrase. What both Warlock and Moeran do is to develop Dowland's chromaticism as a means of intense emotional expression. In both, long soaring melodic lines are coloured by the changing harmonies beneath. But Moeran has a further characteristic – his harmony alternates between major and minor, often by false relationships, so that his music mirrors the constant contrast between the pain and the pleasure of love which is at the heart of the poem.

Warlock dedicated a setting of 'Sigh No More, Ladies' to Moeran in 1928, and a comparison with Moeran's setting reveals some indebtedness to Warlock's earlier setting. But Moeran's treatment is arguably more sensitive to the poem than is its model. Warlock gets himself into some tortuous modulations which make his melody sound contrived – and, incidentally, make it very difficult to sing in tune. Moeran's melody is rather more diatonic in shape, with the subtle word rhythms more faithfully matched. The constant flattened seventh of the melody and also the juxtaposition of major and minor thirds both in harmony and melody, produces a 'blues' effect, fitting for the bitter-sweet words. A response to popular music is not marked in Moeran, but it does seem in evidence here; it would not have been surprising if there had been more, for it affected other members of the Eynsford set, such as Lambert, and is apparent in the early work of Walton. The 'Hey, nonny, nonny' refrain shows one of the Moeran's basic melodic shapes – a theme of three steps up and a leap.

The apparently simple setting of 'Spring, the Sweet Spring' (later to be set by Britten in his *Spring Symphony*) conceals Moeran's greatest art. The art is revealed by a comparison of the treatment of the three verses, where the rhythms are continually modified to meet the different word stresses. It is in this song that one is most aware of the transience and the bitter-sweet nostalgia of Spring, achieved, perhaps, through the 'blues' style, Ellington-influenced harmonies (Ex. 18).

Doke
Ellington

Constant Lambert dwelt lovingly on Duke Ellington in
Music Ho!, published in 1934 (the year after the publication of
these songs). Lambert and Moeran were acquainted through
Warlock and in a roundabout way Ellington and Delius are
linked, since improvised negro harmonisation is an important
element in the harmonic style of both.

Ex. 18

(lips closed)

   The melody of the drinking song, 'Good Wine', fits the words
like a glove, with the result that the music almost sings itself. Its
simple diatonicism is reminiscent of a number of songs to be
found in Warlock, and indeed its roots may be traced to the
song, *Maltworms*, that Warlock and Moeran composed together
in February 1926. This song used, as Moeran put it, the 'steps
up' – a series of ascending thirds, and the principal melody of
Good Wine also has these 'steps up', although 'Good Wine' is in
E major and *Maltworms* is in D minor. The third and fourth line
of each song will also bear comparison – and Gerald Cockshott
has shown that Moeran contributed the third and fourth lines
of *Maltworms*.
   But there is another possible influence on this song. Just a
few years before its composition, Moeran was working on the
set of James Joyce songs, the second of which ('The Merry
Greenwood') deals with the idea of the blitheness of spring. The
melodic resemblances to 'Good Wine' are really very striking –
an echo from the earlier song is heard quite naturally in the
later one. 'Good Wine' is a brilliant song when sung with crisp
diction; its last page, with the soprano and alto lines moving in
$\frac{2}{4}$ against the $\frac{6}{8}$ of the tenor and bass is almost orchestral in
effect. Why did not Moeran end the cycle with it?

For Moeran, as for Shelley and right back to the Elizabethan poets he has chosen to set, all beauty must die. This is Herrick's meaning in 'Fair Daffodils'. Spring, as with the sick rose, carries within its erupting vitality and loveliness the seeds of its own decay. Spring is therefore the time of bitter-sweet acceptance of transitory joys. The placing of 'Fair Daffodils' last in the cycle casts a shadow over the whole work, which is the more penetrating for this projection of the philosophical meaning of rebirth.

The *Songs of Springtime* are difficult to bring off satisfactorily in performance because of the problems of intonation posed throughout. While he must have had some singing ability (presumably he joined in the folk singing in the local pub), Moeran was incomparably more experienced as an instrumentalist. The inner vocal lines are, on occasion, ungrateful, very often because of modulations which have the appearance of having been worked out at the piano. Polyphony is limited to the most elementary voice-leading. Yet in so far as Moeran is known at all outside a small band of devotees, it is probably through these songs, which have always held their well-loved place in the repertory of the small choir.

Whythorne's Shadow

The short orchestral piece *Whythorne's Shadow* is usually coupled with *Lonely Waters* to form the *Two Pieces for Small Orchestra*. The two pieces really have very little in common, for *Lonely Waters* was certainly sketched some years earlier, and is markedly different in idiom. It does not even share the same orchestral requirements, for *Whythorne's Shadow*, in addition to the strings, requires only one each of flute, oboe, clarinet and horn where *Lonely Waters* requires these instruments plus a cor anglais, second clarinet, bassoon and cymbal. Both works are in their respective ways fine examples of Moeran's work, but their linking is merely a publishing convenience.

In 1925 Heseltine had published a pamphlet *Thomas Whythorne – an Unknown Elizabethan Composer*. In 1927 he brought out an edition of Whythorne's SATTB partsong *As Thy Shadow Itself Apply'th*. The published version of Moeran's *Whythorne's*

Shadow[19] dates from 1931 and thus was written a year or so after the Joyce songs and after the Sonata for Two Violins. It is roughly contemporary with the String Trio. Nothing is more remarkable in Moeran's work than his apparent capacity to work more or less simultaneously in two different styles: the Sonata and the String Trio are contrapuntal works looking forward to Moeran's ultimate maturity, while *Whythorne's Shadow* is a retrospective work singing nostalgically of an idyllic, if non-existent, past.

But there is evidence that a work based on Whythorne had existed some years before 1931. It is mentioned by Philip Heseltine in a letter to Colin Taylor dated 19 January 1929. Taylor, in the University of Capetown School of Music, had clearly asked for details of orchestral works by young British composers for possible performance:

> The only tolerably good orchestral work of Moeran (Rhapsody No 2) is still in manuscript; his last composition – a fantasy for small orchestra on a theme by Whythorne – was unfortunately not picked up by the kindly Brussels gendarme who found its composer in a state of beatific coma in the gutter some years ago; and nothing more has been heard of it since that occasion.

It is not possible to say to what extent, if any, the published work is based on or reconstructed from the Fantasy mentioned in Heseltine's letter. It may indeed be an entirely new work.

Moeran's preface and the words of Whythorne's song are quoted in full:

> This piece is based on a part-song by Thomas Whythorne published in 1571.
> The nature of the present work cannot be better expounded than by quotation of the poem of Whythorne's song.

[19] Stephen Wild, *op. cit.*, p.66. *Whythorne's Shadow* was based on a part-song published in 1571 by Thomas Whythorne. This part-song, *As Thy Shadow Itself Apply'th*, transcribed and edited by Peter Warlock, appeared in the series *Oxford Choral Songs from the Old Masters* (No. 362, O.U.P., 1927). Heseltine was probably the first critic to discern anything of value in the works of Thomas Whythorne and the appearance of his transcriptions of the best of that composer's songs, and his pamphlet on them and their creator, did much to discredit the poor opinions previously held of this 'unknown Elizabethan composer'.

As thy shadow itself apply'th
To follow thee whereso thou go,
And when thou bends, itself it wry'th
Turning as thou both to and fro:
The flatterer doth even so;
And shopes himself the same to gloze,
With many a fawning and gay show,
Whom he would frame for his purpose.

Christopher Palmer comments on this preface:

If Moeran is hereby giving us to understand that he regards
himself as a 'fawning flatterer' by way of his treatment of
Whythorne's part-song, he is showing himself in an unneces-
sarily discreditable light.[20]

A 'fawning flatterer' of Whythorne? Possibly, but as the music
develops it flatters not so much Whythorne as Warlock –
'Warlock's Shadow', in fact. In 'Pieds en l'Air' (*Capriol Suite*,
1926), Warlock had taken a gentle diatonic dance from Arbeau
of 1588, and had subjected it to some of his most poignant
chromatic harmony. Whythorne's tune is mainly diatonic and
has similar rhythmic characteristics. Moeran's 'flattery' is to
clothe it in harmony at first in the idiom of Whythorne, but
gradually growing in chromaticism to encompass the harmonic
language he had in common with Warlock.

Warlock's death in December 1930 effectively released the
'shadow' from impotent thraldom. In a sense, the published
version of *Whythorne's Shadow* is Moeran's 'In Memoriam' for
his friend. This speculation (for it is no more than that) gains
some credence from the use in the harmony of that progression
associated with the idea of transience (Joyce songs, *Loveliest of
Trees*, etc.) and its use here (Ex. 19) may be the evidence that
this passage, at any rate, may date from after the Joyce songs.

In *Whythorne's Shadow* Moeran returns to his favourite rondo
form. The trochaic rhythms are those used by Delius and
Warlock so often, carrying with them the seeds of possible
monotony – but Moeran is adept at avoiding this danger; for
example, one appearance of Whythorne's tune is given a varied
accentuation simply by the addition of a minim at its com-

[20] *op. cit.*

Ex. 19

mencement. For its last appearance, the tune is given to the solo violin – a shadow, perhaps, of that definitive image of farewell all Delians know from the conclusion of the *First Dance Rhapsody*.

In assessing the achievement of this poignant and moving miniature masterpiece, I can do no better than quote Christopher Palmer again:

> What he does here, in fact, is to gather together in a single brief movement the whole complex chain of technical and spiritual affinities relating Delius, the folklorists and the Elizabethans. Here is the English Delius movement in a nutshell.[21]

Mr Palmer, however, does not include Warlock in his 'complex chain'. I should like to do so because it seems to me that in the period 1930 to 1932 Warlock and his tragic fate were central to Moeran's thinking. For him, it was a period of crisis – one part of him looked forward but, struggling equally for expression, another part looked back to his late friend and all he represented. It is to this prolonged farewell that we owe the *Songs of Springtime*, the *Seven Poems of James Joyce* and *Whythorne's Shadow*. In them, and particularly in the last piece, Moeran tapped that vein of sweet lyricism which extended back to Whythorne and Byrd (*Will You Walk the Woods so Wild?*) through Delius (*On Hearing the First Cuckoo in Spring*) and Warlock and on past him to Walton.[22]

---

[21] *ibid.*, p.171.

[22] I am indebted to my wife for pointing out the resemblances of melody, rhythm and mood to the Moeran piece of Walton's *Touch her Soft Lips and Part* (Incidental Music for the film, *Henry V*).

In a letter to Warlock dated 23 November 1930, and written at Ipswich (from which I have already quoted), Moeran wrote:

> ... It is an excellent discipline in trying to break away from the mush of Delius-like chords, which I have been obsessed with on every occasion I have attempted to compose during the last two years. Perhaps some good has come of being abed and unable to keep running to the keyboard for every bar.

The 'discipline' was that necessary in writing a Sonata for Two Violins and a String Trio; the other significant information here is that Moeran, up to this point, had apparently been in the habit of making extensive use of the piano for his composition. Gradually he was gaining the confidence to dispense with it, and he used it little for his later work.

The re-appraisal was proceeding apace. From this point onwards, the bulk of his output would be in larger forms and would be instrumental rather than vocal in medium. The principal harvests of the concentration on contrapuntal styles at this period were the Sonata and the String Trio mentioned above. While the discipline or 'purgative' involved can be seen as preparatory to the symphonic and concerted works to come, these two earlier works are rather more than mere exercises, and one of them, the Trio, is a work of considerable distinction.

A leaning towards attenuated forces was already apparent in British music by the late 1920s and early 1930s. It can be seen in the work of Holst as early as 1916 in the *Four Songs for Voice and Violin*, and in the *Terzetto* for flute, oboe and viola of 1925. And one member of the Moeran circle, Alan Rawsthorne, also wrote a work for two violins, the *Theme and Variations* (first performed in 1938). The adoption of such limited forces, and the rejection of the lush harmonies was, as far as Moeran was concerned, an early manifestation of anti-Romanticisim (which the rest of the musical world had espoused some years before). But there is no clear-cut line of progress to be drawn. The most obvious successors to the Sonata for Two Violins are the *Sinfonietta*, which shows Neo-classical tendencies, and the Sonata for Cello and Piano, which explores more consistently the harmonic language proposed tentatively in the earlier work. But the Cello Sonata and *Sinfonietta* come considerably later: the *Sinfonietta* in

1944 and the Sonata in 1947. In between came the Symphony, the Violin Concerto and the Third Rhapsody, all of which, while exploiting the new-found contrapuntal skill, seem less adventurous in harmonic language, and a regression in the one sense that a large Romantic orchestra is preferred. A possible explanation for the Symphony is that it was commenced and almost completed in 1924; what is not yet known is how much of the original version was retained in the final one of 1937.

The Sonata for Two Violins and the String Trio were nevertheless conceived with the intention of stylistic cleansing and technical exploration and all of the works that come after them benefit in some degree from this. Interestingly enough, the two works show some correspondence of thematic material and possibly provide an example of a single joint conception. This would not be unique in Moeran for there is some evidence that this pairing may also occur with the Symphony and the Violin Concerto and with the Cello Concerto and the Cello Sonata.

Sonata for Two Violins

The Sonata for Two Violins is a three-movement work. The first movement is in sonata form, to be followed by a scherzo and a passacaglia. There is thus no slow movement and it is this which helps give the work its lightweight character. It is the choice of passacaglia for the last movement which perhaps tells us most about Moeran's intention, for this is an 'academic' form, and a searching test of compositional skill.

What is immediately striking about the work is the superbly idiomatic string writing, together with the composer's marked skill in balancing the interest between the players. While the ideas lack distinction (the one which opens the work is oddly reminiscent of the somewhat mundane style of Alec Rowley[23]) they do exhibit a striking unity. This unity is not paraded; the method is one of some subtlety for, while there are parent cells, the unit which links all the principal material, and therefore all the movements, is the interval of a fifth (with occasional extension to a sixth).

[23] Alec Rowley (1892–1958) taught composition at Trinity College of Music. While his creative talent was not of the first rank, he wrote much worthy teaching music and some songs and organ music which remain deservedly popular.

Certainly in this work, Moeran succeeded in purging the 'mush of Delius-like chords'. The lean, muscular polyphony which took its place could hardly offer a starker contrast. While Moeran on occasion admired the work of such noted polyphonists as van Dieren and Reger – both highly regarded by the Gray/Heseltine/Sorabji circle, they were hardly the models for his new style. For this we have to look further back in time. In the passacaglia, he seems to have taken a great *vocal* polyphonist as his model – he has chosen William Byrd, and in particular the Byrd of the four- and five-part Masses. Here truly is a legacy of Heseltine, for without doubt it would have been his late friend who inspired the knowledge of and love for the Tudor master. The aspect of Byrd's polyphony which evidently fired him was its sprung rhythms freed from the tyranny of the bar line. Thus the organisation of the phrases of the passacaglia theme ensure that there will be stimulating rhythmic interaction with the upper part.

The Sonata for Two Violins is, in its harmonic language, a prophetic work. Ideas which are basically clear in their tonality are given arbitary harmonies; there is the occasional passage of bitonality. In the middle movement, for example, the first violin seems to be firmly in D major, while the second violin, with its folk song-like melody, seems equally firmly to be in a modal G minor. The use, incidentally, of pastiche folksongs, (discussed in Chapter III, pp. 58–59) becomes quite a feature from this point onwards of Moeran's work, and further examples can be found in the Symphony, the *Sinfonietta* and the Cello Concerto.

In this Sonata the final impression is of technical skill not always motivated by inspiration, of harmonic arbitrariness – the detail not always justified by its context. It was probably necessary for Moeran to go through this phase, and the newly explored style seems altogether more secure in the String Trio than in the Sonata. In the last movement of the Sonata, in particular, the part-writing seems to be without pattern – even aimless on occasion. For the stimulating nature of Byrd's lines is their organic logic, and it is this that is missing in Moeran's passacaglia.

String Trio

In the Trio, he recovered his lyrical vein and the balance of
lyricism with superb part-writing now produced the happiest
results – and the first masterpiece of his mature style. There are
four movements. The first and fourth balance one another in
style, mood, and, to some extent, content. The emotional core
of the work is an intense *adagio*, to be followed by a fugal *molto
vivace*. In the first movement, Moeran set himself the additional
technical problem of writing an entire movement in $\frac{7}{8}$ time. The
groupings within each bar are of the utmost subtlety, using
every permutation of 3-2-2, 2-2-3, 1-3-3, 2-3-2, etc., with the
groupings varying by instrument as well as bar by bar. Sonata
form is used, but there is in its use something of that seamless-
ness already noted in the Piano Trio. This is brought about in
part by principal ideas which are complementary rather than
contrasting – ideas which naturally produce the serene optimistic movement suggested by the direction *giovale* at the head of
the score. The open-air, pastoral lyricism of this movement
extends in ancestry back to the Elgar of the *Introduction and
Allegro* for strings, and looks forward to the *Concerto for Double
String Orchestra* of Tippett. One passage, however, is strikingly
at variance with the rest of the movement. This occurs at the
start of the development, where, over a cello ostinato based on
minor thirds in the key of C sharp minor, the viola proceeds in
the key of A minor while the violin has a free passage in what
appears to be F minor/major (Ex. 20). The passage is deeply
disturbed. Something similar will happen in the last movement
of the Cello Sonata. The present passage is not one of Moeran's
processionals, whereas that in the Cello Sonata is, and there are
similar passages elsewhere – the one in the last movement of the
Violin Sonata also takes place over prominent minor thirds. It
is the minor third which appears to be the link, and this interval
seems to be reserved by Moeran for 'dark sayings'; this particular 'saying' – a sudden madness, almost – echoes that in the
scherzo of Elgar's Second Symphony, just as the surrounding
serenity is of the same order as that rare Elgarian 'spirit of
delight' found, say, at the commencement of Part Two of *The
Dream of Gerontius* (which sings less of an other-worldly heaven
than of the woods and vistas around his beloved Birchwood
Lodge).

Ex. 20

What is merely a moment of disturbance in the first movement is developed in the *Adagio* into a statement of profound
pessimism. Now the texture is shot through with minor thirds,
and with much use of false relation; all the phrases seem to fall.
In contrast with the soaring writing of the first movement, the
instruments appear to be placed for much of its course in their
low and middle registers.

A gradual ascent from these psychological depths is made by
way of the fugal scherzo – whose mood is nevertheless somewhat grim and clouded. The subject is a long one – so long that
the third voice does not enter until the sixty-fourth bar. Harmonically, there is still a prevalent impression of minor thirds, and
the two climaxes are dominated by them. The first hammers
out the elemental shape of falling minor thirds whence the
disturbed passage in the first movement had been fashioned;
the second simply condenses this image into unrelated triads,
most of which are minor.

The Scherzo is joined to the last movement by a short

passage which begins to outline the shape of that movement's principal idea. Something similar will happen at the start of the last movement of the Cello Concerto. The last movement of the Trio brings with it a return to the gentle lyricism of the opening of the work. Knowing by now the composer's approach, we might suspect he would, in some way, attempt to link thematically the material of the first and last movements. Sure enough, the linking is there (Ex. 21). This very free variation technique

Ex. 21

(a) **Last movement**

(b) **First movement**

is but one more example of the manner in which these two experimental works explore methods and styles to be used later in such works as the Symphony, Violin Concerto, *Sinfonietta* and Cello Sonata.

The last movement has a ternary shape, but it has a delightful surprise in store. As a coda, there is an exhilarating *Presto* – rather like a traditional Irish fiddle dance (Ex. 22) – and the

Ex. 22

work ends in a riot of double-stopping for the cello and across-the-strings work for the viola – the party spirit, the anonymity of the crowd, as Moeran remarked some years later to Arthur Hutchings.[24] Had not Tchaikovsky said something about learning enjoyment from the crowds, à propos of the meaning of the last movement of his Fourth Symphony?

At the very least, the String Trio is a work of consummate technical mastery in which the polyphony is not paraded academically but is effortless, both in the distribution of material between the three instruments, and in the interest and subtlety of the accompanying textures. Harmonically, Moeran has so transformed his style as to make comparison with, say, a work of the fairly immediate past such as the *Songs of Springtime* a matter of some wonder. It is not that he has expunged 'the mush of Delius-like chords' altogether; rather he has exercised more control over his style, so that, within a basically diatonic idiom, the chromatics are used at points of intensity – not from habit, in other words, but for specific point. Further, the chromaticisms now derive from the natural movement of the parts.

The speed with which Moeran assimilated the new style is astonishing. The Sonata for Two Violins is an interesting work but the Trio is a masterpiece revelling in the freedom bestowed by newly acquired technical skills. The composer was indeed approaching the point where the long-awaited Symphony might be reconsidered.

There was, however, something erratic in Moeran's progress, and the works which followed show a bewildering stylistic regression.

Songs, 1934

The *Four English Lyrics* for voice and piano were dedicated to the tenor Parry Jones and date from 1934. There is about them a professional facility and ease, an almost contemptuous imitation of the best popular models, which they in fact surpass. Quilter might well have been proud of the first song, 'Cherry Ripe' (Thomas Campion), while the fine setting of 'The Passionate Shepherd' (Christopher Marlowe) matches a sustained melody of quasi-*bel canto* quality with an accompaniment wrought with craft worthy of Brahms.

[24] See Chapter III (p. 49) and note 17 of that Chapter.

The 'Willow Song' (John Fletcher) is one of Moeran's funereal sicilianas (another example can be heard in his setting of *Come away, Death*). As I have noted, the key of G minor is reserved by Moeran for his most personal utterance. It is, for example, shared by 'Love is a Sickness' (*Songs of Springtime*) and the Symphony, and the intense harmonic language of the *Springtime* song is to be found here.

Most revealing of Moeran's thought process is 'The Constant Lover' (William Browne) which returns us to the world of Peter Warlock, and in particular to Warlock's 'Passing By' (Anon.). Why would one of Warlock's weakest songs make any impression? Possibly because the two poems have such marked similarities:

> *The Constant Lover*
> For her gait, if she be walking;
> Be she sitting, I desire her
> For her states sake; and admire her
> For her wit if she be talking;
> Gait and state and wit approve her;
> For which all and each I love her.

> *Passing By*
> There is a lady sweet and kind,
> Was never face so pleased my mind,
> I did but see her passing by,
> And yet I love her till I die.
> Her gesture, motion, and her smiles,
> Her wit, her voice, my heart beguiles,
> Beguiles my heart, I know not why,
> And yet I love her till I die.

Warlock set 'Passing By' for the last time (of four) a year or so before he died. 'The Constant Lover' dates from 1934. The settings are so similar that it is possible to proceed from a verse setting of one into one of the other with little discrepancy of style. Both are in G and both move in a basic four pulses per bar, Warlock in $\frac{4}{8}$, Moeran in $\frac{4}{4}$. That of Warlock is frankly popular, if not vulgar in style. The stresses and rhythms of Browne's poem help Moeran to an altogether more subtle song and, not for the first time, he has taken a model and improved on it (the comparison is, of course, here with inferior Warlock; with some notable and honourable exceptions, Moeran's songs in general but rarely approach the standard of Warlock's finest work).

Why, then, is there a nagging doubt about the *Four English Lyrics*? They do not progress along the path explored by the Joyce songs. In their deliberate pursuit of popular appeal, they seem a reaction to that feeling of disillusion with singers to which Moeran gave vent throughout his life. Singers had no interest in his work. Singers bore responsibility for the death of Warlock. Just as Warlock would on occasion attempt to combat apathy with work of sedulously cultivated popular appeal, so here does Moeran, with the added assistance of four popular texts.

But popularity is illusive and unpredictable – and in any case transient, for the heyday of the ballad had already passed. The *Four English Lyrics* are rarely heard today, while the *Seven Poems of James Joyce* grow slowly in favour. But the *Lyrics* go some way towards explaining how Moeran was seen in the early 1930s, when *The Musical Times* praised him somewhat obliquely 'for his modesty and sensitiveness . . . that quality in us which is often overlooked by foreigners'[25] – an appraisal which suggests that, in the England of the 1930s, pretentiousness, bombast and overstatement were cardinal sins of artistry.

Nocturne

No charge of following popular fashion could be made of the other major composition of 1934, which is certainly one of Moeran's least practical works. The *Nocturne* for baritone, chorus and orchestra is a setting of words from *Don Juan Tenorio the Great*, a play by Moeran's friend Robert Nichols, who himself asked Moeran to set them.

The passage chosen is the 'Address to the Sunset', which begins:

Exquisite stillness! What serenities
Of earth and air! How bright atop the wall
The stonecrop's fire and beyond the precipice
How huge, how hushed the primrose even-fall!

[25] Arnold Whittall, *The Musical Times*, March 1964, quoting criticisms from earlier editions – in this case, of 1934.

The work was written for the Norwich Philharmonic Society, who first performed it in 1935 under Dr Heathcote Statham, but it is inscribed 'To the Memory of Frederick Delius'. Delius had died in 1934, and the words have a singular appropriateness – the sunset image is a Delian characteristic, appearing at its most potent in Delius' *Song of the High Hills*. Jelka Delius, already herself mortally ill with cancer, wrote to Moeran:

> The poem is beautiful and I am sure it must have inspired you to give the best and most intimate and tender . . . you have in your heart. Please dedicate it to the memory of Frederick, it is a tribute which I know would have given him great pleasure.[26]

Critics were quick to point out that the Delius connection went well beyond the dedication. Vaughan Williams, in a letter to the composer, pointed out the absurdity of this:

> Many thanks for the copy of the Nocturne – I thought it beautiful – I think the references to Delius in the Press are absurd. Doubtless if Delius had not existed it might not have been written just as Delius would not have been written without Grieg or Grieg without Schumann and so back to Tubal Cain . . . .[27]

Perhaps Vaughan Williams himself proved his point when he came, a few years later, to write his *Serenade to Music*, which owes something to both Moeran and Delius.

Nevertheless, the *Nocturne* is something of a curiosity. It is performed but rarely, and despite its ravishing beauty, it is not difficult to see why. It will not fit easily into concert programmes and demands choral and orchestral resources and rehearsal provision which in cost both of time and money are hardly justified by the awkward timing of thirteen to fifteen minutes. Despite the sensitive word-setting, the effect is less that of a choral work than of an orchestral tone poem with chorus *obbligato*; much of the chorus, indeed, is wordless. The work is a final piece of self-indulgence which, like some similar Delius works, would well justify recording where concert performances may be impracticable.

Nichols' White Crane wheels and soars to exquisite wood-

[26] In a letter dated January 1935.
[27] In a letter dated 8 February 1935.

wind melismata in that brief moment of transient evening
which, inevitably perhaps, draws from Moeran the obsessive
harmonic progression of the Joyce settings (Ex. 23), recognis-
able still, but further refined with a subtle, grave colouring.
Similarly, the aspiration of 'Now spirit, find out wings' so
naturally accepts the archetypal Moeran melodic figure (Ex.
24).

Ex. 23

Ex. 24

Moeran, too, had now found out wings. The exercise of them
in the years remaining would enable him at least to touch
greatness.

VI. THE SYMPHONY IN G MINOR

So far, of the twin strands of Moeran's heritage, only his Norfolk roots have been considered. In the second part of his life that other part of his parental heritage grew more and more dominant. As Bax said in his obituary of Moeran, 'During his first thirty years he was an Englishman and a diligent collector of East Anglian folk tunes, whilst for the remainder of his days he was almost exclusively Irish'.[1] If Bax is here taken literally, the change would have begun to be apparent round about 1924. Further on in the same obituary, Bax says: 'It was, I would say, about twenty years ago that his consciousness of his Celtic heredity was suddenly aroused'. He was here writing in 1950 so he has in mind the early 1930s. The two dates are not necessarily in conflict and a crystallisation of identity by the 1930s seems likely.

By the middle years of his life, Kerry had become as necessary to him as Norfolk had been in his early years. His environment was all important to his creativity and for Moeran folk music had become an aural representation both of that environment and of the people who lived in it. His own music became a response to this – his only articulate response and therefore his natural language.

The transition from Norfolk rurality to Irishness and Celticism was by no means as bizarre a progress as it might seem. There had always been a tenuous link between Ireland and the Eastern seaboard of England, brought about in part by visiting fisherfolk from Ireland who called regularly at the East Anglian fishing ports. They brought their own music with them and took away the songs they learnt in Norfolk. Moeran himself wrote:[2]

Another thing which bears out the idea that folk song is

---

[1] 'E. J. Moeran, 1894–1950', *Music and Letters*, Vol. XXXII, No. 2, 1951, pp. 125–127.
[2] 'Some Folk Singing Today'.

connected with whose who 'follow the herring' is that in my recent researches on the sea coast of S. W. Ireland I have come across songs that seem to be more prevalent in England among the East Norfolk people near the port of Great Yarmouth than elsewhere. The Yarmouth trawlers used to fish frequently in Irish waters. In bad weather, the crews would go ashore and meet the local people in the back kitchens of Cahirciveen. Then they would spend a convivial evening singing songs and telling stories. In this way, songs would change hands without being written down, for these singers for the most part have extraordinary [*sic*] retentive memories.

Later in the same article, Moeran cites examples of East Anglian songs well known in Kerry, and vice versa. Thus, given Moeran's dual Celtic-Norfolk heritage, the journey from one culture to the other was (at least musically) a natural one.

Moeran delighted in the Irish scene, the Irish people and Irish life. The yearning for the Celtic twilight may today encourage amused, if tolerant, smiles. The disguise of the poet William Sharp as 'Fiona McLeod', or that of Bax as 'Dermot O'Byrne' may well strike sophisticates as a matter for ridicule; yet with Moeran, at least, we might well feel, with Aloys Fleischmann,[3] that he *became* Irish. Certainly, he was accepted as such, as Bax makes clear:

> The people of Kenmare adored him. One of them remarked to me: 'If ever there was a move to elect a mayor of this town Jack Moeran would be everyone's first choice'. His popularity was immense, even, it must be admitted, sometimes to the point of embarrassment.[4]

He needed to return to Ireland at frequent intervals, to savour the landscape in which he took an almost proprietary interest, the delights of Puck Fair and of the saloon bars. At the root of this was what Michael Bowles described as:

> ... a close sympathy for country people, whether in East Norfolk or North Roscommon, and he remembered his socialite days in Boyle with a light and totally irreverent distaste. This conditioned his attitude to The Plain People of Ireland (a cant

[3] In 'The Music of E. J. Moeran': 'two of the foremost composers of the English school, Sir Arnold Bax and E. J. Moeran, have found in Ireland a spiritual home'.
[4] *loc. cit.*

Sir Hamilton Harty in 1935.

phrase nowadays [thanks, perhaps, to the writings of Flann O'Brien]) and, as he pointed out to me, also his life style when he went to live near Kenmare.[5]

So absorbed did Moeran become in his Irish identity that we may well consider Aloys Fleischmann to be justified in claiming him as an Irish composer.

A work to bridge both English and Irish cultures was the Symphony in G Minor. The work had a chequered history, as we have seen: commissioned in 1924 by Harty and almost completed, it was withdrawn as the composer was unhappy with it. He resumed work on the Symphony in 1934 and with Harty's encouragement was occupied with it for another two-and-a-half years. Harty received news of its progress from time to time; Robert Nichols had spoken to him of it, and Harty wrote to the composer:

> He spoke of your Symphony as being partly completed. This was good news, and I am looking forward so greatly to seeing the work fully completed with the orch. parts ready – and the score lying between us as we discuss various points of inter-pretation! Good luck to your pen and may this summer bring you the necessary inspiration and lucky moods for work so that the Symphony may be finished.[6]

According to a pencilled note on the autograph score, the

[5] In a letter to the author dated 26 January 1981.
[6] Letter dated 29 March 1935.

1/24/87 / 2:45 pm

Symphony was finally completed 'on Jan. 24th 1937, 2.45 p.m.
Valentia Island'. Its composition had spanned some twelve
years and two environments – those of Norfolk and of Kerry.

In the event, the work did not receive its first performance
under Harty – that honour fell to Leslie Heward, who conducted it at a Royal Philharmonic Society concert in January
1938. Why not Harty? The misunderstanding and handling of
this episode provide some insight into Moeran's clumsiness in
dealing with fellow professionals, although it is possible to
sympathise with him in what appears to have been a dilemma.
According to Harty's secretary, 'Harty grew very impatient
with Moeran's erratic and, at times, embarrassing behaviour'.[7]

On 8 September 1937, Moeran wrote to Harty to explain
that, because of Harty's recent illness, Messrs Novello and the
BBC had fixed up the first performance by Heward, as they had
not thought Harty would be recovered in time. Nevertheless, he
yet wanted Harty to accept the dedication:

> It would be a great honour and pleasure to me if you would
> accept the dedication of the Symphony. I had from the very first
> intended to ask your permission to do this when the work would
> be finished, and I very much hope you will agree. May I write
> your name at the head of the score?[8]

This letter mentions the work progressing on the Violin Concerto, and continues:

> I should very much like you to see my completed score one of
> these days i.e., if you won't feel inclined to shoot me . . . .

Now, this is open to misinterpretation: it is clear that Harty
thought he was being offered the Violin Concerto instead. We
do not have his reply, but it must have been fairly salty, for
Moeran's next letter has the air of affronted and aggrieved
innocence:

> I had no intention of bothering you with the score of my Violin
> Concerto . . . . It is a terrible disappointment to me that you do
> not feel inclined to accept the dedication. I have no wish to
> dedicate it to anyone else, so it must stand as it is without one. I

[7] David Greer, in a letter to the author dated 12 August 1981.
[8] Letter dated 8 September 1937.

cannot see that there is any valid reason or precedent whereby a
large work should be inscribed to the conductor who directs its
first performance.[9]

In the end, Moeran had his way, and the dedication to Harty
stands at the head of the score. Heward, however, not only gave
the first performance but also made the first recording.
Acquainted with Heward since the early 1920s, Moeran had
come to share the almost universal view among musicians that
the modest, cloth-capped conductor, with his awesome technical and musical resources, was the finest British conductor of
his day. He heard a number of performances of his Symphony
and never made any secret of the fact that he considered
Heward to be its finest interpreter.

Although critical reactions were mixed, the Symphony
prompted much discussion and made an impression – Moeran,
at the age of 44, had scored his first major success. It was the
first symphony to be recorded under the auspices of the British
Council, and *The Music Review* published an extended analysis
by Heathcote Statham.[10]

The Symphony is in four movements: an *Allegro* in sonata
form, *Lento*, *Scherzo* (*Vivace*), and Finale (*Lento – Allegro Molto*).
At a first hearing the most noticeable feature might well be the
responses made to other composers. Certainly, it was the very
obvious influences that were seized upon by the earliest critics.
Since the choice of models may well reveal to an extent the kind
of symphony the composer envisaged, some of these models are
considered here before we examine the structure of the work.

The influence of Sibelius on the work was noted early; later
Arthur Hutchings was to perceive that a style such as that of
Sibelius will not necessarily fit too well on a temperament such
as that of Moeran:

> It's useless to pretend that he commanded an epic style with a
> purposeful forward tread – even the brilliant Bax didn't manage
> that; moreover, unless he were merely to present a meditative
> and improvisatory pastoral work, he felt there should be mena-
> cing and wintry moods which in Sibelius are thematic, part of

[9] Dated 17 September 1937.
[10] 'Moeran's Symphony in G minor', *The Music Review*, Vol. 1, No. 3, 1940, pp. 245–254.

Leslie Heward, conducting the BBC Northern Orchestra in November 1942.

the slow harmonic tick-over that is utterly alien to the nervous Bax or Moeran.[11]

Sibelius was enjoying a peak of popularity in the 1930s. Constant Lambert promoted his work in the thought-provoking *Music Ho!*,[12] as did Cecil Gray in his *Survey of Contemporary Music*.[13] Bax and Vaughan Williams both dedicated works to him (the latter his Fifth Symphony 'without permission'), and Harriet Cohen describes Bax listening to *Tapiola* with tears of emotion streaming down his face.[14]

Moeran joined this general eulogy; he certainly knew *Tapiola*, and the evidence of his Symphony supports the view that he was well acquainted with the Sibelius Symphonies – especially Nos. 2, 3 and 4.

The Finnish master had, perhaps, more influence on the

[11] *loc. cit.*
[12] Published in 1934.
[13] O.U.P., London, 1924.
[14] *A Bundle of Time*, Faber, London, 1969, p.65.

English composers than on anyone else outside his own country. This influence can be seen in Walton (the Symphony No. 1 in B flat minor), in the later Bax symphonies and in those of Vaughan Williams from the Fourth onwards. For Moeran he seemed a natural model. And even if such responses were unconscious, they point to Moeran's path of thought. The stylistic reappraisal in which he had been engaged had armed Moeran with the necessary contrapuntal technique, although he had not written instrumentally on a large scale since the early 1920s. He had not, indeed, written in any extended way for a large orchestra since that time. Sibelius seemed to provide the key, to show the way forward. Moeran had from early days used a Sibelian method of construction, which I have called the 'parent cell' technique. What now appears to be added are certain Sibelian characteristics of melody, orchestration and texture.

But Moeran showed other responses, and 'response' spotting now becomes almost too easy a game to play. Gradually, the suspicion dawns that perhaps Moeran is developing what would be, for him, a new technique – a further phase of the stylistic reappraisal discussed in Chapter V. What if his music were to work by using our knowledge of other, *specific* works, and ones which are accepted *loci classici* for particular emotional gestures? In this event, our listening would take account not only of the Moeran passage, but also of its model; the total listening experience would be compounded of Moeran heard in the light of the model – on occasion, indeed, the Moeran might make ironic comment on the model. Against this, it must be said that he was not always conscious that he had used a model. Arnold Bax recalled a case in point: 'I well remember his perturbation when I pointed out to him that a passage in his Symphony bore a remarkable resemblance to the famous whirlwind in *Tapiola*'.[15]

Although I am unable to substantiate that the referential use of models was a technique Moeran used consciously, I offer it as a working hypothesis. Nor would I expect that the effect of intensification of meaning in these works, which I feel in performance, is felt by all others. But I do believe that this body

[15] *loc. cit.*

of specific musical instances taken collectively is sufficient to justify the view that in the Symphony and Violin Concerto 'derivation' goes considerably beyond normal influence.

I do not consider that Moeran's achievement in these and other works is lessened any more by this than is Wagner's by his borrowings from Liszt and Meyerbeer, or Dvořák's by his from Brahms. For only the manner is borrowed; the idea is unique to the composer.

The composers called on in the Symphony, consciously or unconsciously, include – apart from Sibelius – Tchaikovsky, Elgar, Brahms and Mozart. These are readily identified – there are possibly others awaiting a musical sleuth. *models*

The Moeran Symphony has been variously described as 'rather wild but not unimpressive',[16] 'cloud-hung and windswept',[17] and (of its conclusion) 'bitter and disturbed'.[18] It also has marked elegiac qualities, and to an extent these moods have determined the referential points taken from its predecessors.

Moeran much admired Tchaikovsky, especially for the clarity of his orchestration. Here, the reference work is the Symphony No. 6 in B minor (the *Pathétique*), and it is the opening movements of each work which are comparable. In both, the secondary ideas are pentatonic in construction. Both *Chaik* secondary ideas – almost concepts of an ideal beauty – are *# 6* isolated in their respective contexts, and die away dynamically and rhythmically. In both, the central development commences with an orchestral explosion of some force, to be followed by nervous string writing which obliterates memory of the recent encapsulated moments of serene repose.

The music of Elgar had similarly evoked a continuing response from Moeran, who lost no opportunity to defend him at a time when his critical stock was low:

> I have unbounded admiration for . . . Elgar's Second Symphony . . . . I, too, remember the first performance of Elgar's *Falstaff*, as I was one of the few enthusiasts who was present at

[16] Stephen Lloyd, 'E. J. Moeran: Some Influences on his Music', *Musical Opinion*, February 1981, pp. 174–177. Mr Lloyd quotes 'Britten's cautious description'.
[17] Colin Scott-Sutherland, *Arnold Bax*, J. M. Dent, London, 1973, p. 131.
[18] Stephen Lloyd, *loc. cit.*

the Queen's Hall, and I was shocked at the rows of empty seats on that occasion. It was difficult to square this with the public acclamation with which repeated performances of the First Symphony and the Violin Concerto had been hailed only a short while before.

In conclusion, let me express the hope that the recent report that Sir Edward Elgar is 'at it again' after nine years' silence, and is writing a large work, may prove to be true, and that he may succeed in adding yet another masterpiece to an honourable series.'[19]

As far as Moeran's own Symphony is concerned, the referential work is the Elgar Symphony No. 2 in E flat. The 'Spirit of Delight' does indeed visit Elgar's Symphony but rarely, and much of it is elegiac in character. For the slow movement there is a funeral march, which became an 'In Memoriam' for King Edward VII. It is this movement which is reflected by Moeran in his slow movement, particularly in style and scoring in the closing pages. A further reference occurs in Moeran's last movement rondo, where his central episode is related to the parallel structural point in Elgar's last movement (Ex. 25 (a) and (b)).

Ex. 25

(a)
Elgar

(b)
Moeran

---

[19] In a letter to *The Musical Times* of February 1933; undated, but probably January 1933.

While there is no specific evidence to indicate Moeran's view of the music of Brahms, he clearly knew it well and would in his youth in all probability have played much of Brahms' chamber *Brahms* music. The reference here, however, would appear to be to a Symphony, and specifically to Brahms' Symphony No. 2 in D, and in particular to its third movement. One of the episodes in Moeran's Scherzo is related to those in the Brahms third movement (Ex. 26).

Ex. 26

(a) Moeran

(b) Brahms

But it is to Sibelius that the G minor Symphony is chiefly indebted. There is first of all a structural influence, absorbed *5,6* probably from a study of the first movement of Sibelius' *2* Symphony No. 2 in D major. In Sibelius' design, the climactic point of the movement is reached just before the recapitulation, which itself is considerably condensed. Moeran follows this precedent (so, incidentally, does Walton in his First Symphony).

The slow movement of the Sibelius Second Symphony also provides a point of departure for that of Moeran. Even more *2:2* striking than this, however, is the referential connection with the opening of the *Andantino con moto* of the Sibelius Symphony *5:3* No. 3 in C. Sibelius' *Andantino* opens with sustained horns over a soft timpani roll, with the melody commencing in the flutes at the fourth bar. Moeran closely follows this texture.

His Scherzo, too, is patterned on Sibelius – on the scherzi of both Third and Fourth Symphonies. Interestingly enough, these two Sibelius scherzi are themselves related; both commence with oboe themes, which are tied over the bar and which descend scalically. Moeran's oboe theme is similar in shape but is approached scalically. The scherzo in Sibelius's Fourth Symphony has a *divisi* viola accompaniment, which Moeran echoes with his violin accompaniment (Ex. 27(a) and (b)). Moeran, however, phrases it in twos, to create a syncopation across the bar. For his first episode, Sibelius moves into $\frac{2}{4}$ time; so does Moeran.

Ex. 27

The Sibelius Fourth Symphony is the most grim and forbidding of the seven: it came at a period when the composer was suffering from cancer of the throat and contemplating an early death (in the event, he lived to be 92). While Moeran's Symphony is generally a grim affair, the scherzo is something of an oasis – it is warm and spring-like, whereas the Sibelius is cold and impersonal. Only the manner is shared.

When Bax pointed out the indebtedness of parts of Moeran's fourth movement to the climactic storm in *Tapiola*, the passage he had in mind is to be found between references 107 and 115 of the Novello score. Bleak implacability appears to be the mood of both Moeran and Sibelius in their respective works, but the Second and Fifth Symphonies of Sibelius are also echoed in the Moeran last movement. Towards its climax, considerable tension is generated by the repetition of a passage over and over again. The referential passage in the Sibelius Second Symphony occurs in its last movement, before its final peroration.

In the Sibelius, however, the tension achieves its release in that triumphant peroration. The tension in Moeran achieves no such release; after a short retrospective passage, his Symphony ~~M~~ ends in a sequence of abrupt, angry chords. Again, there is a reference point in Sibelius for this. His Fifth Symphony had ended thus, but his breath-taking sequence of chords is trium- $S:S$ phant, not bitter. The Symphony No. 1 of Walton has a similar ending – and a similar ancestor. Sibelius achieves his triumphant resolution; Walton *appears* to achieve his; but there is no such resolution for Moeran, whose comment on Sibelius now seems to possess a savage irony.

That Mozart should provide a point of reference – or even a point of departure – for a 20th-century work may occasion some surprise, although one does not have to look further than Stravinsky for another example. It is the key of Moeran's Symphony (G minor) which points to the relationship for it is very difficult to think of many symphonies written in this key. There is the First Symphony (*Winter Daydreams*) by Tchaikovsky, and the second of the two by the Swedish composer, Vilhelm Stenhammar (1871–1927),[20] as well as the Haydn Nos. 39 and 83 G M ('The Hen'), the *Symphonie Sérieuse* of the earlier Swede, Franz Berwald (1796–1868), the First Symphonies of the Russian Vassily Kalinnikov (1866–1901) and of Carl Nielsen (written in 1892, three years before Kalinnikov's; the Nielsen, however, moves away from G minor to C major), and Albert Roussel's Third (1930); but most people would think immediately of those by Mozart, and in particular No. 40, к.550 (the other one in G minor – No. 25 – is very close to No. 40 in several respects). This Symphony, and specifically its opening, stands as a musical symbol of disciplined emotion – the emotion of elegiac melancholy. Is it too fanciful to postulate that Moeran deliberately directs our attention to the Mozartian parallel by his choice of key? If this is hard to accept, a comparison of the opening statements of the two Symphonies may make it easier to swallow. Essentially, the Mozart is about a poised and

[20] Colin Scott-Sutherland (in a letter to the author, June 1983) finds 'very definite points of contact' between the Moeran and Stenhammar G minor Symphonies. The Stenhammar work dates from 1915 and pays it own respects to Sibelius. Mr Scott-Sutherland draws attention to certain similarities of woodwind figuration and accompaniment patterns to those of the Moeran.

balanced melodic statement of some emotional distress, which is nevertheless contained or gripped within the relentless rhythmic drive of the accompaniment. Moeran's opening statement is really concerned with the same concept, and is expressed in similar musical language. These referential models point us towards the meaning of the Symphony. Further conjecture concerning the nature of that meaning must be deferred a while until the structure of the work has been considered, since the structure is itself an integral part of that meaning.

It is the structure of the Symphony which has tended to attract criticism, and much of this criticism has centred on the last movement. Possibly, such criticism was unwittingly encouraged by the composer. Michael Bowles writes:[21]

> I remember clearly his opinion that the last movement was 'five minutes too long'. I have never seriously examined suitable points for cutting. Unfortunately, I did not question him there and then about where the cuts might be.

Professor J.A. Westrup wrote:[22]

> He has realised the importance of logic, but he is also willing to allow himself to be diverted from his argument. We find this tendency again in the Finale, where there seems to be an excess of material. Moeran has sometimes been criticised for not knowing what to reject.

Even Professor Fleischmann, one of Moeran's most penetrating critics and one of his staunchest defenders, finds problems with the Finale, and defines precisely what the problem *seems* to be:

> The finale, however, would seem to be the stumbling block of the Symphony. After an exceptionally spacious slow movement, and a scherzo which, for all its incipient playfulness, keeps slipping back into that wistful, forlorn mood which is at the heart of the whole symphony, a firmly knit finale would be needed to sum up all the foregoing elements and balance the whole design. But the materials which go to make up the finale . . . do not cohere sufficiently, and the movement loses momentum more and more as it draws towards a close.[23]

[21] In a letter to the author dated 26 January 1981.
[22] *loc. cit.*, p. 181.
[23] *loc. cit.*, p. 64.

This view of the finale is at the least contestable; but Professor
Fleischmann does then come close to seeing a possible reason
for the course taken by this music:

> One can imagine poetic justification for the design of the finale,
> but the fact remains that towards the end of three-quarters of an
> hour of concentrated listening, the average hearer needs the
> stimulus of a more sustained rhythmic build-up.[24]

These are weighty criticisms. Yet it may be possible to show
poetic *reason*, if not 'poetic justification', for the design. Indeed,
there may be a poetic basis for the design of the Symphony as a
whole. It may also be possible to show that there is in this last
movement a convincing summary, without 'loss of momentum'
of the 'foregoing elements' of the entire Symphony.

For, to Moeran, structural coherence was vital. As Aloys
Fleischmann said, 'it was Moeran's habit to work out his basic
material with the utmost exactitude, so that almost every detail
can be related to one or other of a few parent ideas'.[25]

Whatever else was retained from the original structure of
1924, we may safely assume that the essentials of the second
movement – a brooding *Lento* – date back to then, since Moeran
said that the material for this movement was conceived among
the sand dunes and marshes of East Norfolk. According to
Professor Fleischmann,[26] the rest of the work was written in
Kerry, chiefly on Valentia Island.

Thus the Symphony brings us to the heart of Moeran's
Irish/English dichotomy, since we learned from Bax that, in his
view, Moeran's awareness of his Celticism dated from the early
1930s; if true, the creation of this work spans the two cultures
and environments. By Moeran's own admission,[27] the environment of nature was essential to his inspiration. One might then
expect major stylistic inconsistencies unless the essentials of the
four movements in fact date from 1924. And the work does
impress by its unity and 'wholeness'. Why is this?

To find out, we must look again at those Norfolk tunes

[24] *ibid.*, pp. 64-65.
[25] *ibid.*, p.64.
[26] *ibid.*, p.64.
[27] Quoted in Leonard Duck, 'Inspiration: Fact and Theory', *The Musical Times*,
January 1953, p.13.

arranged by Moeran in 1924. One of the six songs was the hauntingly beautiful *Lonely Waters*, subsequently turned into the short orchestral piece of that name. Another was *The Shooting of his Dear* – and on this tune Moeran based the Symphony in G minor.

2ⁿᵈ mvt

O come all you young fellows that carry your gun,
I'd have you get home by the light of the sun,
For young Jimmy was a fowler, and a-fowling alone,
When he shot his own true love in the room of a swan.

Then home went young Jimmy with his dog and his gun,
Saying, Uncle, dear Uncle, have you heard what I've done?
Cursed be that old gunsmith that made my old gun.
I have shot my own true love in the room of a swan.

Then out came bold Uncle, with his locks hanging grey,
Saying, Jimmy, dear Jimmy, don't you go away,
Don't you leave your own country till your trial come on,
For you never will be hanged for shooting a swan.

So the trial came on and Pretty Polly did appear,
Saying, Uncle, dear Uncle, let Jimmy go clear,
For my apron was bound round me and he took me for a swan,
And his poor heart lay bleeding for Polly his own.

The melody was included in the collection published by Moeran in the *Folk Song Journal*. It had been sung to him by Mr W. Gales at Sutton, Norfolk, in October 1921. In the *Journal*, it is annotated very fully, the gist of which is that there are many variants of the tune known. Most interesting of these is the comment of a certain L.E.B.: 'I have noted a tune in the Western Highlands of Scotland, the text of which turns on the same subject as this and the Irish *Peggy Bawn*'.[28] Michael Bowles comments: 'I first knew the song under the title *Young Molly Ban* (Joyce's Old Irish Folk Music and Songs)', and adds that Moeran was interested in Irish folk music considerably before the time when his interest in Ireland itself was properly kindled: 'His stay in Boyle during the last of World War I interested him in Irish Folk Song and the people who sang it'.[29]

[28] EJM, 'Songs collected in Norfolk'.
[29] In a letter to the author dated 26 January 1981.

The melody *The Shooting of his Dear* is set out as Ex. 28.

Ex. 28

O come all you young fel-lows that car-ry your gun, I'd

have you get home by the light of- the- sun, for young Jimmy was a

fowl-er, and a-fowl-ing a- lone, when he shot his own

true love in the room of a swan.

*The correspondence of this passage with the opening of the Folksong becomes clear when the passage is transposed down a fifth.

Because the slow movement is the one which irrefutably dates from 1924, our discussion of the structure begins with this movement, moving outwards thereafter to the other movements. One reason for this approach is that the slow movement is the core of the Symphony, from which the necessity for the other movements grows. Another is that the slow movement holds the clue left by the composer as a key to the structure and possibly, therefore, to the 'meaning'.

Creative musicians do not, as is commonly supposed, necessarily have an overwhelming desire to communicate to the world in general – and specially to communicate their innermost thoughts. For example, a vast amount of Schumann's work, as Eric Sams has shown,[30] enshrined coded messages which could have been understood only by Clara Schumann – the person for whom they were intended. More immediately relevant is the case of Elgar, whose irritability whenever anyone came too near to the explanation of his *Enigma* is well known. Moeran laid a clue and then covered his tracks.

Professor Fleischmann has described the slow movement of the G minor Symphony as 'one of the finest pieces of nature music ever written',[31] a bold, but not unreasonable claim. Perhaps it may be more than just 'nature music'. First of all, the clue to which reference was made above is this: in his 1924 arrangement of *The Shooting of his Dear* (hereafter referred to as the Folksong) Moeran provided a few bars of piano introduction (Ex. 29). This piano introduction is quoted, with altered rhythm but with substantially the same harmony, in the slow movement. A comparison of Ex. 29 with the passage for divided cellos heard at 35 plus 5 in the score (Ex. 30) will demonstrate the point. This introduction itself derives from bars 8 – 10 of the Folksong.

With this clue, we might reasonably proceed on the assumption that the Folksong itself will be used; and so it proves to be. The movement is a free meditation on the Folksong, and as such we would not expect it necessarily to follow any of the standard forms. In fact, it falls into two sections. These sections are not separated in any sense and the thought is so sustained that nothing impedes the flow to a climax of searing intensity.

---

[30] 'Did Schumann use Ciphers?', *The Musical Times*, August 1965, pp. 584–590; and 'The Tonal Analogue in Schumann's Music', *Proceedings of the Royal Musical Association*, Vol. 96, 1969–70, reprinted in Alan Walker (ed.), *Robert Schumann: The Man and his Music*, Barrie & Jenkins, London, 1972.

[31] *loc. cit.*

Ex. 29

FS

2ⁿᵈ MVT

Sec 1 - short phrases & motifs

Sec 2 - extended melodies

Ex. 30

Ritornello

5:2

The first section consists mainly of short phrases and motives, the second of extended melodies. This method of structure owes little to the forms traditionally used in symphonies – sonata form, rondo, ternary form, etc. Rather, it derives from the practice of Sibelius as seen, for example, in the first movement of his comparatively early Symphony No. 2, where the fragmentary and apparently unconnected ideas presented in the first part of the movement synthesise into a sustained flight of melody. Throughout Moeran's movement, the 'clue' phrase (Ex. 30) acts as a kind of ritornello, marking off and introducing paragraphs.

The ideas which form the mosaic of the first section of the movement can all be related to the Folksong. Ex. 31, heard at *Sec 1* the outset in the divided cellos and basses, corresponds to bars 9 and 10 of the Folksong. The example appears to be a

Ex. 31

Sec 1

Bars 9 and 10 of the Folksong

reduction to its basic outline of those Folksong bars. This brooding phrase recurs throughout the movement, and ultimately provides its climax.

The second idea (Ex. 32) is heard first in the flutes in the fourth bar. It corresponds to bars 1 and 2, and 8 and 9 of the Folksong and is thus also related to the 'clue' phrase (Ex. 30).

Ex. 32

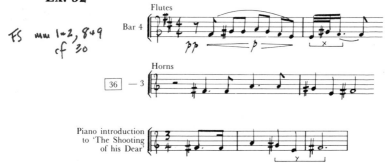

The third idea (Ex. 33) corresponds to bars 13 and 14 of the Folksong and is heard first in the woodwind at the eleventh bar,

Ex. 33

over a timpani roll. It is a classic example of a basic Moeran shape – three upward steps and a leap – characteristic of Irish and Norfolk song. Indeed, it is here a rationalisation of those bars in the Folksong from which it came, and in due course blossoms into a soaring arch of melody (Ex. 34). Moeran was to remember it years later when he came to work on the (unfinished) Symphony No. 2.

The second part of the movement begins with a reminder in the horns of the 'clue' phrase, heralding perhaps the most striking passage in the Symphony. The strings adopt the

Ex. 34

accompanimental across-the-strings figure used just previously for Ex. 34. The woodwind enrich the texture almost in the manner of Smetana at the opening of *Vltava*. Beneath this watery onomatopoeia is buried far below in the cellos and basses what appears to be a complete melodic variation of *The Shooting of his Dear*. At this point, Moeran brings the music to the key (E minor modal) in which he set the song in his 1924 arrangement. Underneath Ex. 28, which gave the complete Folksong, is set this cello and bass passage from the Symphony so that the correspondence of the two lines may be compared. It may be noted in passing that, while the first phrase of the Folksong is repeated (with minor modifications), this repeat is ignored in the Symphony variant.

The first seven notes of the Folksong are transposed in the Symphony version. Why this is done we cannot say with any certainty; the transposition produces a melody shape inferior to that of the original. Since it would have been possible to use the untransposed version here, it is difficult to escape the conclusion that the motive was disguise, although why he should choose to disguise the Folksong is something only for conjecture. In my view, it was a matter of emotional reticence – the reason for the choice of this folksong in particular may have had such profound significance for the composer as to dictate in turn that this emotional core be concealed.

It is given two further treatments. The first, incomplete, is still in the cellos and basses, but the accompaniment is if anything rather more 'aquatic', with rapid arpeggio figures in the woodwind and strings. After a climax of real power, the music crystallises into a mood of elegiac beauty and restraint for a final statement (complete) of the disguised Folksong. Now, the feeling is unmistakably that of a funeral march while the manner is unmistakably Elgarian – the Elgar of the slow movement of the Second Symphony. A final withered reference to the three-steps-and-a-leap melody serves as a poignant reminder of its great blossoming now past, and the movement is over.

The next step is to establish whether or not the Folksong is used in any of the other three movements. The big opening melody (Ex. 35) of the first movement is neither heard again in its entirety nor in the style of its first appearance (Moeran thus appears to have learnt a lesson never really learnt by Elgar, and only fitfully by Tchaikovsky.) It is possible that this fine melody, which constitutes the primary idea of the movement, is itself a very free variant of the Folksong. In this case, however, the process would appear to differ from the slow movement in that the repetition of the first phrase of the folksong is used in the melody structure. As in the case of the slow movement, I set out one melody under the other (the Folksong transposed up a minor third). What appear to me to be points of identity are marked with asterisks; the reader must judge for himself the extent to which the suggestion is probable. Moeran's work does appear to be melodic rather than harmonic in structural basis, and whether or not this melody is entirely a variant of the Folksong, there is no doubt that it is extensively quarried for ideas. Prominent among these ideas is one of the three parent cells which determine the outer movements of the Symphony. This cell is shown under brackets in Ex. 35, and is designated parent cell *A*.

Ex. 35

On its appearance a few bars later, the primary idea is announced by a fanfare-like figure for four horns (Ex. 36), which also acts as a counterpoint to it. Embedded in this fanfare is the second of the three parent cells – cell *B*. These two cells have a common ancestry – while they feature respectively in the primary idea and in its accompanying fanfare, they can in addition both be traced back to the Folksong. Ex. 36 shows not only the Folksong phrase which supplied them, but also the way in which the cells themselves are linked. The words of this phrase of the Folksong may be noted: 'For young Jimmy was a fowler'.

The secondary idea is shown as Ex. 37. It, too, finds a place for cell *A* – albeit an obscure one (shown under brackets in Ex. 37). The third parent cell – *C* – can also be traced to this secondary idea. At this stage it is not a prominent figure, but it is nevertheless a seed which grows mightily in importance. Further, it can stand as a symbol for the secondary idea – that is to say, as a symbol for whatever meaning it may have. The fact

Ex. 36

For young Jim-my was a fowler.

Horns

Outline   yields

i Cell B

ii Cell A

iii Moeran 'root' cell

that *C* has no link with the Folksong may have significance
when we come to consider meaning. The secondary idea itself is
of real beauty – it must have required either some courage, or
perhaps some innocence, to write a pentatonic melody of such
disarming simplicity for a symphony in the sophisticated '20s
and '30s. While it would stand as a stereotype for the concept of
folksong, it does not suggest any particular folksong. Here in
the exposition, the melody blooms radiantly, and is isolated in
treatment and in distance of key (B major from the prevailing G
minor). Linked only tenuously to the primary idea by the
common cell *A*, it otherwise occupies a world of imagined
beauty vastly different from the rigour of the opening of the
Symphony.

While these three cells dominate the two outer movements,
they have no apparent influence on the two middle ones. Thus
the third movement (a scherzo) is in particular structurally

Ex. 37   Pentatonic

Cell A

Allargando molto   *a tempo*

etc.

Cell C   Cell C

Cell C

isolated from the rest of the Symphony, while the slow movement offers a structural paradox, since none of the parent cells
themselves appear to be used other than in the Folksong itself.
This would support the view that the slow movement is the
oldest surviving part of the Symphony: if this movement has
been salvaged from the original version more or less intact, it
would seem inevitable that the only way of relating or welding
the new outer movements to the existing movement would be
by cellular relationship – the cells being derived from the
existing movement.

Thus the relationship of the slow movement to the rest of the
Symphony seems logical enough. But what of the Scherzo? This
movement has claims to be unique in British music. The
creation of a real scherzo – a movement light in meaning,
movement and texture – is something that very often eluded
British composers. Certainly the scherzi in the two Symphonies

uniqueness of scherzo

of Elgar are hardly comparable, the one ferocious in energy and the other overshadowed by its awesome centre section. Bax favoured a three-movement form, omitting any kind of scherzo. Those of Vaughan Williams tend to suffer from a certain lumpiness of rhythm, only compounded by the complex syncopated rhythmic textures adopted by the composer in his attempts to escape it. That of Walton in the First Symphony is ephemeral enough, but is sardonic and, in his own marking, *con malizia*. The Moeran scherzo is a true, light innocent interlude – a contrasting relief in an otherwise passionate and dramatic work. Since contrast is its function, and isolation its protection, it seems only logical that it should not use those cells so deeply identified with the storm and stress of the outer movements.

These outer movements, however, are shot through with the three parent cells. In the first movement cells *A* and *B* are set in antagonism to *C*, the development and coda sections being their battlefield. In the last movement, cell *A* is at the heart of the primary idea (Ex. 39, below), but it is cell *B* which gains ascendancy over both *A* and *C*. That figure (Exx. 29 and 30), which Moeran had used as his piano introduction for *The Shooting of his Dear* in its version for voice and piano, also plays an increasingly dominant part in this movement. Each movement has a specific role. The first movement is an exposition of conflict – a conflict between the rigour and discipline of the primary idea, together with its attendant martial fanfare, and the pastoral vision of the secondary idea. No resolution of this conflict is achieved by the end of the movement. The slow movement, bleak and elegiac by turns, is the fulcrum, and indeed the fountainhead, of the Symphony. In its progress it gradually achieves the quality of a funeral march. The scherzo is an interlude; it is a point at which tension is momentarily relaxed, although even here there is that slightly forlorn mood never too far away in Moeran. The tension and struggle return in the last movement.

From the beginning of the 19th century onwards, there is a tendency in the symphony for the main weight of argument to be placed in the last movement – in comparison, that is, with the 18th-century symphony where the last movement might well have been lightweight. It was this tendency which created the 'last-movement problem' which has bedevilled symphonic composers from (and including) Beethoven, and which has been solved with only varying degrees of success. Moeran's attempted solution is more successful than has been allowed in past criticism. His rondo is so drastically modified from the traditional rondo that it, and the symphony as a whole, reaches its climax towards the end of the last movement – no mean achievement, for the traditional rondo shape is not naturally conducive to such a sense of climax.

S.'4

But there is still no resolution to the conflict.

An imaginative and creative approach to problems of structure is characteristic of Moeran. In the first movement, there appears to be a poetic need that the muscular, leaping primary idea should seem in recapitulation but a shadow of its original self. In this recapitulation the material is so transformed as to alter its meaning – or rather, to make ironic comment on its original meaning. If there is a homecoming here, it is a homecoming chastened by experience. The key (A minor) is 'wrong', (i.e., not in the original 'home' of G minor) the accompanying quavers, once relentless, are now languid. The horn fanfare, so brazen in exposition, no longer swaggers, and all the primary material now peters out in a death rattle of soft percussion. What had covered some 53 bars in exposition is here dismissed in 15. In much the same way, the secondary idea, which bloomed so radiantly in the exposition, is here withered – whatever meaning it had on its first appearance is now distorted.

S! 1 RₑCₐₚ

All this has dictated the placing of the movement's climax which (following the example of Sibelius in the Second Symphony) is reached just before the recapitulation begins. Here for the first time in his orchestral work, Moeran achieves a coincidence of both tension and dynamic climax. The tension results from the massive effort required to re-impose the discipline with which the movement had opened on a convergence of two major ideas – the crowning one being derived from cell *A* (Ex. 38).

cₗᵢₘₐₓ bₑfₒᵣₑ ᵣₑcₐₚ.

The same adventurous approach is seen in the last movement, in which traditional usage would require a final appearance at the end of the movement of the rondo idea. Moeran

Ex. 38

dispenses with this, and in its place he introduces a further hearing of the central episode of the movement (Ex. 39 (a)). This departure from the formal stereotype has two drastic *effects of departure from style* effects. First, a much stronger sense of climax at the end of the movement is engineered, and this is itself enhanced by a notable inspiration. The central episode idea, which had been in $\frac{3}{2}$ time, now gains an extra beat, thus lengthening each bar into $\frac{7}{4}$ time to heighten the labouring, dragging impression produced by the processional at this point. Again, Sibelius (last movement of the Second Symphony) is the model for the way in which tension is increased by repetition of the key phrase over and over again. This leads to the second drastic effect of the modification to the formal rondo stereotype, for all the sympho-

Ex. 39

Piano introduction to 'The Shooting of his Dear'

This episode had been introduced thus:

etc.

Primary Idea

Allegro molto

(b)

etc.

Cell A

nic resource is now concentrated on this phrase. It is a phrase which is derived from cell *B* which in turn is derived (as shown in Ex. 36) from the Folksong at the words 'for young Jimmy was a fowler'. Here, in the placing of the most striking of all the Moeran processionals with all its now-loaded meaning, is 'poetic reason' for the design.

The music dies away, and in a remarkable piece of sound metamorphosis, the woodwind (Ex. 40) gradually melt the 'Jimmy was a fowler' phrase into parent cell *A*. Thus, at the end of the Symphony, Moeran gently shows us, if we had not grasped it before, how the two most fundamental cells *A* and *B* are but aspects of the same thing, and how they both came from contemplation of one song – perhaps even just one phrase of one song.

Ex. 40

Most commentaries on the Symphony in G minor have remarked on the bitterness of its conclusion. On the last page, a peremptory drum roll heralds a last passionate statement of the 'Jimmy was a fowler' phrase (parent cell *B*) and the Symphony is stopped short with six rough *fortissimo* chords. So troubling is this dramatic, even frustrated ending to a disturbed, bitter and elegiac work that I have felt bound to explore a conjectural hypothesis of meaning for the music, which may go some way in explanation of the otherwise apparently inexplicable.

We have a symphony begun in 1924 by a man who had only recently experienced the horror of the 1914–18 War and who was so severely wounded in it that he carried the marks of it to his death. The Symphony is based very largely on a folksong about a shooting accident. In it are to be found blossoming melodies, brave fanfares and symbols of discipline – all of which either wither or sound hollow on repetition. There is a slow movement in which a folksong appears disguised and buried beneath complex textures and which is transformed into an elegiac funeral song. There are sad processionals in both the first and last movements – processionals which can be traced directly to that Folksong phrase ('Jimmy was a fowler') on which the Symphony ultimately pins its full weight.

While Stravinsky may be correct in his view that music is powerless to express anything outside itself, the fact is that over the last few hundred years composers have frequently ignored the communicative limitations of music as a medium and have attempted to run counter to this interpretation of its nature. They may work through onomatopoeia, through a psychological association of idea, or through symbolism. Composers tend not to be illuminative about their work when writing about it: if they could express in words what they have to express, there would be little point in writing the music. It is possible to illumine what actually happens to the music – points of imitation, key change, melody structure, etc., and the music will have a purely musical meaning more or less apparent to the listener in proportion to his aesthetic appreciation. But if the composer was motivated by an extra-musical idea and yet left no note as to what this might be, we can either offer conjecture about that idea or give up the attempt to know the composer's intention. If we conjecture, the best we can hope for is unproven hypothesis; if the hypothesis is wide of the mark, the composer is fatally misrepresented.

Yet the attempt should be made. A language is being used and that language must be translated – or else the idea behind the music will be forever locked in the mind of the composer. There have been attempts to codify musical language in terms of universal music symbols and to identify the way in which music communicates to the emotions. The whole area is necessarily in shadow, and precise statements do not at present seem possible.

Sometimes a composer may help with a title – a *War* Requiem, for example, or a *Pastoral* Symphony. Yet he may be more reticent, even hope to conceal his meaning. A good

example of this might be the Sixth Symphony of Vaughan
Williams. In his own programme note, the composer osten-
tatiously discusses only the technicalities of the music, offering
no concrete support to those commentators who have professed
to see the last movement as a graphic portrayal of a world that
has seen the birth of atomic conflict. Moeran, too, wrote a programme note for his Symphony, to accompany its 1943 release
on 78s. It is concerned equally exclusively with musical matters,
and appears as Appendix 6 on p. 274.

In Moeran's case, my belief is that the Symphony in G minor
is some kind of Requiem or In Memoriam. This hypothesis can
hardly be proved. Neither is it possible to say with any certainty
whether it is a requiem for a person, a generation or an ideal.

One of the supports for my conjecture must be the use, in
three of the four movements, of *The Shooting of His Dear*, which
seems beyond reasonable doubt. Why he used it is less clear. It
is not a particularly striking or beautiful melody and Moeran
alters its opening for its use in the slow movement, making it
rather less attractive. We are led therefore to consider that its
use may not necessarily be for the melody as such but rather for
the significances of the words and especially of that third line
phrase most used in the Symphony: 'For young Jimmy was a
fowler'. Could there not be a loose allegory here of a young
soldier – Jack rather than Jim – called by duty to the war, his
illusions of military chivalry and nobility to be shattered by the
awesome reality of the sordid carnage and its bleak aftermath?

The Symphony presents a succession of images and symbols
which in their potency might well support such a hypothesis.
The first movement has images of grim determination lit by
other images of chivalry. These are contrasted with peaceful
pastoral music. The grim determined music exhausts itself; the
chivalric music has a reverse image – that of a funeral march.
The peaceful pastoral music is distorted and spoiled. The slow
movement musically and therefore symbolically buries its
Folksong, and underlines its point towards the end with a
stylistic reflection of the funeral march of the Second Symphony of Elgar.

The final movement has a mood predominantly of anger, a
feeling shared by many who served in the 1914–18 War. The

pastoral bliss of the first movement secondary idea never returns, and the music is obsessed with the reverse image of the first movement fanfare; what had in the first movement seemed funereal suggestions grow here – ultimately to dominate the entire finale. The nostalgic reminder in the last few bars of the first movement is bitter. The chords which end it are bitter.

Thus the Symphony ceases, but is hardly finished. The music ends, but the impulse which generated its power is hardly exhausted. The sublimation of bitterness would require another work for its expression.

VII. THE VIOLIN CONCERTO

The Symphony had seemed to fuel Moeran's confidence, and can now be seen as the first in a succession of more extended works than had been his wont, continuing with the Violin Concerto. Henry Wood waited for it patiently (Moeran was not to hurry it, 'because I know how letter perfect your work always is'[1]) and when it was completed, Wood was elated: 'Your letter has made me wildly excited, and I am terribly happy to know you have finished the Violin Concerto – Splendid! Bravo!'[2] In the summer of 1942, two years before his death, Wood conducted the first performance of the Concerto, with Arthur Catterall as soloist.

One of the earliest sources for information concerning the Concerto is an article by the critic and writer Edwin Evans which appeared in *The Musical Times* for August 1943. Evans states that the Concerto was begun on Valentia Island in 1938, the first movement being written

> during the summer calm. The rest of the work was composed at Kenmare, South Kerry, which lies at the landward end of the long fjord-like inlet of the Atlantic.[3]

The second movement

> a rondo – expresses the spirit of the summer fairs of Kerry, and particularly of the famous Puck's Fair of Killorgin, which lies to the north, near Castlemain Harbour and Dingle Bay. The retrospective third movement originated during the Autumn of 1941. In its concluding pages it reflects the calm experience in Southern Ireland at this season before the gales begin to burst in from the Atlantic.[4]

Evans was wrong, however, in stating that Moeran com-

---

[1] In a letter dated 18 March 1942.
[2] In a letter dated 10 April 1942.
[3] 'Moeran's Violin Concerto', pp. 233–234.
[4] *ibid.*

menced the Violin Concerto in 1938. On 24 January 1937 he had completed the Symphony: in his letter to Hamilton Harty dated 8 September 1937, Moeran wrote that he was 'now engaged on a concerto for May Harrison'.[5] We get some idea of the importance of the environment to the composer from the continuation of the letter:

> I propose going back to Kerry on Sept. 30th. Having started my concerto there, I want to finish it in the same surroundings. I am glad to say it is progressing well – far easier to write than a symphony, but then I am an ex-violinist, which helps a lot.

Subsequently, he wrote again to Harty:

> It is not yet finished and it may be a year or more before I am sufficiently satisfied with it to think of the question of performance.[6]

The essential point of this correspondence is that it shows Moeran to have been working on the Violin Concerto in September 1937; clearly, therefore, it had been commenced some while before this. The Symphony, in fact, can barely have been completed before he was occupied with his first thoughts on the Concerto. The point is of some importance, for I believe that the Symphony and Concerto are complementary – possibly even to the extent that the Violin Concerto may be considered as a completion of the Symphony. For the Symphony – noble, disturbed, elegiac and bitter by turns – is a questioning work. The Violin Concerto seeks to find and provide answers. Some of the 'reference composers' noted in the Symphony carry over into the Violin Concerto, although the actual 'reference' works differ considerably – and inevitably.

I imagine that Evans would have had the sanction of the composer for the observations he makes on the correlation

---

[5] The first performance of the Violin Concerto was in fact given by Arthur Catterall. According to Lionel Hill (*loc. cit.*) this was at the insistence of Arthur Bliss (then Director of Music at the BBC). Moeran told Hill that he had Sammons specifically in mind when writing the Violin Concerto. Sammons did perform it, but it was towards the end of his career, and despite strenuous efforts by Hill he never recorded it – a real loss, because Moeran thought Sammons' performance ideal.

[6] In a letter dated 17 September 1937.

A view of Valentia Island, Co. Kerry (courtesy of E. Myles Hook).

between the various movements of the work and the Kerry
scene, particularly the linking of the Rondo movement with the
Kerry fair days. Hubert Foss goes so far as to say of this
movement that 'one important theme is a tune written by the
composer in imitation of the effect of a tune he heard a young
man playing on the melodeon at one of the Irish fairs'.[7]
Something of what the fairs meant to Moeran is revealed in a
letter to Tilly Fleischmann:

> I particularly look forward to the ceremony of the crowning of
> King Puck; for various reasons, I have never been able to be
> present at the opening day of the fair.[8]

And subsequently the fair at Kenmare:

> I write this with considerable interruptions on fair day – the
> famous 'twintieth [*sic*] of October'. The place is howling with
> the squealing of pigs, the blaring of cattle and the various noises
> all going on together incidental to the October fair.'[9]

[7] *op. cit.*
[8] Dated 25 July 1938.
[9] In a letter in Peers Coetmore dated 20 October 1943.

The Concerto is very close to Ireland, its people and, indeed, the land itself. As Colin Scott-Sutherland has observed,[10] even the Violin Concerto of his friend Bax (significantly close in date: 1937) does not so betray its Irishness as does the Moeran work.

It was an *Irish* concerto that Moeran intended to write, a concerto which saw Ireland as a haven (which, to him, it was). And he signalled this intention with musical gestures. There is, for example, an Irish 'signal' in the first movement – an idea which, even when considered only melodically, suggests an Irish traditional dance (Ex. 41). The instrumentation underlines the point, for the tune is given to those two instruments which are in themselves traditional in Ireland – the flute and the harp.

Ex. 41

Moeran had a deep love of the Irish poets, and in particular for the work of James Joyce, to whose poems he returned for settings time after time. One Joyce poem, set in 1929 as the last of the *Seven Poems of James Joyce*, is perhaps the seed from which grew the Violin Concerto.

> Now, O now in this brown land
>   Where Love did so sweet music make
> We two shall wander, hand in hand,
>   Forbearing for old friendship's sake
> Nor grieve because our love was gay
> Which now is ended in this way.
>
> A rogue in red and yellow dress
>   Is knocking, knocking at the tree;
> And all around our loneliness
>   The wind is whistling merrily.
> The leaves – they do not sigh at all
> When the year takes them in the fall.

[10] *op. cit.*, p. 172.

Now, O now we hear no more
The villanelle and roundelay
Yet we will kiss, sweetheart, before
We take sad leave at close of day.
Grieve not, sweetheart, for anything –
The year, the year is gathering.

The music with which Moeran had opened his setting of these words is used, in varied form, for the openings of both first and last movements of the Concerto. As Stephen Banfield has pointed out, this passage, which is never played by the solo violin in the first movement, 'runs through it like an inarticulate thought'.[11]

Here the reference composer is Moeran himself; clearly, the thematic connection is deliberate, and the poem, in its bittersweet poignancy, must be relevant to the 'meaning' of the Concerto. Yet there is a discrepancy between the prevailing mood of the poem and the serene conclusion of the Concerto. Banfield suggests that lullaby ending – in D major, not the key of G in which it began – may well indicate a calmer acceptance than is felt in the setting of the poem; 'possibly some new understanding of his temperament is here achieved by the composer'.[12]

Possibly in the thought-process of many composers, and certainly in that of Moeran, the first step in writing a new work might well be the study of some admired model. This process will be most clearly seen in the Cello Concerto, but it is nevertheless also readily apparent in the Violin Concerto, where the admired models seem to be the Violin Concertos of Mendelssohn, Bax, Elgar, Delius and Harty. The parent-cell method of construction used by Moeran was shared, as Deryck Cooke has shown,[13] by Delius in his Violin Concerto. Just as in the Delius and the Mendelssohn, Moeran's soloist enters after only a few bars of introductory material. Moeran's solo theme here may be fruitfully compared with both Bax and Elgar (Ex. 42). The Bax (from the Ballad in the first movement) is in the

[11] Sleeve note for a recording of the Violin Concerto (Lyrita SRCS 105).
[12] *ibid.*
[13] Deryck Cooke, 'Delius and Form: A Vindication', *A Delius Companion*, ed. Christopher Redwood, John Calder, London, 1976, pp. 249–262; reprinted from *The Musical Times*, June & July 1962.

The pencil sketch of the first movement of the Violin Concerto. The photograph has had to be darkened to bring out the rather faint pencil line (courtesy of Colin Scott-Sutherland).

minor key where Moeran is in the major. Would Bax have
pointed out this graceful tribute as he had pointed out the
Tapiola reference, one wonders? According to Colin Scott-
Sutherland,[14] Bax deeply admired his friend's Concerto. The
Elgar reference is the first movement of the B minor Violin
Concerto, at the appearance of the secondary idea. Elgar's
basic melodic shape is the same, but there is a difference in
melodic emphasis. It is the mood of both Elgar and Moeran
which is so telling, for they seem to say something very similar.

Ex. 42

**(a)
Moeran**

**(b)
Bax**

**(c)
Elgar**

One further passage which appears to show response to both
Bax and Elgar must be mentioned. Moeran's Concerto concludes in an atmosphere of peace, and Stephen Banfield's
description of it as a lullaby is not inappropriate. The Elgar
reference is to the conclusion of the oratorio *The Dream of
Gerontius* – at the point known as the Angel's Farewell. Comparison of this with Moeran (Ex. 43) reveals an identity of key,
and similarities of melodic shape and texture. Three bars after
the commencement of Moeran's passage, the solo violin enters,
superimposing a new image of serenity on that already established by Moeran/Elgar. The referential material for this solo
idea is, I would suggest, the violin theme (Ex. 44) which occurs
in the Epilogue of the Symphony No. 3 by Bax. Thus Moeran
has welded a Baxian melodic shape to an Elgarian texture.
Both sources are images of tranquillity – one of them (Elgar) a
widely accepted image. Elgar's tranquillity is that of the faith,

---

[14] *op. cit.*, p. 170.

Ex. 43

Ex. 44

while that of Bax is shadowed in the Celtic twilight. Moeran's is the sunset tranquillity of the hedonist. All three are lullabies – either for transient or eternal rest.

The references to the Mendelssohn E minor Concerto are twofold. Mendelssohn's first movement cadenza, which in due course settles into a pattern of rapid across-the-strings figuration, carries over to provide an accompaniment to the recapitulation of the primary idea. It is a passage of real originality and superb technical accomplishment. Moeran's cadenza settles into a very similar figuration, and also carries over to

provide an accompaniment – but it is placed far earlier in his
movement – before even the appearance of any secondary idea.
When this idea does come, its superficial resemblance to that of
Mendelssohn is striking (Ex. 45). The Mendelssohn, however,
has a kind of bland serenity, whereas the serenity of the Moeran

Ex. 45

(a) Moeran

(b) Mendelssohn

is more apparent than real. It is fed by the somewhat Delian
harmony. In Delius, the chord of the added sixth is almost
always used (overused?) in situations of serenity and repose –
endings of movements, for example. The Moeran added sixth,
(bars 1 and 3 of Ex. 45) have this effect cancelled by the chords
which follow. There is thus an image of flawed, or false,

serenity, enhanced by the marriage of serene diatonic melody to intense chromatic harmony, and by the memory of the reference point – the bland, untroubled Mendelssohn passage. Moeran's central movement (the Rondo) can also show an interesting pedigree. This is the movement that reflects the Ireland of the fairs, with their bustle, noise and roistering crowds. In looking for referential works, I naturally had by this time some idea in which direction to look. Armed with Moeran's rejoinder to Arthur Hutchings that 'you can escape into a crowd', and remembering that Tchaikovsky had attempted exactly that in his Symphony No. 4 in F minor,[15] it seemed possible that the Russian composer might be a source. The Symphony No. 6 in B minor had, after all, proved a reference point for the Moeran Symphony; my belief that the march from the *Pathétique* Symphony was a source for Moeran's Rondo was re-inforced when I discovered subsequently that Stephen Banfield had come to the same conclusion. Additionally, Moeran's descending bass resembles that in the Tchaikovsky – although Tchaikovsky's bass moves in triplets.

There is, however, another source. The Ulster composer and conductor Hamilton Harty had helped and encouraged Moeran from the earliest days. As John Barry wrote of Harty:

> . . . there would not be the smallest possibility of his thinking of himself as anything other than Irish, specially if he was reared (as Harty was) in a house on the edge of a street which gave him a ring-side seat at the twice-monthly fair days.[16]

There seems little doubt that Moeran's principal rondo theme has some relationship to the principal idea of the last movement of Harty's Violin Concerto (Ex. 46), and while we do not know that Harty had any pictorial intention in his Concerto, fair days were undoubtedly a source of inspiration for him – there is a 'Fair Day' movement in his *Irish* Symphony.

[15] In a letter to Nadezhda von Meck, dated 1 March 1878, Tchaikovsky outlines the programmatic basis of his Fourth Symphony. Of the fourth movement, he says 'If you have no joy in yourself, look around you. Go to the people. See how well they know how to be merry . . . . The people do not trouble about you. They do not look at you; they do not notice that you are alone and sorrowful . . .'. The entire letter is reproduced in Edwin Evans, *Tchaikovsky*, J.M. Dent, London, 1906, pp. 113–117.

[16] 'Hillsborough Years' in David Greer (ed.), *Hamilton Harty*, Blackstaff Press, Belfast, 1978, p.19.

Ex. 46

(a) Moeran

'Root' cell
(*cf.* Ex. 36)

(b) Mendelssohn

When an imagery of despair seemed necessary, Moeran
would make reference to Tchaikovsky. But for Moeran of all
composers, the supreme masterpiece of one other artist would
stand out as pre-eminent in the expression of desolation and
despair – the song-cycle, *The Curlew*, by his close friend Peter
Warlock. Sure enough, the characteristic melismatic cor
anglais phrases of that work find echo in Moeran's last movement, at a point of maximum intensity just before the work
achieves its release with the 'Angel's Farewell' passage mentioned above.

The design plan of a fast central movement flanked by two
moderately slow outer ones was not, of course, new. Brahms
had introduced a scherzo into his Second Piano Concerto,
while Tchaikovsky had gone a stage further by introducing one
into the middle of the slow movement of his First Piano
Concerto. Most likely, however, the design models for Moeran

would have been Prokofiev and Walton – and specifically the latter's Viola Concerto. What *is* new in Moeran is the very tight cellular and thematic relationship between the movements, going far beyond the mere repetition of first-movement idea as a peroration of the final movement found in the Walton. The first movement, in a very loose sonata form, is notable structurally both for its unusual proportions and for the placing of its cadenza. The exposition occupies well over half the total length of the movement, while the recapitulation is correspondingly condensed, holding on a tight rein what had on first hearing been discursive. The principle cadenza, already noted to be influenced by that in the Mendelssohn Violin Concerto, is placed not as in the Mendelssohn just before the recapitulation but in the exposition immediately before the secondary idea. Against all odds, this works well in performance – Moeran had an instinctive feeling for sequence and flow.

The central scherzo is a rondo of some complexity, which ends in a waltz only to be described as somewhat tipsy.

The last movement – a moving and original *Lento* – is difficult, if not impossible, to analyse in any traditional sense; broadly, it consists of a highly rhapsodic contemplation and distortion of ideas from the first movement resolved into an epilogue of real beauty and serenity.

Once more the parent-cell technique is used. The cell in its most basic form consists of melodic steps and a leap (Ex. 47);

Ex. 47

the leap is usually a third, but may on occasion extend to a sixth. The diversity of the material generated by this cell is quite remarkable: of the four separate ideas which make up the primary group of the first movement, three derive from the cell – yet in their expanded melodic versions they show little apparent similarity.

Even more striking is the cunning by which the principal unit at the heart of the rondo idea is constructed; for, as Ex. 46(a) shows, it too comes from the same parent cell. The steps-and-leap figure is hidden there and the kinship with both primary and secondary ideas of the first movement is also evident. Additionally, the cell becomes a kind of brass refrain at the end of the melody. If sheer invention is the hallmark of a fine composer, then the numerous variants conjured from this exuberant rondo theme show Moeran to be in a exalted class. It does seem as if the rondo structure stimulated him to his highest flights of fancy.

There is also that innate or instinctive sense of appropriateness, shown best by that part of the rondo heard just before the 'waltz-coda'. By this time, the listener knows the theme well – there is no need for a complete statement of it, and so just enough hints of its characteristics are given to satisfy the needs of the formal stereotype. The passage is crowned by the trumpets playing their refrain, but this time in augmentation. The mastery has been in knowing what to leave out.

Equally remarkable in the last movement are some of the distortions of ideas heard earlier. The serene opening of the Concerto (Ex. 48[17]) is distorted into the anguish of the opening

Ex. 48

[17] Note the harmonic ambiguity of this passage:
(i) delayed approach to the tonic in bars 1 and 2.
(ii) tonic major immediately cancelled by the B flat in bar 2;
(iii) B flat cancelled by B natural in bar 3;
(iv) B natural to B flat in bar 4;
(v) B flat to B natural in bars 5–6.

Ex. 49

of the last movement (Ex. 49). The Elgarian sweetness of the soloist's first thoughts (Ex. 42 (a)) is twisted into the passionate distress of his first appearance in the last movement (Ex. 49). Technically, the method is readily apparent: it is accomplished by increasing the amplitude of key intervals in the melodic line so that the line swoops and soars disturbingly. The manner has in it echoes of Walton, but something of the distortion technique has been seen already in the Symphony in G minor; here in the Violin Concerto there is virtually a re-interpretation of the original ideas. It is as if Moeran were saying that all apparent reality is illusory – that apparent peace and beauty may yet reveal its alter ego of distress and pain.

In the case of the surpassingly lovely passage[18] for the horns in D major towards the end of the work (Ex. 50), distortion seems a poor word in its loaded implications; transfiguration is more apt for this luring siren call. Perhaps the inspiration for this marvellous moment is to be found specifically in the

Ex. 50

[18] A comparison with Ex.42(a) will show how this passage is linked to the first movement.

contemplation by the composer of the Kenmare River he so loved – the river whose outflow only a few years later would claim him. The horns slowly recede leaving a moment of quiet brass in which time seems suspended.

In these pages are to be found the resolution and dissolution of those tensions at the heart not only of this Concerto but also of the Symphony in G minor. Admittedly the relationship between the two works is something felt rather than manifest in provable analysis. The frustrated, angry conclusion to the Symphony solved none of the problems posed by that work and something like exorcism was needed. The composition of the Concerto commenced scarcely before the ink was dry on the Symphony. In addition, there is the undoubted fact that a number of Moeran's compositions come in pairs. It had, after all, become by no means unusual for a composer to spread a 'meaning' over more than one work; we have only to think of the symphonies of Mahler or, nearer to Moeran, those of Bax.

There is, however, some tangible evidence to support the contention of a relationship – the evidence of cellular links. One melodic unit is present which can be traced directly to two of the parent cells in the Symphony – of which cells it may be considered a synthesis (Ex. 51). The process of this synthesis is suggested in Ex. 36. Now it may be objected that the result is a mere musical commonplace, and indeed the figure is common

Ex. 51

enough in the language of Norfolk and Irish folksong. Commonplace or not, it is at the heart of some of the most significant and striking ideas of the Concerto: it is found in the principal idea of the Rondo (Ex. 46) and in the tipsy waltz towards the end of that movement (Ex. 52). It is at the root of the 'Irish

Ex. 52

Alla valce [sic] burlesca

signal' (Ex. 41) in the first movement. In his music as a whole it becomes an obsession, generating, for example, much of the Cello Concerto and Cello Sonata yet to come. The last note has only to be raised an octave to reveal the basic Moeran utterance (Ex. 53). And is it only coincidence that the 'Irish Signal' (Ex. 41) harbours that dominant cell *A* which had been so prominent in the Symphony?

Ex. 53

These cellular links provide some evidence of continuity of thought between the two works but are hardly sufficiently convincing of themselves. Moeran's tonal scheme helps us a little further. The three movements of the Concerto are in G major, D major, and A and C minor, with the concluding epilogue in D major. Certainly there are many instances of composers working in progressive tonality, but most of these, working within traditional tolerances, finished a work in the key in which it started. Few have cast their work in the form of an extended plagal cadence – which in the tonal progress of the Violin Concerto is just what Moeran has done. The loaded associations of this cadence, as it has been used in sacred contexts down the ages, are very powerful indeed. The final balm of peace and inner calm, so hard won, required nothing less than a symbolic 'so be it'.

Finally an assessment must be made of the inter-relationship of the Symphony and Violin Concerto with the *Seven Poems of James Joyce* already mentioned as a starting point for the Concerto, and another illuminating work – *Phyllida and Corydon*.

A comparison of the opening of the last movement of the Concerto (Ex. 49) with that of the last movement of the Symphony – in particular the phrase in the horns (Ex. 54) – shows that, in effect, Moeran is giving a reminder of the core of the emotional situation. It is this situation which is illuminated by the remarkable parallel with the Choral Suite *Phyllida and Corydon* at the setting of the line 'so vain desire was hidden' in the song 'Beauty sat bathing by a spring' (Ex. 55) which clearly uses the same concept. Moeran interrupted work on the Con-

Ex. 54

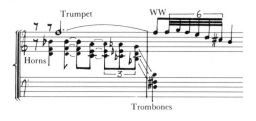

Ex. 55

certo to write this suite of madrigals. Why would he use here
such a prominent idea from both Symphony and Concerto? If
its use is deliberate, what 'vain desire' is enshrined in the two
major works – a desire, a yearning even, for ultimate peace?

The Joyce poem the setting of which provided the opening
phrase of both first and last movements of the Concerto and the
'inarticulate thought' running through it suggests the object of
that desire, and thus the resolution of the Symphony's tension
and bitterness:

> Now, O Now in this brown land
> Where Love did so sweet music make.

It may be that this very Irish concerto suggests and finds a
haven from the bitter world of the Symphony in the 'Brown
Land' of Ireland. Haven or Heaven? The plagal manner and
the 'Angel's Farewell' of the ineffably peaceful epilogue suggest
that the two are inextricably intertwined in the mind of the
composer.

Between them, the Symphony and the Violin Concerto
justify a place for Moeran among the greatest of British composers. The greatness of these works lies in the sustained
intensity of their expression, set in structures which re-interpret
traditional forms in an entirely novel manner. The manner, in

other words, is directly at the service of the matter, which is how all great creative effort should be. With Moeran, the matter is some deep-rooted anguish. It can be drowned by alcohol in some bucolic festivity; it can be calmed only by the contemplation of some beloved natural scene, such as he found in abundance in South West Ireland. This, in essence, is the Moeran experience transmuted into sound imagery.

Phyllida and Corydon – Madrigal postische

What of *Phyllida and Corydon*, the work for which Moeran put aside his Concerto? It cannot compare in range with it or the Symphony but familiarity with it is nevertheless essential to a fuller understanding of Moeran's thought.

It consists of nine settings for unaccompanied chorus of loosely related pastoral poetry. The poems comprise:
'Phyllida and Corydon', Nicholas Breton (1545–1626);
'Beauty sat bathing by a spring', Anthony Munday (1553–1633);
'On the hill there grows a flower', Nicholas Breton (1545–1626);
'Phyllis Inamorata', Lancelot Andrewes (1555–1626);
'Said I that Amaryllis', Anon. (16th century);
'Treasure of my heart', Sir Philip Sidney (1554–1586);
'While she lies sleeping', Anon. (16th century);
'Corydon, arise', Anon. (16th century);
'To meadows', Robert Herrick (1591–1674).
The work was completed in 1939 and is dedicated to Constant Lambert.

Superficially, the nine songs are madrigal pastiche; each type of madrigal is included – Ballett, Canzonet, Pastoral, Ayre and Madrigal proper. 19th-century imitation madrigals, by such manufacturers as Hatton, were in reality four-square part-songs at worst and glees at best. By contrast, Moeran's pastiche is of very high quality. He has absorbed thoroughly the idioms of Wilbye, Benet (or Bennet) and, in particular, Morley. The characteristic shapes of their themes, and their sprung rhythms with accent freed from the bar line, are used as to the manner born. There would, however, be little point in writing imitation madrigals in the 20th century; there would have to be some justifying twist. Sure enough, the madrigals of *Phyllida and Corydon* feature passages of chromaticism and modulations which would never have occurred in even the most advanced work of the 'Golden Age'.

It is precisely here that the problem lies. Commentators have tended to dismiss the work as stylistically inconsistent. Westrup, for example, thought the imitations of Elizabethan idioms somewhat self-conscious, and he was worried by the chromaticisms.[19] The latter also worried Aloys Fleischmann, who thought they sat uneasily with the strictly conventional 16th-century styles of much of the work.[20]

Despite these reservations of respected musicians, the work is highly characteristic of its composer, and valuable therefore precisely because of the stylistic inconsistency. For we are continually made aware, throughout his music, of a kind of divide or dichotomy. Within it lyricism has two faces – major/minor tonality is split in false relation, passages of pastoral diatonicism are dispersed in polytonality: and here, in *Phyllida and Corydon* strict Tudor polyphony is set against extreme chromaticism.

A fairly mild example occurs in the first madrigal (Ex. 56).

Ex. 56

[19] *op. cit.*, pp. 175–184.
[20] Fleischmann, *loc. cit.*, p. 62.

Here, the music makes a sudden shift to E minor at the words 'there I spied all alone'. More extreme is Ex. 57 (from the Canzonet, 'Treasure of my heart'): at the words 'to her sweet sense, sweet sleep some ease impart' the music shifts quite brutally from the basic tonality of G to that of B minor, whence it moves on to a passage of extreme chromaticism, featuring several striking false relationships.

Ex. 57

Because in *Phyllida and Corydon* the music sets and attempts to illustrate words, it throws light on Moeran's musical language when applied in other, instrumental, circumstances. The passage quoted above from the second madrigal ('Beauty sat bathing by a spring') was a case in point, illuminating as it did the Symphony and the Violin Concerto; in the next chapter, another madrigal in the work will be seen to illustrate a later piece (the *Overture for a Masque*).

It is undeniable that some of the passages in *Phyllida and Corydon* which worry because of their inconsistency nevertheless contain music of overwhelming intensity. That these passages are often associated with ideas of 'vain longings', unease or loneliness may give pause for thought in probing the deeper strata of meaning in Moeran's music.

The final image of the work, in the last madrigal ('To Meadows') is one of utter loneliness, bereft of consolation (Ex. 58). I know of only one work, Delius' *Sea Drift* (to which Moeran's conclusion here perhaps owes something), to compare with its emotional desolation.[21]

Ex. 58

And Moeran broke off in the middle of the Violin Concerto to write it.

[21] At Whitman's words, 'O darkness, O in vain!'

VIII. COMMISSIONS
AND A KIND OF POPULARITY

In 1930, while visiting the painter Augustus John, Moeran had met a young cellist. Her name was Peers Coetmore (originally Kathleen Coetmore-Jones; 'Peers' was derived from a family name of Pierce). Peers had been a brilliant student at the Royal Academy of Music, winning both Piatti and Vallange prizes. Nothing came of this casual meeting at the time, but some years later, in 1943, she was touring for CEMA (the Council for the Encouragement of Music and the Arts, the fore-runner of today's Arts Council) with the pianist Michael Mullinar and gave a concert in Leominster. Moeran was in the audience, their acquaintance was renewed and this time their relationship grew, on Moeran's part at least, into love. In Peers' company he was to some extent able to escape 'this miserable loneliness, which is a thing I have tried in the past to fight against and have more often than not been beaten by'.[1]

In the intervening years since that passing meeting of 1930, she had studied abroad with Eisenberg and Feuermann, and had made a name for herself as a solo cellist of some distinction. She would become one of the finest interpreters of Moeran's music. At the time of their second meeting, Moeran was 48, and Peers some eleven years younger.

The effect of Peers' playing was comparable to that of Mühlfeld the clarinettist on Brahms, or of Peter Pears on Britten. We have her to thank for two major masterpieces, the Cello Concerto and the Sonata for Cello and Piano. His first offering to Peers, however, was a Prelude for Cello and Piano, which she took with her as a 'keepsake' to play on her ENSA (Entertainments National Service Association, which in war-time organised tours of artists who performed to the armed

---

[1] In a letter to Peers Coetmore dated 19 October 1943.

Moeran with Peers Coetmore in the mid-1940s (courtesy of Walter Knott).

forces) tour of the Far East. She had to wait until 1945 for the first of her major works.

On 26 July of that year Moeran and Peers Coetmore were married. It was to be an uneasy marriage which, for a few years, endured after a fashion, but which did not so much end as peter out. He required solitude amid nature for his work, while her professional touring meant all-too-frequent long separations. In the last year of his life separation became permanent, if unspoken, as Peers' work led her to Australia.

Always in the background was the drinking problem. Gradually he brought himself to acknowledge it, but he was never finally to overcome it. Peers may not have understood that alcoholism is a disease – not just 'a liking for drink', which is how his parents saw it.

His letters show clearly that he loved Peers deeply; hers to him have not survived. His requirement of freedom was, perhaps, stronger than his love, and on the night before the wedding he told his close friend Dr Dick Jobson that the marriage would be a disaster; he was undertaking it only because he had given his word.

Peers had had one previous marriage, and would have two more after Moeran's death. All except the last were failures. The word we would use for Peers and Moeran today would probably be 'incompatibility'. But, for a while, there was a kind of happiness.

At the outset of the 1939–45 War, Moeran was too old for service, and was in any case in receipt of a disability pension. He could thus take no active part.

We have only glimpses of Moeran over the years 1939–42; he would go out of circulation for long periods and friends would be concerned for his well-being, among them Arnold Bax:

> Any news of Jack? . . . What state of repair was he in when last you met him?[2]

Unfortunate accidents continued to plague him:

> Walking in my sleep, of all things, I sprained my left wrist and bruised some ribs.[3]

Four Shakespeare Songs

It was an uncertain time for Moeran as for everyone else; musically, the Violin Concerto was hanging fire and, apart from *Phyllida and Corydon*, the only work of consequence to emerge from the years 1939–40 was the collection of *Four Shakespeare Songs*. All four poems have been set repeatedly by other composers – two of them ('The Lover and his Lass' and 'When Daisies Pied') by his friend Warlock – yet Moeran could find, in two of the poems at least, a fresh approach to the well-worn words. Admittedly, his setting of 'The Lover and his Lass' bears more than a passing resemblance to that of Warlock, yet it has become one of his most popular songs – a staple of music festivals and being adapted easily into two-part and four-part arrangements. Although modelled on the Warlock setting, Moeran's is arguably superior, for his melody flows more easily for the voice.

[2] In a letter to Tilly Fleischmann dated 19 July 1939.
[3] In a letter to Aloys Fleischmann dated 30 August 1940.

The relationship of 'Where the Bee Sucks' to the Joyce songs was mentioned earlier.[4] Suffice it here to say that Moeran's sense of irony tinges Shakespeare's blithe and careless rapture with bitter regret. Neither of the last two songs ('When Daisies Pied' and 'When Icicles Hang by the Wall') approaches the first two in interest. Indeed, 'Daisies' seems to be a throw-back to that innocuous style of so many Moeran songs of the pre-Warlock period.

Fanfare for Red Army Day

Moeran's experience in the previous war had been horrific; yet there is no evidence that these experiences had soured his patriotism. While he never turned his hand, as had Elgar, to the conveyor-belt manufacture of patriotic music, he did attempt the occasional piece. One such work was the *Fanfare for Red Army Day*:

> The Ministry kept ringing me up at Glasgow telling me different each time as to the instrumentation required. Finally, since I got back here, I have contacted Flash Harry on the telephone and got down to final brass tacks, so I am writing it for three large brass bands, two of which will be on the stage and one in the auditorium.[5]

The *Fanfare* was performed at a Red Army Day concert at the Royal Albert Hall in February 1944. I have found no trace of it. The presentation, entitled 'Salute to the Red Army', also included a choral setting by Arnold Bax of words by John Masefield, *To Russia*. Moeran had to turn down work, including incidental music:

> I couldn't tell the BBC Features Department that I am unable to write music for a show about a destroyer in the Atlantic on the grounds that I am doing a Prom piece unless I had a definite assurance from the music department that that is the case. It seems there was a conference with Wood this morning at which the matter was settled . . . .[6]

---

[4] Chapter V, p. 83.
[5] In a letter to Peers dated 8 February 1944; 'Flash Harry' was the name by which Sir (then Dr) Malcolm Sargent was generally (if not unfairly) known to musicians.
[6] In a letter to Douglas Gibson dated 23 February 1943.

A possible venture into film music is revealed in a letter to Leslie Heward:[7]

> I am taking on a contract for a M.O.I. film. Anyhow, it will save all risk of being called up for factory work

but it came to nothing.

Quite obviously, with the completion and performance of the Symphony and the Violin Concerto, Moeran was becoming well known and the war and post-war years were indeed the high point in his career, as far as public recognition was concerned. To crown all, the Symphony was receiving a first recording:

> it has had such a performance as it never had before – 12 solid hours rehearsal![8]

Rhapsody No. 3 in F sharp

Partly as a result of this growing publicity, he was receiving more commissions. They included the Rhapsody in F sharp for piano and orchestra (the 'Prom piece' in the above letter), the *Overture for a Masque* and the *Fantasy Quartet* for Oboe and Strings. None of these three works really exercised him. The composition of at least one (the *Overture*) he found irksome and his attitude to the completed work was, to say the least, ambivalent. A fairly typical response was that, on completion, he would find the work acceptable, or even likable; subsequently its faults would loom ever larger in his mind. With the Rhapsody, however, the reverse was the case. Shortly after its completion, it provoked the following comment:

> to my certain knowledge, it contains more than its fair share of tripe.[9]

A few months later (and after a particularly good performance) he was to write:

[7] 14 December 1942.

[8] EJM, in a letter to Tilly Fleischmann dated 2 December 1942. Leslie Heward was the conductor. By this time in Heward's career, the tuberculosis which was to kill him a few months later was well advanced, and there was doubt as to whether he would be able to undertake the task. The recording (HMV C3319–24; recently reissued on HMV EM 29 0462 3) is a monument to a conductor who, in the opinion of Sir Adrian Boult, had 'no one to touch him'.

[9] In a letter to Peers dated 10 October 1943.

I find I was wrong, and I really think that after all it is a very good effort on my part. It seems now all so virile and logical.[10]

It had been some while before that Bax had asked Moeran to write a work for piano and orchestra for Harriet Cohen to play.[11] In 1942 Douglas Gibson (then the proprietor of the publishers, J. and W. Chester), was endeavouring to extend his Moeran representation. He was given the Second Rhapsody which had been written many years before and which was now revised and moved to Chester from the Boosey catalogue. The new Rhapsody (No. 3 in F sharp) is first mentioned in a letter from Gibson to Moeran dated 2 October 1942. The publisher hoped the 'new orchestral work' might be given to him. Despite the self-doubts expressed to Lionel Hill[12] that he 'seemed to have lost the knack of writing piano music', Moeran worked rapidly –

14 December 1942 (Moeran to Gibson):

> I arrived back yesterday and got out the preliminary version of the piece for piano and orchestra, as far as it goes.

15 December 1942 (Gibson to Moeran):

> I have just been approached by Sir Henry Wood regarding the Promenade programmes and I of course mentioned the work for piano and orchestra which we were speaking of the other day.

15 December 1942 (Moeran to Gibson):

> Harriet Cohen some time ago asked me to let her play a new work for piano and orchestra should I write one. . . . I cannot avoid calling it a Rhapsody, for it is that and nothing else . . . Today I have reached the end of the middle section.

5 February 1943 (Moeran to Gibson):

> I am now at the end of the composition of the Rhapsody for Piano and Orchestra, but only in the form of a shorthand version. The full score will take another six weeks.

[10] In a letter to Douglas Gibson dated 10 September 1944.
[11] 'I had to do it in order to carry out an old promise; also because of my friendship (of many years standing) with Arnold': EJM, in a letter to Peers dated 10 October 1943.
[12] *loc.cit.*, p.7.

Sir Adrian Boult in 1937. Although Boult conducted performances of Moeran's music during the composer's lifetime, his long and fruitful association did not begin in earnest until several years after the composer's death (courtesy of the Royal College of Music).

Gibson received the score and corrected parts by the end of May. In mid-June, anxieties were growing as to whether or not Harriet Cohen would be able to play it–
16 June 1943 (Gibson to Moeran):

> By the way, have you heard how Harriet Cohen is getting on with the piano part? I do hope she will make a success of it. The last time I spoke to her on the telephone a few weeks ago, she gave me the impression the work was rather much for her.

In the event, Miss Cohen learned it and played it. She gave the first performance at the Proms on 19 August 1943, with the BBC Symphony Orchestra under Sir Adrian Boult. But the fears expressed above had some substance: Moeran had little enthusiasm for her interpretation and much preferred those of later exponents – in particular, that of Iris Loveridge.

The F sharp Rhapsody seems in some ways stylistically reactionary. Harmonically, formally and pianistically it would more logically sit with the music Moeran was writing in the pre-Heseltine days than it does into its real date, following the Symphony and Violin Concerto. In harmony, the principal influences are those of Ravel, Ireland and Delius; formally, Moeran returns to the ternary structures of his early piano music, while the piano technique is very much that of John Ireland.

When all this is considered, and when the time Moeran usually needed to complete a large work is compared with the six months or so taken over the Rhapsody, it is reasonable to ask if it had perhaps been started some years before. When, one wonders, was that 'old promise' to Arnold Bax made?

In effect, the Rhapsody in F sharp is a large-scale waltz for piano and orchestra. A response is being made here to another composer of waltzes – not an obvious one such as Johann Strauss, but the French composer Ravel whose influence had been so potent many years before. In the main it is to *Valses Nobles et Sentimentales* that the Moeran work is chiefly indebted – the influence is to be heard not only in the harmony, but also in some of the rhythmic shapes. Perhaps the work owes something also to *La Valse*, although there is a marked contrast between the piquant indoor sophistication of these ideas and the rugged outdoor simplicity of Moeran's principal theme, which has a pronounced folksong brogue. The contrasting idea of the middle section (Ex. 59) has that wistful, retrospective quality — a kind of withdrawn musing – into which Moeran was wont to slip in much of his music about this time.

As one would expect in such a work, the writing for the solo instrument is of considerable virtuosity, that is, it is difficult, and both sounds and looks so in performance. Lest it seem

Ex. 59

strange to remark on the visual aspect of performance, we need to remember that during the 1939–45 War, symphony concert audiences contained many who would not ordinarily have been attracted to what was loosely called 'classical music'. The mainstay of such concerts would be the piano concerto, those of Grieg, Tchaikovsky and Rachmaninov becoming especially popular. In due course, this new interest was reflected in 'concerto' films, like *Love Story*, *The Seventh Veil* or *Brief Encounter*. The Third Rhapsody is frankly popular in style and none the worse for that. Strangely enough, Harriet Cohen apparently thought parts of it discordant (this from an exponent of Bartók!), to which Moeran nonchalantly replied that this was to be expected as it was inspired by the four-ale bars of Kerry.

It is light music of an attractive tunefulness written in that 'romantic concerto' style that was beginning to be expected by wartime audiences. In it are the massive chordal passages, the double octave bravura work, the Chopin-like arabesques – all the trappings of a manner as much visual as aural. One can see why Moeran would feel some of it was 'tripe', for there is here a degree of self-indulgence he had otherwise eradicated from his music from the mid-1930s onwards. In a short while, he would tighten up his style again. But for this work and one or two others of about the same time, there was to be a looseness of construction and relaxation of manner which was not inappropriate to the aim – a popular work for the delectation of Prom audiences in wartime.

The F sharp Rhapsody received a number of performances in its first few years and was taken up by some of the most prominent pianists of the day. It contributed not a little to Moeran's wartime popularity.

The last weeks of 1943 found Moeran making the first sketches for an orchestral overture. This was to be the *Overture for a Masque*, referred to as 'Legge's Overture' in Moeran's letters. Walter Legge held a position at that time in ENSA, and commissioned composers to write works for performance at concerts for the troops. Bax and Rawsthorne received similar commissions for overtures.[13]

[13] The Bax work was the overture *Work in Progress*, and the Rawsthorne the overture *Street Corner*.

Legge at first specified that the work should be for a small classical orchestra, but must have changed his mind, since, in the event, large forces were required.

Unfortunately for the embryo Moeran overture, between receiving the commission and carrying it out, the composer had become infatuated with Peers Coetmore; above all else, he wanted to settle down to the composition of cello works for Peers to play, and the overture became a chore.

Prelude for Cello and Piano

All he could manage, as a kind of promissory note or declaration of intent was the 'keepsake' mentioned above – Prelude for Cello and Piano, which received its first performance, somewhat improbably, in the city of Alexandria. Sad to say, it is a work of little distinction; the cello melody is shapely enough, but the piano part is frankly dull. It is a retrogressive piece, doomed to a humble place in grade examination lists.

Overture for a Masque

Something of the drudgery of commissioned work for an artist of Moeran's somewhat wayward nature is shown by comments in letters to Peers over the winter of 1943–44. Yet, as 'Legge's Overture' took shape, a moderate enthusiasm for it was kindled, and finally he seemed pleased with the result.
10 October 1943:

> I'm supposed to knock up an overture for his ENSA concerts.

16 November 1943:

> Blast Legge, his overture must wait till I have had a session with you and your cello this week.

30 December 1943:

> I think I must do the overture for ENSA. Then I shall get down to writing cello music for you.

2 January 1944:

> Well, I shall have to thrash away at Legge's overture during all the week.

4 January 1944 (he has had no news of Peers, who is aboard ship for the Middle East):

> It is a mockery trying to compose this (snappy?) overture for ENSA in my present state of anxiousness.

5 January 1944 (after the tonic of a cable from her):

> Today I have actually approached my ENSA overture with zest and the idea that I am going to make it really snappy and exciting for the troops to listen to.

9 January 1944:

> It is getting on slowly at the moment, but that is not for lack of energy on my part. I am just at an awkward bit and once I am over that, I expect to go ahead pretty fast. But I am longing to finish it and then get at the cello sonata.

12 January 1944:

> Honestly, I wish the overture were finished with, and I were on to something else. It is a commissioned work, as you know, and it is not my top notch. The fact is I am doing it as a duty engendered by the war and working to a time-table I am not able to follow my normal method of extreme self-criticism.

26 January 1944:

> My overture has made a spurt this last two days, so much so that I hope to finish the composition of it comfortably before I go to Glasgow next week.

12 February 1944:

> As for the overture, now that it is getting into full score, it is turning out really well.

20 February 1944:

> I think it turns out to be quite a good little work – what you might call athletic in style. Consequently, it has reams of long string passages in semiquavers and in consequence it takes the devil of a time to write out.

The *Overture for a Masque* is truly a very good little work. Perfectly tailored to its function (although what it has to do with a masque is not apparent), it demonstrates that facet of Moeran's art which is all too easily overlooked – his thorough professionalism. One aspect of this is the clarity of the textures and of the orchestral sound; in orchestration the overture may well be a response to the work of Tchaikovsky and the Russian school. This is most immediately obvious in the building of the climax over a pedal A towards the peroration of the work; the manner here is reminiscent of Tchaikovsky towards the conclusion of his Symphony No. 4 in F minor (a fitting model, given Moeran's particular outlook).

Superficially episodic in construction, the music is nearest in structure to Moeran's favourite form – rondo. The growth and relationship of the ideas is not immediately obvious, but closer familiarity shows all the ideas except one to develop organically and sequentially one from another. Thus Moeran sets himself a typically Sibelian paradox to solve – the building of a structure whose basis is contrast yet with most of the ideas deriving from a single source. This source is the opening flourish, which yields the parent cell (Ex. 60). Except for one interlude, the key scheme has a logic to enhance the unity: B flat major, G major, C major, G minor, F major, C sharp minor, D major and B flat major.

Ex. 60

Opening flourish

yields motivic outline:

suggesting fanfare:

The key which sits uneasily within this scheme is that of C sharp minor; it is used for that one idea mentioned above which defies any attempt to relate it to its fellows in their organic sequence (Ex. 61(a)). Both the melodic style and harmonic treatment of this idea are foreign to the rest of the Overture, which in the main leans stylistically towards the *Sinfonietta* to be written a few months later. Moeran really makes no attempt to

Ex. 61

(a) = **Overture for a Masque**
(b) = **Phyllida and Corydon**
(c) = **Sinfonietta (second movement)**

1. On a hill there grows a flower, Fair be-fall the dainty sweet;
2. O fair eyes yet let me see   One good look and I- am gone;

By that flower there is a Bower,   Where the heaven-ly muses meet.
Look on me,   for   I am he,   Thy poor silly   Cor-y-don.

In that Bower there is- a chair,   Fring-ed all a-bout with gold,
Thou that art the   shepherd's Queen,Look upon   thy sil-ly   swain;

integrate this interlude into his structure. It is an instance of a familiar Moeran procedure – the encapsulation of a moment of beauty and the isolation of it by key. There are similar examples in the Symphony and the Cello Sonata. There is here a psychological withdrawal – a rapid transition from extroversion to introversion which is perhaps the musical equivalent of those sudden disappearances made by the composer and remarked on by all who knew him.

Any further attempt to interpret the meaning of the passage must remain pure speculation. Nevertheless, a comparison of the idea with two similar ones – from *Phyllida and Corydon* and from the second movement of the *Sinfonietta* – has been made in Ex. 61. All three are folksong pastiche; the comparison may guide us to a pertinent area of musical experience, or to some very private thought or special memory. All three are expressed in Warlock/Delius terms regardless of any other circumstance and, indeed, these ideas are caricatures almost of that type of Warlock song in which the melody is little more than commonplace, since the emotional impact is made in the supporting harmony.

While there are general resemblances between all three ideas, there is only one specifically identical relationship, and that only for two bars. But that there should be an identical relationship, however small, is in itself remarkable. The bars are 7 and 8 of the Overture idea, and the same bars of the *Phyllida and Corydon* song 'On the hill there grows a flower' (Nicholas Breton). These two bars are extracted as Ex. 62,

Ex. 62

(a) Overture

(b) Phyllida

where they are given their respective supporting parts which are closely related. The words of the Breton poem start:

> On a hill there grows a flower,
> Fair befall the dainty sweet:
> By that flower there is a bower
> *Where the heavenly muses meet.*
> In that bower there is a chair,
> Fringed all about with gold,
>
> Where doth sit the fairest fair
> That ever eye did yet behold.
> It is Phyllis fair and bright,
> She that is the shepherds' joy,
> She that Venus did despite
> And did blind her little boy.
>
> O fair eyes yet let me see
> One good look and I am gone;
> Look on me, for I am he,
> *Thy poor silly Corydon.*
> Thou that art the Shepherds' Queen,
> Look upon thy silly swain;
> By thy comfort have been seen
> Dead men brought to life again.

The words italicised in the poem are set to that phrase used in the Overture passage (bars 7 and 8 of Ex. 61). It is not possible to say whether or not the quotation of these bars is deliberate or unconscious, but earlier instances already discussed have shown quotation to be an intermittently recurring feature of Moeran's technique.

Perhaps this carefully insulated and isolated interlude is an orchestral love song. The words of the poem seem remarkably allusive, for if ever a dead man had been brought to life by love it was Moeran – the 'silly Corydon'. He and Peers, themselves the heavenly muses, would together create great music. The background to their love was the hill:

> How I wish you would be with me like you were when we walked up to Hergest Ridge and Bradnor. Don't say this will never be: if you do I really think I would walk up the mountain and never come down.[14]

[14] EJM, in a letter to Peers dated 21 October 1943.

The *Overture for a Masque* fills a logical place stylistically between the Violin Concerto and the *Sinfonietta*. Its syncopated rhythms, first heard in the String Trio, are here expressed in those Stravinskian terms which the *Sinfonietta* would fulfil. It is thus no surprise to find such a work at this stage of the composer's career – and it serves to strengthen my belief that the F sharp Rhapsody (completed only three months before the *Overture*) must contain material dating from much earlier, so stylistically inconsistent with the other works of the time does it seem.

Six Poems of Seumas O'Sullivan

Among his friends, Moeran numbered the Irish poet Seumas O'Sullivan (whose real name was James Starkey). Over the period 1943–44, he was to set seven of O'Sullivan's poems:

> I have been practising my songs all the afternoon with the singer Violet Burne,[15] who is going to do them on Friday. We have decided to do only two of the new ones this time, one a James Joyce setting, and the other a Seumas O'Sullivan poem. As soon as I shall have had a day or two at a piano there will be a whole cycle of the latter gentleman's verse, but so far, of the four I have done, it seems more feasible to do the one separate one 'Invitation in Autumn' and to leave the rest for a subsequent recital.
>
> There are two more poems I want to set and actually I have got the music of them in my head, so it will be mainly a matter of committing it to paper.[16]

Invitation to Autumn did appear separately. The Joyce song mentioned is probably *Rahoon* – not published until 1947. The other O'Sullivan poems mentioned in due course made up a collection or cycle – the *Six Poems of Seumas O'Sullivan*, published in 1946. By the end of December 1943, five had been written and Moeran thought

> there will have to be two more. . . . The one I have done today is strange; it is called The Herdsman and is about slow moving cattle. As the vocal part is very largely on one note, it is possible it will not find favour with our brilliantly intelligent English singers!

[15] The *Six Poems of Seumas O'Sullivan* are dedicated to Violet Burne.
[16] In a letter to Peers dated 10 October 1943.

I think these are my swan songs so far as solo songs are concerned.[17]

There was to be only one more song in the set, and 'The Herdsman' was the last of those published. But another O'Sullivan setting survives, in a faint pencil manuscript which Peers sent to Colin Scott-Sutherland almost twenty years after the composer's death. Its first page (of two) appears overleaf. The poems set comprise: 'Evening', 'The Poplars', 'A Cottager', 'The Dustman', 'Lullaby' and 'The Herdsman'. They have a haunted, fey feeling about them; autumnal in mood, they constantly invoke an imagery of aging and transience:

The rafters blacken year by year

I will go out and meet the evening hours
and greet them one by one

Over my heart too, the shadows are creeping.

In these songs, thirteen years after his friend's death, Moeran at last exorcised the ghost of Warlock. The 'mush of Delius-like chords' so characteristic of much of his early songwriting is here refined into a style at once more simple, yet growing in pungency as it looks towards the manner yet to come in the Cello Sonata. The accompaniment figurations, however, in such songs as 'Evening' or the central part of 'The Herdsman' hark back to those of Schumann, whose keyboard style was at the root of the piano part of some of the early chamber music.

Melodically the songs range widely in style. 'Evening', for example, is pentatonic while 'The Poplars' reaches back to the shapes characteristic of Norfolk folksong. The opening phrase of 'A Cottager' bears a striking resemblance to a phrase in Ireland's 'The Holy Boy', but the most notable responses of all are, as we noted in the Joyce songs, to Moeran's own work. It seems that a phrase in the poetry sometimes prompted lateral thought, suggesting music for it from an earlier work. An example occurs in 'The Cottager', where the words

---

[17] In a letter to Peers dated 30 December 1943.

*The faint pencil manuscript of the first page (of two) of the unpublished
Seumas O'Sullivan setting, 'If there be any Gods': This is its first
appearance in print (courtesy of Colin Scott-Sutherland). The full text of
the poem runs:*

> Wild birds flying across the moon,
> Sedges singing beside the pool,
> Long hills quiet for mile on mile,
> Water ruffled by winter wind,
> All that the fields in their silence tell —
> These are the gifts of Gods to men.

And Spring again and the fields are green

are set to a phrase (Ex. 63) already used in the Third Rhapsody.

Ex. 63

(a) Six Poems

And Spring a-gain and the fields- are- green.

(b) Rhapsody

The O'Sullivan songs were a considerable advance in Moeran's song-writing technique and together with the *Seven Poems of James Joyce* they represent Moeran's finest work in accompanied song. Such a song as 'The Dustman' shows, in its subtle observation of a child's psychology, a marked extension of Moeran's concept of setting poetry. The songs of the earlier 1920s contented themselves with a generally appropriate melody supported by generally appropriate piano textures. In the present songs, sounds are well considered and chosen carefully. Again, 'The Cottager' well illustrates this more discriminating aural palate: various poetic images of the passing of time are paradoxically reflected in a harmony of timelessness. There has always to be a technique through which an effect is achieved; in this case, the technique involves a preponderance of second-inversion-based chords and it is these which help give the song its static quality.

The closing two pages of the last song, 'The Herdsman', are a fitting summary of Moeran's song-writing achievement:

O happy meadows and trees and rath and hedges
The twilight and all its flock will pass you by.

The first line is set to a fragment of melody used a few years before at the conclusion of the Violin Concerto (*cf.* Ex. 43). The poetic image is one of serenity;[18] the gentle reference here to the

[18] See the discussion in Chapter VII, pp. 138–148, of responses in the Violin Concerto. The passage in question was shown to echo images of serenity in Elgar's *Dream of Gerontius* and Bax's Third Symphony.

Irish serenity of the last moments of the Concerto – Ireland and
serenity being linked symbolically in that work which was itself
linked back to the Joyce songs – reinforces the meaning of both
passages.

But for the second line, the music moves into a world of

'Evening': the pencil manuscript of the first of the Six Poems of
Seumas O'Sullivan (courtesy of Colin Scott-Sutherland).

shadow. The enigmatic harmonies, while not really bitonal are yet ambiguous – F sharp in the right hand against E minor in the left, for example – and their flavour was increasingly to dominate Moeran's last music. In few other passages are the two sides of Moeran – the light and the dark – so starkly opposed as here (Ex. 64).

Ex. 64

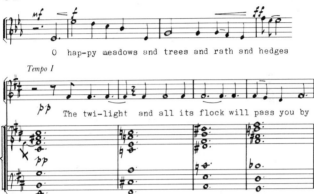

O hap-py meadows and trees and rath and hedges

The twi-light and all its flock will pass you by

Sinfonietta

Despite his irritation with the chore of 'Legge's Overture' and his insistence that all that mattered to him was the creation of great music for the cello, one other work appears to have been squeezed into 1944. This was the *Sinfonietta*, completed in September of that year, to receive a first performance by the BBC Symphony Orchestra under Barbirolli, at the Corn Exchange, Bedford, on 7 March 1945. Thus the period 1944–45 was one of exceptional activity, for the *Sinfonietta* is no hack work (as he appears to have considered the *Overture*), but a major three-movement work ranking high in his output. It even received the accolade of performances by Sir Thomas Beecham[19] – a gesture of some eloquence, for Beecham's forays into contemporary music had became all too rare.

The *Sinfonietta* was inspired by rambles over the hills of the Welsh Border Country – especially the second movement,

[19] 26 April 1947: Royal Philharmonic Society concert in the Royal Albert Hall, with the Royal Philharmonic Orchestra.

which he complained was often taken at a slower speed than the
brisk walking pace he had in mind. The work shows considerable stylistic advance, all the more remarkable in that it slightly
pre-dates the Cello Concerto, which is in a traditional mould
and does not maintain these new stylistic features. That
Moeran was consciously experimenting in the *Sinfonietta* is
confirmed in a letter to Peers:

> I shall have to find out a new idiom, as I did temporarily when I
> wrote the Sinfonietta.[20]

Here, he is writing apropos the Cello Sonata a few years later.
Why should a composer 'find out a new idiom'?

Moeran was subject to the same critical pressures as his
fellows, and in addition English composers were always open to
the charge of insularity. The mainstream of European contemporary music – Stravinsky, Hindemith, Bartók and the Second
Viennese School, for example – had been little enough reflected
in the work of the leading English figures of the 1940s. Admittedly the younger generation – Lutyens, Searle, or Arnold
Cooke, for example – looked to continental models, but the
Moeran generation would have had little defence against criticisms of parochialism. The Neo-classical movement in Europe
was a product of the anti-Romanticism that followed the First
World War in the 1920s. Such movements tend to make their
real impact on British artistic circles a generation or so after
their first flowering on the Continent. At one time it was a
matter of convenience to date the so-called 'English Musical
Renaissance' from the first performance of Parry's *Prometheus
Unbound* at the 1880 Three Choirs Festival at Gloucester. But
posterity has since tended to undervalue the sterling work of
Parry and Stanford – and several others – and to place more
emphasis on the achievement of Elgar and Delius. Both were,
in Bax's memorable phrase, 'brazen romantics' and, by the
time of their deaths in 1934, they had firmly established the
musical importance of their country. But Elgar had made no
attempt to come to terms with the new musical world of the
1920s, and Delius, physically and musically incapacitated
since 1922, enjoyed a brief creative Indian Summer with the

[20] Undated, but thought to be late 1946.

help of Eric Fenby, but attempted no extension of his natural language.

Of the principal figures of the succeeding generation – Vaughan Williams, Holst, Brian, Ireland and Bax – the last two had written most of their important music by 1940, and scarcely modified their traditional and Romantic approach to composition. Holst had died in 1934, but his last decade had shown an acute awareness of continental trends in such works as the Double Concerto or the *Terzetto*. Vaughan Williams lived on beyond Moeran and remarkably, after periods in which his style was dominated successively by Parry, folksong and, in the 1920s, a mild rapprochement with Neo-classicism, he moved on to such questing works as the Fourth Symphony (1935) and the Sixth Symphony (1948). Havergal Brian, of course, was writing music even more questing, but it was not to become known until after Moeran's death.

The composers most nearly of Moeran's own generation included Howells, Rubbra, Bliss and Walton. Both Howells and Rubbra show mastery of polyphony, although their work has little in common apart from this. Neither appears to have been touched by continental trends – in their mature work, at any rate. Both Bliss and Walton, however, went through an *enfant terrible* phase in the 1920s, during which their work showed most of the features of anti-Romanticism while not espousing the more positive attitudes of Neo-classicism. By 1940, both had given up the struggle and lapsed into a Neo-Romanticism – well marked in, for example, the Piano Concerto by Bliss and the Violin Concerto by Walton. Both works date from shortly before the 1939–45 War.

The youngest generation of composers – that is, those under 40 in 1940 – included Lutyens, Searle, Britten, Tippett and Berkeley. Of these, the first two did not even rate a mention in the standard survey of some ten years later – *British Music of Our Time*.[21] Of the five, Lutyens and Searle adopted the serial technique of the Second Viennese School, and of the other three only Tippett (in 1940) could be said to show an affinity with the English tradition. At that time, Britten seemed a clever young man whose eclectic style fed on many sources among which were

[21] Ed. A. L. Bacharach, Pelican, London, 1951.

the works of such Continental masters as Mahler and
Berg – Britten would have studied with Berg if he had been
able. Berkeley, on the other hand, looked to France where he
had been a pupil of Nadia Boulanger.

Thus, in 1943, Moeran was to an extent isolated as a
composer. The true Romantics with whom his affinities lay
were either dead, or creatively dying down. His younger col-
leagues looked to the Continent, as indeed on occasion he had –
but they took very different models. In these circumstances, a
composer might well feel pushed to adapt his work – to get up to
date.

He had an additional motive; not a lot was written about his
work during his lifetime, but within this small corpus of
comment, a recurring criticism concerns his allegedly limited
technique. We have seen his attempts in the early 1930s at a
more polyphonic style, which resulted in such works as the
String Trio and the Sonata for Two Violins. There was now to
be a conscious effort to achieve terseness and economy. The
earlier influences had included the work of his teacher Ireland,
and of Ravel, Warlock, Delius and Sibelius. With Moeran, a
review of style tended to mean a review of influences, or rather,
of models. In the *Sinfonietta*, certain Stravinskian methods are
in evidence – methods, however, of the Stravinsky of *Petrushka*
and of *The Rite of Spring*. There is also something of the
cleanliness of texture and clarity of line which are such features
of the later Stravinsky. Even more important is the unlikely
(because so distant in time) influence of Haydn. Moeran knew
his Haydn thoroughly,[22] and the smiling ambience of the
Austrian master suffuses every moment of the *Sinfonietta*.

What Moeran appears to be trying to achieve is the clarity
and economy of the Classical era, although this is in no sense a
pastiche period piece like, say, the *Classical Symphony* of Prokofiev. Rather it is a re-interpretation of Haydn's aesthetic in
terms of Moeran's present-day experience. A good parallel
would be Stravinsky's Symphony in C. The intention is underlined by the scoring, which is that of the late Haydn symphonies. There is no filling, or padding, or unnecessary doubling. The resulting sound is airy and remarkably invigorating.

[22] Michael Bowles, in a letter to the author dated 26 January 1981.

The textures are models of clarity in which bright, unmixed sounds predominate, and the music is lean and wiry with its formal outlines sharply defined. Such was his concern for clarity that he rescored the last few pages after hearing the Bedford performance, to achieve a better balance there between the complex strands.

The *Sinfonietta* is in three movements and as usual in Moeran these movements are melodically linked. The linking unit is a figure of descending fourths which can as easily be fifths (Ex. 65). The outer movements are in sonata form, sandwiching a

Ex. 65

central movement, which is a set of variations. Additionally, the final movement is capped with a fugue; one of the secondary ideas from the first movement is recruited to bubble joyfully along over it. Perhaps Moeran is here recalling Mendelssohn, who does much the same sort of thing in his Octet.

From time to time in his work, Moeran returned to certain melodic shapes, in much the same manner as an artist may be preoccupied with, say, a circle or a cube. Two of these shapes are to be found in the *Sinfonietta*. The first dates from the Warlock days and is the succession of rising thirds which Moeran called 'steps up' – the same basic shape that had first appeared in the Warlock/Moeran collaboration *Maltworms*, and was subsequently used in 'Good Wine' and the Joyce songs. Here in the first movement of the *Sinfonietta* it provides the primary idea. Even this will not be its last appearance in Moeran. The version used here has its fourth degree of the scale raised – a Sibelian characteristic to be seen in the Second and Fourth Symphonies, which may in Moeran be an attempt to avoid the 'old fashioned' sound of the ordinary subdominant.

The other favourite shape is the three-steps-and-a-leap figure, which may progress either upwards or downwards; in the *Sinfonietta* it is downwards (Ex. 66).

The ideas discussed so far are, apart from the raised fourth

Ex. 66

degree, brightly diatonic and as such they cast their sunlight over the work. The set of variations which serves as the middle movement is based, however, on a somewhat wry theme (Ex. 67). The wryness is caused in part by the indeterminate sense of key; the theme could be in A minor, but it seems to finish in D minor. There is something of the feeling of a forlorn march

Ex. 67

about the tune, and this, taken in company with the quasi-military allusions of distant fanfares in the sixth variation, may be a further half-remembered image of the 1914–18 War.

The construction of the principal theme in the last movement, while not novel, is unusual; it is a synthesis of the principal ideas of the first two movements – that is, the linked fourths, and the descending scale which is the basis of the theme of the variations. A well-known ancestor of this technique is the last movement of the Piano Concerto in A minor by Schumann – further evidence of influence.

Rhythmically, Moeran's style in this work involves much syncopation – not only in the principal ideas but also in the patterns in the accompaniment. The bass patterns in the variations seem reminiscent of those in the First Symphony of

Four studio portraits from the mid-1940s (courtesy of Walter Knott).

Walton, while the fugue subject of the last movement (Ex. 68)

Ex. 68

owes something to an earlier Walton work – *Portsmouth Point* – which itself was a product of Walton's anti-Romantic phase. The influence of the early Stravinsky (*Petrushka*) can be seen in, Moeran's phrase-elision, which results in accents being transferred to different parts of the bar.

It is in the harmony that the work shows its most striking departure from Moeran's earlier styles. A determined effort is made to avoid the implications of the diatonic scale: as early as the third bar, there appears a characteristic of Stravinsky's early style – a cadence which sounds simultaneously the harmonic characteristics of both plagal and perfect forms. A few bars later a theme is presented in fifths, omitting one of the symbols of Romanticism – the third. In the accompanimental pattern of fast-moving string quavers, the harmonies are all first inversions which coincide with the theme only occasionally and then on a random basis. Bitonal and polytonal passages abound; Ex. 69 shows a passage from the first movement in which upper strings sound the chord of C and the lower strings sound that of E flat, while above them, the oboes are in G.

Ex. 69

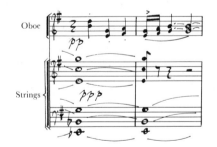

From the late 19th century onwards, the expressive quality of harmony has often been heightened at the expense of its structural functions. Thus a theme may alter in meaning or impact according to the harmonies to which it is subjected. The theme of the variations, for example, has harmonies which are wrong in the sense that they are not the natural ones, and the meaning of the theme itself is thus distorted. The last movement provides further examples of what could be and would have been big, Romantic gestures in earlier Moeran, which in the event are clouded, even soured, by 'wrong' harmonies. In earlier days, such melodies would have been given a lush treatment. Now that early manner becomes the subject of self-comment, for there is a developing sense of irony in which may be seen a potent symbol of the composer's own growth.

Sometimes the departure from Classical habit is simple; in Variation 2, for example, music which moves in perfectly ordinary D major harmony is given an underlying B flat pedal point. Elsewhere the departure is rather more drastic as, for example, in the fugal conclusion to the last movement where bass entries of the subject in the home key of C major are answered in the upper strings with a stretto entry in the unlikely key of G flat major (Ex. 70).

Ex. 70

Orchestrally the *Sinfonietta* must be as accomplished a piece of craftsmanship as anything being written at that time. Moeran profoundly admired the work of Tchaikovsky and, in particular, his orchestration. What he had learnt from Tchaikovsky by this time was that clarity is achieved by adding no more notes or instruments than are absolutely essential. Comparison here with the extravagant scoring of Bax shows the difference between the approach of a Romantic and the more bracing one now being attempted by Moeran. The treatment of the second half of the variation theme demonstrates the point. There is here a gap of anything up to two octaves between the themes and the accompanying harmonies which some composers would have considered empty and might well have filled in with horns; not so Moeran. The result of this and similar passages is the airiness and loose texture which is such a fingerprint in his later work. Orchestral doubling is kept to a minimum and the resulting primary orchestral colouring enhances the impression of brightness and cleanliness.

The one doubling which is used is that of the oboes and trumpets (Variation 2) – significantly a favourite Tchaikovsky doubling. Another instrumental combination is that of the violas and cellos playing in thirds; the cellos, however, are above the violas – a manner of scoring learnt possibly from Brahms, who first used it in the Second Symphony.[23] (It is not without significance that other influences of this particular Symphony had appeared in Moeran's G minor Symphony.) Sibelius, too, is echoed in the orchestration of the *Sinfonietta*. In the last movement, for example, themes are presented in the brass and woodwind against rushing semiquavers in the strings. This idiom is to be observed in the Sibelius Third Symphony, although a similar idiom appears nearer to home in the first movement of the Vaughan Williams Fifth Symphony (dedicated, incidentally, to Sibelius 'without permission' and first heard at a Promenade Concert on 26 June 1943).

The independence of Moeran's timpani writing is notable; at one point in the last movement it is the timpani alone which establish the home key of C major after a passage in G flat major. They are treated with considerable virtuosity – and, indeed, the timpani ostinato which is the basis of Variation 2 seems indebted to Elgar's virtuoso work in 'Troyte' (*Enigma Variations*).

Formally, the work is marvellously concise. It is as if Moeran

[23] In the first movement, at the first appearance of the secondary idea.

wishes finally to lay the ghost of old criticisms and to demonstrate his structural and technical skill – not that these skills, impressive though they are, are the final purpose in themselves, but there is nevertheless a degree almost of academicism here which has hardly been a feature of earlier work. While classic *principles*, such as balance and restraint, are upheld, there is no adherence to classic *models*. There are canons, themes in diminution, clever combinations of themes and all the rest of the 18th-century stock in trade but all wear a decidedly 20th-century face. What the *Sinfonietta* attempts is a synthesis of Moeran's lyric muse with the refinement, balance and economy of admired Classical models filtered through and tempered by a growing awareness of 20th-century Neoclassicism. The work is unique in Moeran's output in that while later works each explore further some of the techniques pioneered in it, none can be seen as a direct step along its path.

IX. THE INFLUENCE
OF PEERS COETMORE

With the completion of the *Sinfonietta*, Moeran was at last able to contemplate the promised major works for cello in which Peers Coetmore was to have an active part. What he seems to have had in mind was some kind of creative partnership with Peers in which she as performer would be as intimately bound up in the composition process as he himself:

> There are wonderful things we could do together in creating music, not only concertos and orchestral work, but chamber music. When I say creating music, I mean writing it.[1]

The trouble was that Peers tended to be away for long spells touring as an ENSA artist, and there were thus separations which were doubly hard for Moeran as they meant his idealistic dream would be only imperfectly realised in practice.

The first mention of some kind of major work for Peers was made in a letter dated 10 October 1943. The wording of the letter suggests that at that stage he had in mind a concerto, for which she would be the soloist:

> My position, such as it is, is sufficiently strong with either the BBC or the Royal Phil. for me to insist on that.

It would be one of his best works:

> I give you my promise that I will put my whole heart into it.

By January 1944, however, he talks of completing a sonata for cello and piano first, and in February of that year wrote:

> I am beginning to work out the shape of the cello sonata.[2]

In the event, the Concerto was completed first, while the Sonata was not finished until early 1947. The apparent confu-

---

[1] In a letter to Peers dated 21 October 1943.
[2] In a letter to Peers dated 12 February 1944.

sion of aim has some significance for, just as in the case of the String Trio and Sonata for Two Violins, and in that of the Symphony and Violin Concerto, there appears to be some kind of joint conception at work which will be considered a little further later in this chapter.

Cello Concerto

There are relatively few cello concertos of quality since, of all forms, a concerto for bass or tenor instrument poses the most daunting technical problems.

For this reason, if no other, it seems unlikely that Moeran would have attempted a cello concerto, were it not for the spur of his devotion to, and admiration for, Peers. The problem was compounded, because Peers' style was elegant and intimate rather than aggressively virtuosic, and her tone was more that of a player of chamber music. Perhaps because of this, the result was a concerto which has few equals for the skill with which the cello is throughout allowed to be heard.

The first performance was given by Peers, not surprisingly its dedicatee, and was conducted by Michael Bowles at the Capitol Theatre, Dublin, on 25 November 1945. Of this intimate present for Peers Moeran was later to write:

> I would not allow anyone else to play it and I will not, while it is still under my control, which will be for a long time until it is published.[3]

The two earlier works for solo instrument and orchestra had been adventurous in construction. The Cello Concerto is much less so, following as it does a traditional pattern of three movements — sonata form, slow movement and rondo. Nevertheless there is a free use of the parent-cell technique and it is this which creates an overall unity possibly more convincing than that of any earlier work, and yet more effectively concealed. In this Concerto, the technique is refined with some subtlety, with the cell itself modified after its first use in the first subject, so that it may be used in later movements (Ex. 71).

The overall shape of the first movement is that of a gentle $\frac{9}{8}$ *moderato* for the exposition and recapitulation, sandwiching a

[3] In a letter to Peers dated 11 January 1946.

Ex. 71

fast and, at times, violent development. Elgar, too, had set the first movement of his Cello Concerto in $\frac{9}{8}$. The all-pervasive opening subject (Ex. 72) is stated by the soloist after two bars of light orchestral introduction. A comparison of the crux of this theme (bracketed as A – a germ which dominates the movement) with the opening idea of the Dvořák Cello Concerto is telling, and the two references together – Elgar and Dvořák – illustrate that method of working noted all along. An admired model (two in this case) is taken as a starting point, and a response to it is made. (This priming is in no sense plagiarism – would the cantatas of Bach, or the early sonatas of Beethoven have been as they are without the models, respectively, of Buxtehude or C.P.E. Bach?)

Ex. 72

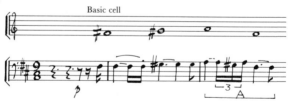

Basic cell

Some nineteen pages of full score are devoted to an extended rhapsody on this idea and, at this stage, no other is used. Even the accompaniment of the secondary idea is worked from it. This secondary idea (a further example, incidentally, of a melody with three descending steps and a leap) is unfortunately somewhat lacking in character; it does not have that quality of memorability to be found at such a crucial part of a cello concerto, in, for example, that of Dvořák.

The orchestra has been kept on a very tight leash throughout this exposition and is now given its head. Traditionally, the ends of sections in a concerto were marked by a *tutti* and Moeran follows the precedent. His *tutti* is a violent *Allegro molto* – its jagged rhythms and changing time-signatures distinctly reminiscent of certain passages in Walton's Violin Concerto.

The development is throughout concerned with ever fresh variations of the first subject; both rhythms and intervals are subjected to a continual process of re-arrangement until one version (Ex. 73) achieves dominance – a version to be retained

Ex. 73

as the core of the principal idea for the soloist in the slow movement (Ex. 75 below). The characteristic rhythm of Ex. 73 is repeated obsessively by the soloist throughout, to culminate in a climax of Sibelian intensity. This second *tutti*, with hints of the principal idea in the brass, marks the end of the development as clearly and in as classical a fashion as the previous one had marked its beginning.

It is here that Moeran makes his most notable departure from traditional sonata form – although here again he follows a precedent established by Dvořák in the first movement of his Cello Concerto. The secondary idea receives its recapitulation first. The craft of its approach is masterly, for the seams are so concealed that the listener is hardly aware of its actual arrival. Inevitably the ensuing placing of the recapitulation of the primary idea at the end of the movement means that its mood of melancholy has dominated the Concerto up till now.

This structural adjustment to achieve a specific emotional end is by no means unique in Moeran; here he follows his own precedent in the last movement of the Symphony in G minor. In this first movement, Moeran has achieved an almost monothematic structure in which the rhapsodic flow of cello melody has, through consummate skill, appeared seamless. It is a further step along a road of refinement and concentration of

The ink short score of the Cello Concerto: the beginnings of the
Adagio *(above) and the* Allegro Deciso *(opposite; both courtesy of*
Colin Scott-Sutherland).

material which will reach its ultimate perfection in the Cello
Sonata.

At the commencement of the slow movement the parent cell
provides the material for an orchestral introduction the key of
which is difficult to define but which seems nearest to E minor.
Shortly a very clear B flat is established and the parent cell
passage resolves into a fine violin melody.

The key change is magical, and its effect is much enhanced
by the muting of the orchestral strings (Ex. 74). The ensuing
cello melody, derived from the first movement (Ex. 75), sounds
as if it ought to be a traditional Irish song, but I have not been
able to identify it as such.

The slow movement is simply a very moving meditation on
these two ideas whose ancestor in spirit is probably the corresponding movement in the Elgar Cello Concerto. The music is
linked to the last movement by a cadenza for the solo cello, but
this is no mere display cadenza for it has a structural function:

in it, Moeran organises the metamorphosis of Ex. 75 into what
will be the primary idea of the ensuing Rondo.

From this point on, there are letters from Moeran to Peers

Ex. 74

Ex. 75

which provide an interesting insight into the problems of writing the Concerto, not the least of which was that a rough score of the movement he had sent her was mislaid. The correspondence, extracts of which are now interpolated, shows that Moeran turned the loss to advantage, incorporating new details.

While the primary idea of the Rondo has grown out of Ex. 75 (phrase *x*) from the slow movement, its core is the parent cell. Comparison with the Dvořák Cello Concerto (Ex. 76) reveals

Ex. 76
   (a) = **Moeran (last movement)**
   (b) = **Dvořák (last movement)**

not only similarities in the shape of the themes, but also the common property of the five-note turn with which Dvořák rounds off his melody. The first episodic idea (F sharp minor) is introduced by the soloist – as, indeed, are all the principal ideas in this movement. It is not in itself a compelling idea, halting as it does in rhythm on the second beat, and a comparison again with Dvořák is inevitable (Ex. 77). At this point, Dvořák's soloist offers only a commentary on what is really an orchestral idea, the main weight of which is placed in the second half of the bar.

Ex. 77

(a) Moeran

(b) Dvořák

*'a lovely bassoon thing'

Ledbury; Thursday, 4 pm[4]

All sorts of touches are in this new score . . . .

    I thought of a lovely bassoon thing this morning that wasn't there before.

Were it not for the 'lovely bassoon thing', the cello part would have nothing to disguise its shortwindedness. Moeran obviously saw this for himself and corrected it with his afterthought.

    Moeran now returns to his primary idea but he rarely makes an unaltered repetition – there will usually be some small touch to provide variety and yet emphasise unity. Here the episode shape just used (Ex. 77) provides a countersubject. For the second episode, the key progresses to E minor and near its end, the horns have a short phrase whose function at this point is to lead back to a further statement of the primary idea. It will be

[4] This letter is difficult to date with precision, but is probably after May 1945.

remembered later and expanded into a long passionate flowering. Both the E minor episodic idea and the horn phrase merit music examples in Moeran's letter of 4 May 1945.

Kington. May 4th/45

The present position is that from

I have inserted a return to the first subject, but in an entirely different way, consisting of 34 bars at the end of which we reach the key of F minor with you on top C after some brilliant passage work which I trust (but feel pretty sure) will be all right for the cello.

The principal idea returns in E minor, but, as Moeran writes, 'in an entirely different way'. He clearly felt that the rondo needed another hearing of the principal idea here, but was well aware of the danger of monotony. Thus, only sufficient material to identify the idea is used, and then more in the nature of a variation.

The letter of 4 May continues:

After this we lead into the new tune

in much the same way as before but a semitone higher. There are reasons for what I have done after much pondering and reflection.

(a) The question of form: the movement as it first was began to sprawl; moreover, the very nature of the main subject seems to call for an insistence on the Rondo scheme. One is, I feel, fully justified in interpolating all sorts of tunes provided the movement is bound together by the main idea which in this case lends itself admirably to the purpose.

(b) The tension wanted keeping up at this point with a longer lead up to the climax and more brilliant work for the soloist seemed called for before settling down for a time to be lyrical.

(c) A change of key seemed essential coinciding with the climax and the new material which follows in the coming lyrical section. The last interpolation in the rondo was in E.

During the weekend ahead I will jot down for you a sketch of how it goes and send it to you. Anyhow, I feel far happier about it now up to its present point. I had been getting very worried. No doubt there will be further snags ahead, but no doubt by 'exploring avenues' I shall surmount them.

For the third episode, that horn phrase mentioned above flowers into a lyrical melody which might easily be taken for an Irish traditional tune (Ex. 11). Clearly, Moeran considered anything was permissible in a rondo episode – as, indeed, his letter above seems to show. It is a trait of Sibelius' technique (as of that of Beethoven) to introduce in the most insignificant way an idea to wax more important later. Moeran here allows his rhapsodic tendency full reign – the 'coming lyrical section' of the above letter. The mention of 'new material' in the letter suggests that the rough score he had sent Peers must have been nearly complete structurally, and that now, therefore, his work is virtually a complete reconstruction. The musings on the 'Irish' tune in this episode extend to some seventy bars and reach a high pitch of intensity.

Ledbury; Thursday.[5]

. . . 4 pm I have reached your entry

7 pages of score since breakfast. I hope you won't mind my saying so but I look upon the loss of edition 1 of the score as some special intervention of what ever guardian genius (or genie?) looks after me. All sorts of touches are in this new score that keep coming to me which were not in the old one. I was, as you know, unhappy about the last and I suppose it was that I did not feel inspired scoring it as I seem to be this time. It is quite another

[5] A later Thursday than that of note 4. No precise dating possible.

thing to what the other would have been. If the other should
turn up, you will see the difference. . . . I am longing to see what
other ideas crop up as I forge ahead.[6]

I think working in bright daylight has more to do with it than
anything, together with the pleasant outlook from the window
facing me to the green lawn.

I work in the dining room, and if, which is only very occasionally, I need the piano, I nip into the next room.

P.S. The concerto is in a position which requires no more
work today but sleeping on tonight plus a lot of thought as to
what is to happen.

I am back again in the tonic (in the major) after a section
which contains probably what is best in the whole work and
ends in soliloquy but the thing is how to round it off so as to
make a satisfying ending.

It will require a little or a lot, so far as I can see at present. It
has got to be a brilliant finish: I have got back to the theme in
quick $\frac{6}{8}$ B ma.

Anyhow, after some days sedentary (barring a hurried trip to
Hereford when I took out a driving licence) I shall have to
summon up energy to go up to the hill and try and think out the
finish.

The passage he thought the 'best in the whole work' is the long,
rhapsodic third episode, just finished.

The rondo stereotype required here one last statement of the
principal idea, but in the event it was to be in the key of B

---

[6] 'I am longing to see what other ideas crop up': the wording of this sentence is
revealing of the creative process as some artists experience it. Haydn, for example,
disclaimed any personal responsibility for the composition of *The Creation* and Stravinsky claimed that he was only the 'vessel' through which *The Rite of Spring* passed.

minor, not B major as the postscript says; comparison of the version in the letter with what finally appeared in the score shows some striking differences (Ex. 78), although the basic concept of turning the idea into a kind of jig is kept. The orchestration here is masterly in its delicacy – Moeran realised that the cello cannot simultaneously produce fast movement and big tone.

Ex. 78

The finish he 'thought out' consists of a brief resumé of the first two episodes to be followed by a fleeting glimpse of the primary idea in a variant of its $\frac{6}{8}$ version, which makes explicit the parent cell on which the whole work has been founded, and *is* in the tonic major key.

The final structure is idiosyncratic – but in it the traditional rondo is still readily apparent:

(principal idea = A)
A (B minor)
Episode 1 (F sharp minor)
A (B minor)
Episode 2 (E minor)
A (E minor)
Episode 3 (F minor)
A (B minor)
Episode 1 (B minor)
Episode 2 (B minor)
A (B major)

The cello is the devil . . . on account of its middle and bass register: frequently you must treat it as a solo, albeit alto or tenor part, and you must be careful not to put too much on top. Hence, I believe, the scarcity of cello concertos owing to the technical difficulty in writing them.[7]

[7] In a letter to Peers dated 8 February 1945.

In a nutshell Moeran here defines the problem in writing a cello concerto. His own Concerto is remarkable for the balance in which the soloist and the accompaniment are held. Generally he tends to pick sounds that will offset the sound of the cello: horns, for example, or woodwind. Characteristic accompaniment textures can be seen in the first movement (Novello score, reference 14) where rapid solo passage work is matched with muted trumpet and trombone, the orchestral cellos being used, but in *pizzicato*. Moeran tends to use the orchestra, when accompanying, as a chamber group, and the orchestral strings themselves are used sparingly in this situation. Where violins are used, they tend to play in a different style from that of the soloist. A fast moving solo passage, for example, might well be accompanied by a sustained melody in the violins – but even in such a case the only other instruments would be orchestral cellos playing *pizzicato*. More especially when there is a tenor or bass instrument as soloist, the problem of clarity in the orchestral bass line – which is always to some extent present in the make-up of the symphony orchestra, even when there is no soloist – becomes acute. Moeran is remarkably successful in meeting this problem, and on occasion he adopts a Mahler-like response in doubling the bass line with the deep notes of the harp.

The writing for the soloist is exacting to a degree, but it is difficult to point to much purely virtuosic music. Naturally, the lyrical nature of Moeran's style is well suited to the cello, and in effect the solo part creates a series of long, sustained, arching flights.

Structurally, the most striking feature of the Concerto is the integration and economy of the basic material, giving an overall unity yet a sufficient contrast within the three movements. Possibly, the secondary idea of the first movement lacks distinction for its purpose; yet even here it could be argued that a more memorable idea would have disrupted what seems to be an intended dominance by the principal idea.

The composition process revealed by such correspondence as there is may show superficially a haphazard approach, but there appears to be no question of adopting existing structural stereotypes and filling them with music. Especially is this true of requirements of formal repetition: where adherence to a pre-existing plan would require the appearance of a theme at a certain point, Moeran tends to trust his aesthetic instinct in reducing the scale of such appearances. The whole structural approach is indeed instinctive, with a willingness constantly to revise, adding details where subsequent re-appraisal suggested they were necessary.

Such revisions could be quite drastic; Moeran had, for example, clearly scrapped most of the first version of the last movement of the Concerto. Far from reflecting uncertainty, the approach shows a determination to work towards perfection, for there is no question but that Moeran consciously put forth his full powers in this work, which came to acquire the character of a love song. It is, therefore, one of the works on which he would have expected his ultimate reputation to rest. Arguably it is a work of such quality as to place it with the concertos of Dvořák and Elgar as the finest written for the instrument. Regrettably, it is hardly known.

Fantasy Quartet for Oboe and Strings

In 1946 Leon Goossens asked Moeran for a work for the oboe. Goossens' playing had always excited Moeran, perhaps because he played the Intermezzo from Delius' *Fennimore and Gerda* so sympathetically. By the beginning of May of that year, Moeran could write:

> I have now decided that the work will be a quartet, definitely not a quintet, also I think I am getting the shape of it. Anyhow, I have more or less decided its opening.[8]

The work must have proceeded with some speed for by the beginning of July he was writing out the score, completing it at Rockland St Mary in Norfolk. In the late summer of 1946 he wrote with some pride:

> Leon only wanted to alter one phrasing mark in the whole quartet.[9]

[8] In a letter to Peers dated 5 May 1946.
[9] In a letter to Peers undated but, from references in the letter, before the end of August 1946.

The *Fantasy Quartet* for Oboe and Strings is an accomplished score. Fantasies have an honourable history in English music, dating back to Purcell and beyond; the form took on a new lease of life in the early 1900s with the institution of the Cobbett chamber music prize, which dictated the style of much chamber music of the period. Moeran's *Fantasy Quartet* is in the line of succession of those works in that it is in one movement, although the music does fall into clearly defined sections which are linked by the monothematic nature of the work. While this structure is dominated by one melodic shape, its appearances are interspersed with episodes which give it the feel of Moeran's favourite rondo form.

The success of such a movement must depend on the interest of the idea, and its susceptibility to metamorphosis. In this case, the idea (Ex. 79), which is played at the outset of the work,

Ex. 79

reaches back over a quarter of a century in style to the opening of the String Quartet in A minor. It is conceived in a modal F minor, the principal phrases being shaped within the parameters of two minor sevenths – F to E flat and B flat to A flat. In, for example, the Symphony or the Violin Concerto, the parent cells had an anonymity which, paradoxically, assured variety without sacrificing unity. The Oboe Quartet theme has one very striking feature (marked *x* in Ex. 79) which, being impossible to disguise, dominates each section of the work; thus the price of unity here is a degree of monotony.

There are some advanced moments. Ex. 80 shows one, where each instrument is given a different key signature. There is, however, no real feeling of polytonality here, and despite such moments, the work as a whole does seem a stylistic regression, an impression which is intensified by the snatches of Norfolk

Ex. 80

folksong which haunt the texture. Albeit reluctantly, Moeran himself admitted this in a revealing letter to his wife:

> When I was all set to get on with the next movement of the cello sonata, your letter of Tuesday came and literally stopped the clock as regards the composition of that work. I hope it will get going again, but what you said about my being a spoilt child etc. has had the effect of making me feel that you think my present work is no good. Perhaps it isn't, and I shall have to find a new idiom such as I did precisely two years ago temporarily when I wrote the Sinfonietta. I have here the proofs of the Oboe Quartet. This does, on reflection, seem a bit naive and childish. I liked it well enough when I heard it last Saturday, but it certainly does seem to hark back to the idiom of before the Sinfonietta and is, very likely, not the music of a grown up person.
>
> P.S. All this doleful screed is not 'alcoholic remorse', as I haven't had a drink since Monday. I have been feeling it coming on for a long time more or less subconsciously, but your letter brought it to a head as regards the Cello Sonata. What I had already thought of for the second movement just wasn't good enough and now I realise I must think of something else quite different.

This is an extract from a letter dated merely 'Ledbury, Thursday', but it was probably written late in 1946. We do not have the letter from Peers which prompted this response, but it is clear that Moeran was about to start work on the middle movement of the Sonata for Cello and Piano, and that Peers had criticised the Oboe Quartet. Certainly she was by this time deeply worried over his continuing drink problem, and we may conjecture that this is why she had taken him to task for childishness and for behaving like a spoilt child.

Whatever was in Peers' letter, the effect on Moeran was traumatic, for he had come to depend on Peers and her good opinion of both him and his work. He was unable to contain his drink problem and she, seeing it as the root of his inadequacies, was unable to live with it. Without her approval his creative stream would in due course dry up. So it was to prove as a truly tragic situation was played out.

P.C.

Rahoon

Something of his state of mind can be perceived in *Rahoon*, the last of his Joyce settings. This depressing masterpiece is as significant for the fact that Moeran chose to set it at all as for the setting itself. The intense vision of Joyce's sepulchral lovers communing beyond the grave is matched in Moeran's language – language of a sophistication to place it with the Cello Sonata, for song and sonata seem spiritually related and one illumines the other.

The desolation of mind that could pen such a song can only be guessed at.

Sonata for Cello and Piano

There are further tantalising glimpses of the progress of the Sonata from time to time:

> I am at a certain 'parting of the ways' in the Finale and can't decide at the moment. I expect this afternoon's walk may settle it. I am not stuck, but I am not at the moment sure whether I am pretty near the end or if there may have to be a tidy piece more. I am on the eleventh page of this movement and I mustn't make it too long; on the other hand, a lot of it being in quick 2/4 time the pages are soon over. It is turning out in places to be accidentally contrapuntal.
>
> I have just realised in a bit I have done this morning that three of the themes are combined at once (one on the cello and two on the pfte.) but I didn't spot it till afterwards. . . . I am not going to be rushed and spoil the finale of this work.
>
> But in any case it can only be a matter of a few days at the

The first page of Rahoon *in ink manuscript (courtesy of Colin Scott-Sutherland).*

most, then we can spend more time together working out its interpretation.[10]

Finally it was in sight of completion, as he wrote to his wife:

> Ledbury: Monday mid-day
> As things now turn out, there is a good chance of finishing the composition of the sonata next week, as I have a clear run . . . .
> I think the last movement is turning out good but for the rather highly concentrated effort of this sort of music, day to day work is really necessary, hours at a time without break for other engagements.

Peers wrote to Arnold Dowbiggin on the 17 April 1947:

> I expect you will be interested to hear that the cello sonata by my husband is finished and is a very fine work.

With Charles Lynch as pianist, she gave its first performance on 9 May of that year, in Dublin. The work was in due course issued by Novello, and in it Moeran knew that he had produced some of his best work:

> Kenmare: Monday
> I have just spent all yesterday on cello sonata proofs. You know I don't usually boast, but coming back to it, going through it note by note, and looking at it impartially, I honestly think it is a masterpiece. I can't think how I ever managed to write it.[11]

We may well agree with the composer that the Sonata for Cello and Piano is a masterpiece, and indeed it has strong claims to be his most perfectly realised work. Both cello and piano writing is splendidly idiomatic, and the balance between them is masterly. The Sonata is remarkable for the sustained intensity of its mood and for the perfection of its structural proportions. While it does not so consciously explore new techniques as did the *Sinfonietta*, it nevertheless seems altogether more advanced in idiom than that work. Stephen Lloyd[12] professes to see in it the influence of Bax, and if this is allowed it is probably most apparent in the second movement. Unlikely as it would seem from our knowledge of Moeran's musical tastes, the

[10] In a letter to Peers dated 27 February 1947.
[11] In a letter to Peers dating from some point in 1948.
[12] *loc. cit.*

obsessional writing of much of the final movement suggests more than a passing knowledge of Bartók.

The essential point with the Cello Sonata, however, is that with it a point is at last reached where any attempt to identify influences is not only more difficult than in earlier works but is also without profit. For here at last is that mature style and individual voice for which he had been seeking all his life. Sadly, although there is a brave optimism about its concluding pages, the prevailing mood is one of depression mixed with yearning.

When Moeran first contemplated writing cello music for Peers Coetmore, there was some doubt whether the first work would be a concerto or a sonata. In the event, the Concerto came first. But if the primary ideas of the first movements of the two works are examined, resemblances are at once apparent which are too striking to be dismissed as merely coincidental, and it seems at least possible that once more some form of joint conception occurred for the two works (Exx. 72 and 81). At the very least, one of the principal parent cells (Ex. 71) is common to both works,[13] and is already very familiar from its use in the Symphony and Violin Concerto. It is now possible to see that this melodic cell is one which Moeran had been toying with for most of his creative life.

Ex. 81

The three movements of the Sonata are respectively in sonata, ternary and rondo form. In all three movements the prevailing mood is one of depressed tension, to be lightened in glimpses only in the first movement, and generally towards the end of the last. The compositional problem was therefore two-fold:

---

[13] When the final note of the four comprising the cell is raised one octave, the figure of three steps and a leap is revealed — see Exx. 36, 71, 82 and 83.

(a) to achieve without monotony an overall unity of mood, up to a point where the tension thus created could be relieved; and (b) to create satisfactory macro- and micro-structures to contain the thought and feeling.

To achieve unity without monotony it was necessary to evolve leading ideas of considerable plasticity; to create these Moeran made the most far-reaching use he had yet attempted of parent cells. In his earlier work these cells, sometimes of three or four melodically organised notes only, were irreducible units; in the Cello Sonata, the listener is more aware of their intervallic structure. Moeran appears to have refined his technique to a point where the interval, used both melodically and harmonically, is the essential unit of construction, together with certain key rhythms which are used also to unify the structure. The chosen intervals were the third and the fifth – the third may be major or minor, although the minor form predominates. Tension is thus musically inherent from the outset, for there is a conflict between the traditional emotional implications of the two types of third, and also between the third and the fifth. 'Traditional emotional implications' should perhaps be amplified. The falling minor third has come to be used by musicians as a symbol of sadness, depression or gloom and has therefore a pessimistic ambience, while the major third, perfect fifth and its perfect fourth inversion have similarly acquired qualities of optimism.

This primary intervallic material is linked, for two minor thirds separated by a semitone comprise the perfect fifth while also providing for the major third (Ex. 82(b)). Thus in microform is present one of Moeran's most personal idioms – the close alternation of major and minor.

While they have a rhythmically propulsive function of establishing the tolling pattern of much of the music, the opening three bars of the first movement set out the intervallic material of the entire work (Ex. 83). From this material grows the primary idea of the first movement – an idea which, quite apart from its intrinsic beauty provides an almost inexhaustible selection of developmental possibilities (Ex. 81). From it, the two parent cells can be isolated (Ex. 82). They share the interval of a minor third.

Ex. 82

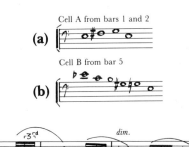

Ex. 83

It is arguable how the composition process worked in Moeran. Did this primary idea evolve from the cells, or were the cells derived and then isolated from the inspirational idea? It is impossible to say, although, as I have suggested, there are remarkable family links with the opening of the Cello Concerto. What is beyond dispute is that the sonata is created from the development, melodically, harmonically and rhythmically, of the implications of this primary idea. In tracing some of the threads of this development, the treatment of some of the possibilities suggested, for example, by just one bar – bar 6 – provides a sample of the method (Ex. 84).

The sequence of linked thirds (cell *B*) in fact so pervades the whole work that there would be little point in quoting every instance of its usage. The fact that the textures are shot through with it means that it is a crucial agent for unity between the three movements, and it appears always to occupy a prominent position. In the second movement it is heard first in the cello immediately before the first point of climax and then in the piano immediately after that climax. It starts the third movement, as if to emphasise that in this movement the argument will centre on matters of interval. Here the cello has the thirds while the piano has the opposing fifths, thus underlining one of the tensions (Ex. 85).

Ex. 84

In the enduing phrase, the fifths are linked
into a descending sequence:

Some of them invert to fourths:

and turn into semiquavers
to accompany the cello:

Ex. 85

The preoccupation with the third becomes quite obsessive –
disturbingly so in later passages. The cello, using major and
minor thirds in the rhythm of Ex. 85, forms a bass ostinato to
the piano in a processional which is in the line of succession to
those in the Violin Sonata (last movement), String Trio and
Symphony (last movement). Both the comparable passages in

the Violin Sonata and Symphony also feature prominently the interval of a third. The comparison with the first movement of the Trio is, however, even more striking – the rhythm of the cello ostinato in each is similar (Exx. 20 and 86).

Ex. 86

The other key interval – the fifth with its associated inversion of a fourth – is important in the secondary idea of the first movement (Ex. 87(a)). I suggested above that it had become a symbol of optimism and to some extent Moeran's acceptance of this symbolism is supported by the aspiration of the other prominent idea to use it in the first movement (Ex. 87(b)). The inversion – the fourth – in particular achieves even more

Ex. 87

prominence in the final movement where it provides one of the primary ideas (Ex. 88). It is here that the obsessiveness is so striking – the melody centres around the note E from which it seems unable to escape, creating a tension all the fiercer because the underlying piano part moves in the antagonistic thirds of cell *B*.

Ex. 88

The harmonic journey Moeran had made in his music had started years before with progressions suggested naturally by the Dorian mode. Subsequently his language had been enriched in turn by the added-note harmony of John Ireland, the diatonic discords of Ravel and the chromaticism of Warlock and Delius. At each stage something of each previous influence was retained, so that at this ultimate stage represented by the Cello Sonata, all the influences are to a degree present – but refined in subtlety beyond anything met with before. The chromaticism, for example, now has little of the lushness of Delius and, indeed, when there is the occasional lush chord it is a matter of aural surprise.

Having chosen his harmonic path, Moeran advanced along it fearlessly. In Ex. 89 the piano chords are clearly identifiable

Ex. 89

triads, but those in the right hand appear at first glance not to be related to those in the left. The effect is not bitonal since some kind of tonal framework is sustained by the cello. Rather is there an effect of harmonic souring – a distortion of a basically tonal language. The chords are not chosen at random, however. There is a pattern – the right-hand ones are generally in pairs a minor third apart. Thus the key interval of a minor third has here a harmonic influence, and since the minor third is so often approached melodically from above by a semitone, it is natural that triads a semitone apart will be a prominent feature.

Melodic interval control of the harmonic process is not carried out systematically (i.e., serially) – Moeran was too lyrical and impetuous a composer for that. But it is a factor of which further instances may be given. In Ex. 90 the falling thirds sequence (cell *B*) suggests the harmonic pattern for the piano accompaniment of the secondary idea. Here the interplay of the major and minor thirds is maintained, but their opposition is not dramatised as it is at the end of the first movement where the cello identifies itself with the major third while the piano assumes the role of the minor third – a struggle which is abandoned in the last chords where both instruments agree on a final chord without a third.

Ex. 90

The alternative principal interval (fifth with inversion of fourth) is the basis of the harmony at the commencement of the second movement. The fourth and fifth are sounded together and in these two introductory bars are placed adjacent to and thus in direct contrast to the thirds and their inversions, the sixths (Ex. 91). This passage, encompassing as it does the main structural unit of the sonata, has an importance seemingly underlined when it furnishes the basis of the processional in the

Ex. 91

last movement (Ex. 86). Thus intervals which work melodically to create structure are now seen to work harmonically to unify it – in this case to tie together the second and third movements. Towards the end of the latter, the secondary idea from the first movement is heard again but in varied form. The mood here is one of optimism associated with this idea and with the interval of a fourth which generates it. Now, however, the piano has just sufficient outline to relate it to Ex. 86, and thus to the concept of fifths/fourths found at the beginning of the second movement. Here fourths, major seconds, fifths and sevenths are the rule while the thirds, throughout associated with pessimism or depression, have only a minor role.

If the harmony is examined in terms of overall effect, we see that throughout the Sonata Moeran has blurred implications, effectively to sustain and heighten a tension which is not released until the clear, unequivocal statement of the tonic major heard in the *Lento* towards the end of the last movement. The phrase, 'blurred implications', perhaps needs some amplification; two examples may help clarify the point.

The dynamic climax of the Sonata – and also the point of maximum tension – (a few bars before Ex. 92) occurs when an apparently triumphant A major is soured by the deep

Ex. 92

bass notes of the piano which are foreign to the tonality. Much of the Sonata is concerned with conflict between the cello and the piano, and this conflict is carried mainly by the harmonic language. One instance of this has already been seen at the conclusion of the first movement where the argument is about major/minor tonality. A further example occurs just before the appearance of the secondary idea in the first movement, where the piano has led the music to a chord of C major, which will be the key for that idea. But the cello is reluctant to agree, and takes a further bar and a half to leave its C sharp for the necessary C natural – in a phrase, a blurring of harmonic implication (Ex. 93).

Ex. 93

If melodic and harmonic intervals are used to build structure, so to a certain extent is rhythm – principally as means of uniting the three movements. The dotted rhythm of the first movement primary idea (Ex. 81) suggests in turn the primary idea of the second movement (Ex. 94), and the closing figure of

Ex. 94

this same first-movement idea (bar 6 of Ex. 81) generates the energy of the last movement (Ex. 85). Rhythm is also an important agent in creating and sustaining the tension between the two instruments. Thus in the long passage leading up to the huge dynamic climax in the third movement, the six quavers are divided into two groups of three for the cello, whereas for the piano they are divided into three groups of two. Similarly in the processional passage, rhythmic tensions are evident

Outside the house on Valentia Island in which Moeran stayed stand his landlady, Miss Margaret Higgins, and her sister. His bedroom is on the left (courtesy of E. Myles Hook).

between the dominating piano chords and the rhythmic ostinato of the cello.

It is illuminating to compare the respective roles of the piano and the cello, for it reveals that the innate character of the two instruments is used to enhance tension just as much as the purely musical elements discussed above. In a sonata for two instruments of, say, the 'First Viennese School', the material would be more or less equally shared between the two instruments. That is to say, no theme was necessarily the preserve of one or other instrument. In the Moeran Sonata, themes tend to be identified with an instrument – not that the composer is dogmatic about it. Thus in the first movement the primary idea (Ex. 81) is heard only in the cello; the secondary idea (Ex. 87(a)) is given at various times to either instrument – but only to the cello in its undistorted optimistic version. The piano has the passage which commences the second movement (Ex. 91) and retains it for the processional in the last movement. It is a moment of massive release of tension when it is given to the cello and turned, for the first time, into music of pure A major (Ex. 92), for up until this point in the movement the cello has been the chief vehicle for the passages involving linked descending thirds with all their emotional implications.

To an extent, therefore, instrumental characterisation plays its part in the structural concept. Can one go a step further and see in this characterisation a reflection of Moeran's and Peers' personal tensions in their troubled relationship? Were we dealing with an author – Hardy, for example – autobiographical quarrying would be so much more explicit and therefore so much more readily acceptable. Yet it is little more than a question of artistic medium – neither musician nor author can hope to work entirely oblivious to their personal circumstance. It would be ironic indeed if Moeran's hope for

The sideboard occupying the part of Moeran's bedroom where his piano stood, decorated by a 1948 photograph of the composer (courtesy of E. Myles Hook).

Peers and himself – the 'wonderful things we could do together in creating music' – had in the end been realised in so untoward a fashion.

The Sonata for Cello and Piano is the ultimate prize at the end of Moeran's long journey and apprenticeship, absorbing and rejecting and eventually crystallising a language and technique fit to express the deeply personal thought of what he knew to be his masterpiece. The concentration of thought is such that it would be difficult to find a redundant sound; whatever criticisms may be sustained of other works, whether of technique or of derivation, they fall to the ground here. If nothing else of Moeran had survived, we would know from this Sonata that he was among the finest composers of his time.

Serenade in G major

With the Cello Sonata behind him Moeran, in the Spring of 1947, appears to have been sketching two orchestral works: first, a movement for string orchestra, described in a letter to Peers (30 May 1947) as 'à la Barber'; and secondly, 'a completely mad and wild scherzo for orchestra. *Denny Island* is its title: this is a famous but lonely pub . . . famous for fiddling, melodeon playing and step-dancing in the kitchen'. Neither appears to have been finished. The only remaining orchestral work to be completed was the *Serenade* in G. Nearer in intention to the *Sinfonietta* than to the Cello Sonata, this unpretentious music is in no way to be compared with those major works. The *Serenade* was completed in 1948 and consists of six movements: Prologue, Air, Galop, Minuet, Rigadoon and Epilogue. It received its first performance at a Promenade Concert on 2 September 1948 (conducted by Basil Cameron). 'The audience was delighted,' said the critic Clinton Gray-Fisk, 'and Mr Moeran was recalled several times to the platform.'[14] At this first performance two further movements were apparently included, but they were omitted from the published score because, according to Lionel Hill,[15] the publisher considered they made the work too long. These two movements are to be

[14] *Musical Opinion*, October 1948.
[15] *Lonely Waters: The Diary of a Friendship with E.J. Moeran*, Thames Publishing, London, 1985, pp.87 and 137.

found, Mr Hill says, in the copy of the score deposited with the Grainger Museum in Melbourne, Australia. In contrast to the classically-scored *Sinfonietta* the orchestration includes trombones. Two of the movements – the Minuet and the Rigadoon – were salvaged, with minor modifications, from an earlier work which had been withdrawn, the Suite *Farrago*.

Farrago had been written in 1932. The composer was much vexed when any later reference to it was made, claiming 'it doesn't exist'. He was particularly annoyed that Professor Westrup included mention of it in the Moeran article in *British Music of Our Time*.[16] But it was performed. The first performance (broadcast from the studio) was given by the BBC Symphony Orchestra (Section C) in April 1933, and it was a Prom novelty for the 1934 season.[17]

In the opinion of Ian Copley,[18] *Farrago* had been made possible by the researches of Heseltine in Renaissance dance music. Certainly Moeran's own interest in this period would have been stimulated by his friend's work. Warlock's own *Capriol Suite* was based on dance-tunes from Thoinot Arbeau's *Orchésographie* (1588). Both *Farrago* and *Capriol* therefore had a similar ancestry in the early dance forms, but Warlock used the tunes of Arbeau whereas Moeran created his own. It was by no means uncommon in the early part of the century for composers to ape their forerunners with pastiche dance suites: Herbert Howells, for example, did so in *Lambert's Clavichord* (1927). So too did Ravel, in *Le Tombeau de Couperin*, which, incidentally, contains both a minuet and a rigadoon.

The link with the *Sinfonietta* is tenuous indeed; it is simply that the *Serenade*, too, looks to interpret an earlier period of music. But the period is not that of the Classical style reflected in the *Sinfonietta*, for in the *Serenade* Moeran looks beyond to the English Baroque, and beyond that again to the Renaissance dance forms which had inspired Warlock. *Farrago* had been a response to Warlock's *Capriol Suite*, and so, too, is its successor, the *Serenade*.

Inevitably, with a gap of sixteen years between the composi-

[16] *loc. cit.*, pp. 175–184.
[17] Sir Henry Wood, *My Life of Music*, Gollancz, London, 1938, p.371.
[18] *op. cit.*, p.149.

tion of *Farrago* and that of the *Serenade*, there are some stylistic inconsistencies. Of the two movements preserved from *Farrago*, the Rigadoon does show a strong Warlock influence, but Moeran prefaces the *Serenade* version with an impish quotation from the central movement of the Violin Concerto. The music seems to echo the 'Mattachins' movement of *Capriol* – both have drone/fifth accompaniments, both share similarities of melody and both conclude with a stepping-up of the tempo, accompanied by increasingly wild harmonies. It is the phrase-endings which are the most telling evidence for the link between the Rigadoon and 'Mattachins'. The link extends also to the Galop. While this was, so far as is known, a new piece, in melodic construction it uses the 'steps up' technique of the Moeran/Warlock collaboration *Maltworms*, and of the Warlock song *Piggesnie*.

The *Serenade* avoids the developmental forms in favour of ternary, rondo and ritornello forms. Thus the Prologue uses ritornello form to make the following shape: Ritornello, Episode I, Ritornello, Episode II, Ritornello. The concluding Epilogue is simply the first Ritornello of the Prologue preceded by a fanfare.

That element of pastiche so cleverly avoided in the *Sinfonietta* is here sedulously cultivated. Where the *Farrago* movements in their rhythms reflected the Renaissance dance idioms, the Prologue and Epilogue seem to represent a somewhat later pastiche; the use of hemiola and the mock-massive style suggest the occasional music of Handel. Yet in harmony the specially composed movements use some of the newly explored techniques of the *Sinfonietta* – but even here, the discords arise naturally through the interplay of the parts, much as they would have done in Purcell (Ex. 95). Against such pungency, the Minuet is harmonically in a much earlier Moeran style and we are back in the tonic minor/subdominant major world of the A minor String Quartet, and of Butterworth in Shropshire. The remaining newly composed movement is the Air, scored for strings only. It is a melody of disarming simplicity and beauty, built on the very familiar pattern of three-steps-up-and-a-leap.

Stylistic inconsistency is very much a part of the work, but it in no way spoils music of charm, boisterousness and quasi-Gallic wit.

Ex. 95

Songs from County Kerry

In the same year (1948), Moeran returned to folksong, adding to his earlier Norfolk and Suffolk sets what proved to be a final set – the *Songs from County Kerry*. His preface to the collection has the following note:

> These arrangements are taken from a much larger collection I noted in Co. Kerry at odd times during a period roughly between 1934 and 1948. They were sung to me by Kerrymen in Cahirciveen, Sneem and Kenmare. The verse by verse variants in some of the tunes are exactly as I heard them from the singers themselves on a number of occasions.

The Kerry arrangements represent a mature approach and masterly touch rarely reached in the earlier two sets. Perhaps this can best be seen through a comparison of the treatment of similar songs. Two such songs are 'The Oxford Sporting Blade' from the Norfolk set and 'Kitty, I am in love with you' which concludes the Kerry set. 'Kitty' is altogether more subtle; the placing of the chords, the restraint in their use, and knowing what to leave unsupported all show complete technical mastery. Nor are the lush chromaticisms which occasionally disfigure the earlier settings present here.

By this time in his career he had become adept at creating a phrase, or perhaps just a motive, that will fix the mood of the

words to be set. This Schubert-like ability is seen in the second
song, 'My love passed me by', with its halting, dour little figure
which seems so appropriate to the tale of spurned love (Ex. 96).

Ex. 96

The diatonicism of Moeran's accompaniment in this song is
striking – no accidentals are to be seen, yet even within these
self-imposed limits he manages a final chord which unites the
essentials of the chords of D, F and G. The blood-spattered tale
of 'The Murder of Father Hanratty' and the misty wraith-like
figures of 'The Lost Lover' both illustrate the spare textures
that Moeran had come to favour for folk settings in his mature
years, while 'The Roving Dingle Boy', a predominantly pentatonic melody, is given piano figuration of a delicacy worthy of
Fauré. 'The Tinker's Daughter' is, with 'Kitty', a jig-like
melody. Moeran spent some time living with tinkers in 1948;[19]
perhaps he collected 'The Tinker's Daughter' from them.

---

[19] An editorial note to Moeran's article, 'Some Folk Singing of Today', *Journal of the
English Folk Dance and Song Society*, Vol. V, No. 3, 1948, reads: 'It is hoped that in a later
number of the Journal Mr Moeran will tell of his travels in Eire, and contribute some of
the songs he collected there – particularly these peculiar to the calling of the tinkers,
among whom and in their tents he lived in the spring of 1948'.

X. DISINTEGRATION AND THE UNFINISHED SECOND SYMPHONY

From the point in 1947 when he completed the Sonata for Cello and Piano, Moeran seemed to undergo a process of gradual but inevitable physical and mental disintegration. In August 1947 there had been talk of a possible job for him. Perhaps Peers hoped by this means to bring some orthodoxy, if not order, into her husband's haphazard existence. It is not clear what form the work would have taken, but it seems most likely that it would have involved some form of lectureship in Cape Town. It came to nothing, and indeed it is difficult to imagine Moeran ever assuming the restrictions necessary for such work. Instead, as we have seen, he went off to live with the tinkers. (One would love to lift a veil on this tantalising piece of information – have *any* other composers gone so far in associating with their sources? Bartók, perhaps?)

Moeran had worked intermittently on a Second Symphony from about 1945.[1] Although it is clear from later correspondence that this would eventually have been a one-movement structure encompassing linked separate sections (on a model, one would think, of the Seventh Symphony of Sibelius), the earliest mention of the work in correspondence (with Peers) suggests something more traditional:

> Kenmare. 7th January, 1946
> The E^b Symphony progresses, but I am a bit stuck over the slow movement also about the finish of the first. However, I have all the material for it and it will only be a matter of time working it out.

Lionel Hill's recollections[2] bear out this view. Moeran played him the Second Symphony in 1948 ('a great deal had been written') but a few years previously he had confided to Hill his

[1] Rhoderick McNeill, 'Moeran's Unfinished Symphony', *The Musical Times*, December 1980, pp.771–777, and subsequent letter, *The Musical Times*, April 1981, p.230.
[2] *Loc. cit.*

problems with the form of the work: 'the three movements don't "gel", so to speak'. Hill suggested a continuous, one-movement work such as the Sibelius.

Moeran must have felt some confidence in January 1946, for in that month *The Daily Sketch* carried a report of his work on it. References in the correspondence to the Symphony in May 1947 show it still progressing well, and a first performance by the Hallé Orchestra was mooted for the Spring of 1949. By March 1948, he is still well pleased with his work, as a letter to Peers reveals:

> Kenmare. 8.3.48.
> I can't write much because I am at the moment in a state almost amounting to stupour [*sic*] at the point I have reached in the symphony. It may be imperfect in its present form but I think that in the last pages which complete the first section, I have reached my high water mark. It is rather luscious and spring-like – or so I hope it will sound on the orchestra. And, incidentally, apart from the lovely Southern spring here, your gorgeous cello playing, on the instrument you are now using which I listened in to last week put me into such extasy [*sic*] that the next morning I *really* got going with a tune for cellos mostly in thirds and sixths. I've tried it out on one or two locals . . . . they say it reminds them of all the Kerry tunes put together. The symphony is taking a peculiar form . . . .

Even in this optimistic letter, the seeds of a problem are already apparent: 'imperfect in its present form' and 'taking a peculiar form'.

The drinking continued, and by October 1948 he had reached a state of total breakdown. At his wife's urging he placed himself in the care of a Dr Hazlett at Cheltenham. She had professional engagements to fulfill in 1949 which involved a prolonged tour of South Africa, Australia and New Zealand. The first performance of the new Symphony was postponed, although by May 1949 it was apparently well advanced.

> Cheltenham. 10th May 1949.
> I am sorry to say that I am by no means satisfied with my E^b Symphony; well on towards the finish. I am terribly depressed about it as I fear it may have to be scrapped in toto.[3]

---

[3] Letter to Peers.

And two days later:

> . . . the form of it is bothering me I set out to write a work in one big movement incorporating the essentials of four, but as I get near the end, I am more and more in doubt whether I haven't failed.

By June 1949, he had decided that what he had written simply would not do.

> Cheltenham. 14th June 1949
>
> . . . This symphony which I started perpetrating in Eire, and which I have been working on here, simply will not stand . . . . I am not inclined to let go what I believe to be second rate. I shall have to scrap this symphony as it now is, nearly finished, and start afresh on something different. As to the writing of it, the 'venue' is wrong. If I were in Southern Ireland, I could work it out and finish it, but it is absolutely and irreconcilably impossible to do it here. It started by being Irish, and if I try and put it right here, it only ends up by being pastiche Irish. So it must go by the board . . . . it's a pity because the first part of the symphony is so good, i.e. what I wrote in Ireland and shortly afterwards . . . . I have had in this symphony to go right back to the beginning, and I find that, if I go on with the idea, it means scrapping the whole of the middle part as it now exists. I find I just don't like it, so I am driven to think it just isn't good enough . . . . There are only three alternatives, one is to tear it up and abandon the E^b symphony and the other is to go to Ireland and complete it, and the third is to write something else.[4]

Why did he not straight away adopt the second alternative and go to Ireland where he apparently felt confident of putting the work right? We may speculate a reason. In this year, his wife Peers was away on concert tours and doubtless constantly worried by her husband's alcoholism. It was at her insistence that he was at this time in Cheltenham, hopefully undergoing a cure. The above letter, read in this light, seems to be a plea to be released from whatever undertaking Moeran had given Peers to remain in Cheltenham. In a desultory way he worked,

[4] Letter to Peers.

spasmodically. In February 1949 *The Jolly Carter* was arranged for chorus. Two months later found him 'seriously considering trying to concoct another quartet',[5] but his Cheltenham lodgings were overheated and uncongenial for creative work.

Throughout the first half of 1949 Peers seems to have tried to persuade him to join her in Australia, where he might teach composition and conduct his own music. He toyed with the suggestion, but always parried. For her part it is quite clear that Peers, after this last effort, gradually extricated herself, to pursue her life in the Southern Hemisphere.

In October anxious correspondence[6] between his brother Graham and Peers (still on tour) shows that Moeran had made another of his troubling disappearances, and again the necessity of persuading him to submit to a proper cure is raised. Once found, it was only too apparent that he was suffering from another breakdown and by December he was submitting to treatment from a Dr Groves.[7]

Work on the Symphony went on fitfully, but no completion was achieved. It had been conceived in Ireland and we have his own testimony on a number of occasions that his surroundings were crucially important for his creative work. Unfortunately, he was incarcerated in England. Thus, history repeated itself; the First Symphony, almost complete, had been withdrawn in 1924, not to emerge until 1937. Now the Second Symphony suffered a similar fate.

Even now, other creative work did not cease entirely, though it was mostly of the lowly order of arrangement. One original piece – the madrigal *Candlemass Eve* for male voices – was completed in May 1949, and was dedicated to the Cheltenham Male Voice Choir. As late as 16 March 1950, when he wrote to Peers, he mentions work on a piece called *The Oyle of Barley*, 'an orchestral fantasia on this tune from Playford 1675, at the instigation of Barbirolli, and Francis, Day and Hunter'. It seems unlikely that this work progressed beyond sketches. Further, in addition to the early manuscripts mentioned in Chapter I, and the sketches of the unfinished Second Sym-

---

[5] Letter to Peers dated 31 May 1949.

[6] Graham Moeran, in a letter to Peers dated 18 October 1949.

[7] Graham Moeran, in a letter to Peers dated 22 December 1949.

Two further portraits of Moeran from the mid-1940s (courtesy of Walter Knott).

phony, the archive of the Victorian College of the Arts, Melbourne, holds also manuscripts of an orchestral overture in short score and a work for baritone, male voice choir and piano – *Rores Montium*.[8] No date for these has yet been established, but it is possible that they, too, date from this late period of Moeran's life.

In February of 1950, Moeran wrote to Douglas Gibson from Ledbury:

> I am returning to Ireland very shortly where I hope to get down to some months of concentrated work. I have found a place to live in where it is very remote, isolated and in lovely surroundings of mountain and sea, though only twelve miles from Dublin.[9]

He had achieved the conditions he thought necessary for the work needed to complete the Symphony – but it was too late, for he was now incapable of the sustained effort needed.

At some time in March 1950, he visited an eye specialist in Dublin, ostensibly for a spectacles prescription. Rhoderick McNeill speculates that he may have been given some bad

[8] Rhoderick MacNeill, *loc. cit.*
[9] In a letter dated 23 February 1950.

prognosis;[10] he did no further work on the Symphony after March 1950.

It is always tantalising to speculate what might have been; it is possible to imagine what a fine work Elgar might have fashioned from the sketches he left of the embryo Third Symphony, and Deryck Cooke and others have actually enabled us to experience somewhat more than the torso of Mahler's Tenth Symphony. But in the opinion of John Ireland, who saw the remaining Moeran sketches, there was not enough material in them to attempt a completion. Since Moeran wrote at one point of the work being almost finished, it seemed that either much material had been lost, or, more likely, that in exercising his highest critical standards, he must have destroyed much of the work.

That the Symphony was nearly complete is attested by Moeran's close friend Pat Ryan, who himself carried out the most searching hunt for the missing score.

> . . . The Symphony was almost if not wholly finished months before his death. Apart from the constant references to the progress of the work in letters to many people including Sir John Barbirolli (for whom it was written), I spent a month in Kenmare last summer, and he not only discussed the work many times with me, but even asked my advice on various passages. I find it hard to believe that a man of E.J. Moeran's integrity would deliberately write for four years about the progress of a fictitious work. It is, of course, possible that he may have destroyed the score himself. But that the score did exist I am positive, and I am sure that this view is also held by all his friends in Kenmare.[11]

After Moeran's death Sir Arnold Bax received from Graham Moeran a parcel of manuscripts. As discussed in Appendix 3 (p. 268, below), when Bax died these manuscripts passed into the hands of the late Julian Herbage.

Among them was a symphonic movement dated 11 February 1948, which could have been all, or part, of the missing Second Symphony. Nothing approaching a symphonic movement is

[10] *Loc. cit.*
[11] Pat Ryan, in a letter to *The Daily Telegraph* dated 17 January 1951.

Moeran with Sir Arnold Bax, probably in 1948 (courtesy of Walter Knott).

among the manuscripts donated by Peers to Victorian College; there are only sketches of the Symphony.

Such manuscript sketches as are available do not suggest a further advance of style, nor a maintenance of quality. The opening subject is brash (Ex. 97), and does not compare in grip

Ex. 97

and originality with the opening of the Symphony in G minor.
Moeran's last creative thoughts, however, were still obsessed
with that melodic shape which had marked almost all periods
of his work (Ex. 98). Was this the tune, one wonders, which
sounded to the locals like 'all the Kerry tunes put together'?

Ex. 98

Moeran wrote no further to Peers after March 1950. It seems
that he was happy in his work and his lodgings until March, but
thereafter he began to drink heavily. For three months he
wandered here and there, eventually appearing in Dublin
where he suffered an attack by thieves. On 16 June he was seen
in Kenmare 'in the company of a cripple',[12] and lived there

[12] Graham Moeran, in a letter to Peers dated 3 December 1950.

The pier at Kenmare, where, in 1950, Moeran met his death (courtesy of E. Myles Hook).

quietly for the next six months, even giving some music lessons. He was, however, unable to concentrate on anything for more than a short while. Worried friends prompted him to write to his mother, which he did a few days before his death. In his letter, he said that his lucid moments were few, and he was afraid of being certified insane.

On 1 December 1950, during a violent storm, Moeran fell off the pier at Kenmare and was recovered dead. Michael Bowles writes:

> Since he died, I have met people who assumed he was drunk when he fell off the pier at Kenmare. The medical evidence at the coroner's inquest was that it was a heart attack: no water was in the lungs; he was dead before he fell in. Actually, as far as I know, he had stopped taking any alcohol at all for six months before he died.[13]

[13] In a letter to the author dated 26 January 1981. The jury at the inquest returned the following verdict: 'That Ernest J. Moeran came by his death from natural causes, namely cerebral haemorrhage, and fell into the water at Kenmare Pier on December 1st'.

A fortnight after his death, his brother Graham wrote to Peers:

> The illness which finally proved fatal was of such a character that nothing, so far as I have been able to gauge, could have been done to give him back his powers of creative thought again.[14]

The cause of death was thus thought to be cerebral haemorrhage. Kenmare honoured him by turning out in strength for his funeral.

[14] In a letter dated 15 December 1950.

XI. PORTRAIT

By far the best character-sketch of Moeran is given, in loving detail, in Lionel Hill's *Lonely Waters: The Diary of a Friendship with E.J. Moeran*. In many ways he seems a reticent, retiring figure, elusive and shadowy. Freda Swain describes him as 'gently spoken and somewhat lacking in confidence – hesitant, as it were'.[1] Yet he had a considerable capacity for friendship and appears to have numbered friends not merely in the musical world but in the arts generally. Poets such as Robert Nichols, Bruce Blunt, James Joyce and Seumas O'Sullivan, painters like Augustus John, performers such as Harriet Cohen, Hamilton Harty and Désiré Defauw and fellow composers like Bliss, Ireland, Warlock and Bax – all appear regularly in his story.

While he did not marry until late in life, he certainly did not remain celibate until then and had friendships, liaisons and affairs of some seriousness with the opposite sex. One such involved the artist Nina Hamnett with whom, according to Jack Lindsay,[2] Moeran lived for a while in the mid-1920s; and another involved the model Eileen Hawthorne – a mistress he shared with Augustus John. According to Michael Holroyd,[3] Eileen Hawthorne was John's principal mistress from the 1920s onwards. John wished

> he could trust more wholeheartedly her ability to hide things: for example pregnancies. Though he shared her favours with the musician E.J. Moeran, it was John who, after some grumbling, paid for the abortions. He had no choice. Otherwise her mother would get to hear of them, and then the world would know.

John's own attitude was delightfully insouciant:

[1] In a letter to the author dated 8 August 1983.
[2] *Fanfrolico and After*, Bodley Head, London, 1962, p.84.
[3] *Augustus John*, Vol.II, Heinemann, London, 1975, p.90.

One day while strolling on the front at St. Maxime I espied two figures approaching: they seemed familiar. It was E.J. Moeran and an old friend of mine, Eileen Hawthorne. What had brought them here I couldn't imagine. Our greetings were politely joyous. . . . I couldn't discover they had any clearly defined plans. . . .[4]

The inconsequence of this is somehow typical both of Moeran and of John.

Moeran's loyalties to those he admired were strong, and he would rush to the defence of any who were wronged. The attacks on Benjamin Britten by the musical press in the 1939–45 War were a case in point. An earlier instance of this loyalty occurred in April 1931 when, in company with fellow musicians, he rushed to the defence of Elgar in protest at 'the inscriptions of that preposterous and wooden headed old bore Professor Dent'.[5]

Yet, while of a gregarious nature, Moeran also needed solitude and seclusion for his work. He put this need graphically to Eric Fenby: 'He used to say that what he really wanted in life was a job minding a railway crossing in some remote spot with two trains a week'.[6] His love of engines, trains and everything connected with railways is attested by, among others, Christopher Le Fleming[7] and Lionel Hill.[8] Railway people on his Hereford branch line were esteemed friends, and his knowledge of railways, from timetables to the characteristic sound of each locomotive, was encyclopaedic.

To the constant concern of his friends he would disappear for weeks at a time. The two elements of gregariousness and desire for solitude went deep in his make-up and are, of course, reflected throughout the music, which may one moment exhibit an extrovert brilliance, and yet within a few seconds may turn inward to a quiet self-communing. Instances of creative artists

---

[4] *op. cit.*, p. 198.

[5] Dent had contributed an article to Adler's *Handbuch der Musikgeschichte* (pp.123–130, second enlarged edition, 1930) in which he had appeared to undervalue and even to denigrate the work of Elgar. Moeran's fellow signatories included Harty, John Ireland, Augustus John, Landon Ronald, Walton, Warlock and George Bernard Shaw.

[6] In a letter to the author dated 7 July 1983.

[7] *Journey into Music by the Slow Train*, Redcliffe Press, Bristol, 1982.

[8] *op.cit.*, p.18.

With a group of local worthies in the grounds of the Windmill Inn, Stalham, probably in 1926, are Augustus John (far left), Peter Warlock (next to John, wearing a beret) and, in the centre, John Goss (with a pint glass in his hand), Barbara Peach (Warlock's girlfriend) and Moeran.

with a dual animus are not hard to find: Schumann is an extreme instance, but Heseltine/Warlock perhaps not nearly as extreme as had been suggested by his biographer Cecil Gray.

Stephen Wild has suggested that Warlock was 'a person with whom [Moeran] shared many common personality and character traits, both laudable and regrettable'.[9] In the latter category was a certain instability, and certainly in Moeran's case there were occasional unfortunate and embarrassing lapses. Michael Bowles writes: 'From my years of acquaintanceship, I would say he was unreliable and unpredictable in drink. This was due, in my view, to the effects of his wound in World War I'.[10] His unreliability seems to be borne out by a letter from Bruce Blunt to Arnold Dowbiggin in 1943[11] about a radio programme on Warlock that Moeran had undertaken to assist:

> He let everybody down and provided neither himself nor anything else . . . . I am told he has now gone to Ireland to hide his shame.

[9] *op.cit.*, p.14.
[10] In a letter to the author dated 26 January 1981.
[11] Dated 20 May.

Moeran had perhaps been closer to Warlock than had anyone else. But after Warlock's death he would not speak of him if he could avoid it, and could have agreed to take part only in a moment of weakness.

Freda Swain found him 'a weaker character than some', and felt 'he was not a happy person, at any rate when we knew him'.[12] Others, too, held Moeran to be ineffectual; the letter from Bruce Blunt quoted above shows Blunt to be among these, and Jack Lindsay writes that 'Moeran merely bubbled in red-faced confusion',[13] when a member of the Eynsford house party, Nina Hamnett, suffered a fall and was injured. Yet there was a streak of Norfolk obstinacy, particularly where publishers were concerned. He could be a tough bargainer:

> I am not perfectly acquiescent over the terms of the agreement for the oboe quartet – the Royalty of 10% is, after all, only a fraction over a penny in the shilling.[14]

There was, however, the weakness which dogged him; his drinking eventually became chronic alcoholism. Whether this first became a problem during the three riotous years Moeran spent with Warlock or whether, as Michael Bowles asserts, it was attributable to the effects of his war wound, it is not possible to say with any degree of certainty. That it clouded his later life is very apparent. Michael Bowles gives a striking picture:

> I have seen him ready to sing snatches from the slow movements of Haydn quartets (of which he knew a very great deal indeed) after two sherries; I have known him still steady and sober after four or five whiskies. The trouble was that he could be overcome with drink unexpectedly – very often in a public place, which got him some reputation as an alcoholic, instead of merely a World War I casualty.[15]

Gwen Beckett, too, recalls[16] that after a rehearsal she and Sir Adrian Boult (whose secretary she was for half a century) 'had been a little disturbed' at the amount he drank. She added: 'but

---

[12] *loc.cit.*
[13] *op.cit.*, p.84.
[14] In a letter to Douglas Gibson (of J. & W. Chester Ltd) dated 6 December 1946.
[15] In a letter to the author dated 26 January 1981.
[16] In a letter to the author dated 13 January 1981.

he seemed quite sober'. Mr Bowles adds a personal comment
with which many might humbly agree:

> Personally, I would not mind being an alcoholic if I could leave
> behind me the music, in quality and quantity, that Jack did.

Moeran's drinking excesses were clearly well known to all his
friends and tolerated by them if not by the law: one such
encounter mentioned by Peter Warlock ended felicitously, but
suggests there was nevertheless a case to answer:

> Raspberry, who has been pronounced 'not guilty', leaving the
> court without a beerstain on his waistcoat, so to speak, wishes to
> come and help at the end of this week, to recuperate from the
> strain and attendant insomnia, of his period of suspense.[17]

But these excesses became a considerable problem in his
marriage and his correspondence with a worried wife, travel-
ling abroad on concert tours, is littered with promises to keep
away from alcohol. Sadly, these promises could never be kept.
It took a real effort for Moeran to admit his problem even to
himself: he talks of 'real happiness' as opposed to

> the rotten sort of happiness that is engendered by being ging-
> ered up by artificial or other means . . . Let me blurt it out and
> say I mean excessive liquor . . . I can definitely and finally
> promise that I won't any more want to step off the deep end.[18]

Things came to such a pass that Peers suggested that he
should not come to Liverpool for the first performance in
England of the Cello Concerto, in case he were not to 'behave
himself'. He clearly *had* misbehaved at the first performance in
Eire:

> Anyway, my darling, coming to Eire was, I am afraid, like a boy
> being let out of school.[19]

And there must have been several thousand witnesses to the

---

[17] In a letter to Bruce Blunt dated 23 October 1928. I am indebted to Fred
Tomlinson for the information that 'Raspberry' was one of Warlock's nicknames for
Moeran – presumably because of Moeran's florid complexion. Warlock made a habit of
such names for his friends – Cecil Gray (C.G.) became, for example, 'Tympani'.

[18] In a letter to Peers dated 20 October 1943.

[19] In a letter to Peers dated 11 January 1946.

embarrassing scene at the Proms in 1946, when, unable to manage it on his own, he had to be assisted to take a bow after a performance of the Cello Concerto and was unceremoniously marched off the platform with support at each elbow. Moeran was aware constantly of the pain his habits were causing, but this was an area of his life that he was incapable of controlling.

He was nevertheless capable of deep consideration and sensitivity. A small example might be the matter of the dedication of the Third Rhapsody. The work is inscribed to his old friend Harriet Cohen, and the publisher (Chester) had omitted this dedication from the newly printed orchestral score. Moeran was anxious lest this should further add to the problems of a pianist who was going through a difficult period. His persistence (and an unusually tolerant publisher) led eventually to a reprint of the edition.

Moeran acknowledged no religious faith. His few attempts at music for church ritual were occasioned by the hope of earning money:

> that is why I am writing this bilge for the Church. It is very easy to do and it is financially a waste of time to write songs or piano pieces.[20]

Yet the church music is highly regarded, is 'bread and butter' for many choirs and Moeran himself would go to hear it in Hereford Cathedral whenever the opportunity presented itself. A somewhat less cynical attitude to religion is revealed in a letter to Peers:

> [your mother] pointed out to me that you are 'not in our keeping' – in other words that power above disposes of you as to your safety . . . . But as you know, that does not bring much comfort to me although I realise what it must mean to those who can and do honestly believe in those things.[21]

There is no evidence that Moeran had any strong political leanings, apart from a distaste for 'the left wing glue pot

---

[20] In a letter to Philip Heseltine dated 5 November 1930.
[21] In a letter to Peers dated 2 January 1944.

fraternity'.[22] In health and general constitution he does not seem to have been strong, despite a love of the outdoor life and much walking in the hills.

He seemed to be accident-prone and injury would be caused by walking into obstacles or falling over them. Mention of such accidents recur throughout his letters and are often mentioned in the letters of others writing about him. Augustus John recounts, for example, that Moeran slipped on the steps leading to John's villa while visiting him in France.[23] On this occasion, he badly injured his face. At another time, Moeran himself writes[24] that he has sprained his wrist and bruised his ribs – waking suddenly in his sleep. Many of Moeran's accidents have been attributed to drunkenness – but this seems too facile; it is probable that the war injury may have had much responsibility for them.

As a performer, Moeran had sufficient skill as a violinist, at any rate in his youth, to hold his part in a string quartet; he was also a competent pianist. References to him as a conductor are very sparse and it is not possible to judge his competence from them. He certainly conducted the *Songs of Springtime* on at least one occasion,[25] but his reference to 'mugging up the contents of my Sinfonietta score'[26] to conduct at the Cheltenham Festival hardly suggests a man comfortable in the art. In the end he thought he did it competently enough, but his temperament and general unreliability would always have prejudiced his career as a composer-conductor. But it would be unfair for him to shoulder all the blame for his withdrawal from conducting the London Symphony Orchestra at the 1946 Three Choirs Festival in Hereford since the authorities had apparently not checked with him before programming his appearance.

From performers in general he had evidently suffered more than his share:

---

[22] EJM in a letter to Peers. The letter is undated, but is thought to be in the summer of 1946. The 'Glue Pot' was a pub – The George – situated conveniently for the old Queen's Hall, and nicknamed thus by Sir Henry Wood who complained that his players tended to 'get stuck' there.

[23] *op.cit.*, p.198.

[24] In a letter to Aloys Fleischmann dated 30 August 1940.

[25] EJM in a letter to Douglas Gibson dated 30 November 1944.

[26] In a letter to Peers dated 2 July 1946.

the trouble about piano music as a rule is that there are such a lot of damned fools who set out to be pianists; they play our works occasionally and completely misinterpret them and pull them about.[27]

His irritation on an occasion when he had not been informed of a performance of his Symphony is perhaps understandable:

It all makes me depressed. These people who play one's music seem to have no thought that the composer might like to hear it – and it took me two and a half years to write.[28]

Nor did singers escape the lash:

Singers are so stupid and uninterested in music that it seems more worthwhile to conserve one's energies for writing music in other forms.

The pity of it is in my case that I think I am better at songs than anything else; i.e. some of my songs are my very best works, but there is not the slightest chance of much happening about them with the present level of intelligence of singers in this country.[29]

For a handful of artists – Hamilton Harty, Leslie Heward, Leon Goossens, Michael Bowles, Aloys Fleischmann and, above all, his wife – Moeran was always generous and grateful.

His own tastes in music are above all reflected in his work. Elgar and Haydn were fundamental, as ultimately was Sibelius. One may guess that his deep knowledge of the Haydn Quartets derived from that school quartet at Uppingham. Apart from Haydn, however, there is little evidence of a love for the other Viennese classicists; rather his tastes inclined to the late Romantics. Just as the clarity of his chamber music writing owes something to Haydn, so his orchestral writing seems indebted to the example of Tchaikovsky. On borrowing a record of the Tchaikovsky Third Symphony (which he mistakenly calls the 'Little Russian'), he commented:

It is a model of orchestration and old Tsch., when he does go all-Russian, seems to do so to more effect than some of the Nationalist composers.[30]

[27] In a letter to Harriet Cohen, quoted by her in *A Bundle of Time*.
[28] In a letter to Peers dated 5 January 1946.
[29] In a letter to Peers dated 30 December 1943.
[30] In a letter to Peers dated 9 January 1944.

A piano concerto by Medtner is dismissed as 'incredibly dull',[31] while Hindemith's Symphony in E flat is judged 'a most exhilarating affair'.[32] Reger sparks the following crisp comment:

> Here and there are cases of rare inspiration, probably occurring when the old bugger had just broached a fresh cask, or having outrun his daily supply of beer had, as was quite frequent, turned his attention to sparkling hock.[33]

A string quartet by Kodály was

> terribly disjointed and far too orchestral in effect . . . . I must say I find a vertical quartet which is almost devoid of polyphony as this one is, or sounded to be, very wearisome to listen to for three movements on end.[34]

A sonata by Samuel Barber, however, was judged a fine work:

> I shall make a point of missing nothing of Barber's that may be broadcast.[35]

Of the English composers after Elgar, the music of Warlock, Delius and Bax was most akin to his temperament. He was excited by the recording of the Bax Third Symphony;[36] if we did not have this evidence of his knowledge of the work, we would have deduced it from his own Violin Concerto. It is a matter for comment that he is to hear the Delius Violin Concerto played by Albert Sammons,[37] and that he was given records and a miniature score of Delius's *Appalachia* as a birthday present — works he must, in fact, have known for many years.[38]

The contemplation of Nature in solitude was fundamental to Moeran's creative process:

> Speaking purely personally, I find that 'inspiration' arrives as a

[31] In a letter to Peers dated 20 February 1944.
[32] *ibid.*
[33] In a letter to Philip Heseltine dated 23 November 1930.
[34] In a letter to Peers dated 2 January 1944.
[35] In a letter to Peers dated 9 January 1944.
[36] In a letter to Peers dated 12 February 1944.
[37] In a letter to Peers dated 12 January 1944.
[38] In a letter to Peers dated 9 January 1944.

result of concentrated thought in complete solitude amid natural surroundings which seem to be conducive to the germination of musical ideas, such as long rambles over the countryside.[39]

The point echoes one made in an earlier letter, and goes a long way towards explaining the composer's sudden disappearances which so worried friends: he needed isolation, and enforced spells of incarceration in hospital, nursing home or even his own domicile meant inescapable people and in turn creative inhibition:

> I spend a good deal of time writing music, but lack of privacy prevents me doing anything on a larger scale, as I am still too helpless to be free of constant attendance.[40]

In particular, it was the Atlantic seaboard of Kerry that became indispensable to Moeran. Speaking of Kerry, he wrote to his wife:

> I think of my themes when I walk the mountains there[41]

and in another letter to her:

> I am going for a walk to see the sun set to the west over our lovely bay. I shall have paper and pencil with me and I may jot down something for our work together.[42]

He defined his composition practice rather more precisely to Leonard Duck, making a distinction between the conditions necessary for work and the source of inspiration:

> There is one other point of view in my own case. That is that in writing songs or choral works it is the poems themselves that give rise to any inspiration I may be lucky enough to get wherever I may be — not necessarily the solitudes of nature which, on the other hand, usually are the only conditions which provide the kind of ideas I care to use in abstract work.
>
> But I have sketched out songs in all sorts of places when reading poetry. The six Seumas O'Sullivan poems I did a good bit of in the public lounge of Wynn's Hotel in the centre of

---

[39] Quoted in Leonard Duck, 'Inspiration: Fact and Theory', *The Musical Times* January 1953, p.13.

[40] In a letter to Philip Heseltine dated 5 November 1930.

[41] In a letter dated 10 October 1943.

[42] Dated 20 October 1943.

Dublin. Another song, *'Tis time, I think, in Wenlock Town*, I thought out in the train between Paddington and Westbury and then, after lunch at my destination, wrote it straight down as it now stands in print.[43]

It can also be seen from the above comments that Moeran became a composer who could dispense with the keyboard for composition, and the point is confirmed in a letter to his wife:

I work in the dining room, and if, which is only very occasionally, I need the piano, I nip into the next room.[44]

Despite this, independence from the keyboard was not easily won; his prolonged illness in 1930 helped break the habit of using it for composition since he was bedridden for some months.

He had a life-long diffidence about his worth as a composer which could only be overcome in the face of irrefutable instances of creative mastery. According to Harriet Cohen, very little of his piano music satisfied him:

. . . most of my piano music is complete tripe and I wish it were not published. One of the exceptions is *The Lake Island* for which I still have a great affection.[45]

The church music was dismissed as 'bilge', and an early song (circa 1926 and unidentified) is described as 'so bad that I thought "finis". It is published, by the way, obscurely, and I believe it is out of print now'.[46] One letter to his wife is so self-revealing that it is quoted here extensively. Many musicians will know all too painfully the feelings of inadequacy to which Moeran gives utterance here:

I find myself here in Liverpool a kind of 'white headed boy' and I feel all the more conscious that it is difficult to live up to it in the future with my appalling lack of technique and facility.

I sometimes wonder whether I wouldn't be better occupied in wielding the pen in a music-journalistic capacity.

Perhaps I am not a composer at all.

[43] Leonard Duck, *loc.cit.*, p.13.
[44] Undated, but probably after January 1945.
[45] Harriet Cohen, *op.cit.*, p.261.
[46] In a letter to Peers – undated, but probably 1948.

I have been again through the experience lately of (a) either sitting blankly for hours and being incapable of writing two decent consecutive bars or (b) writing with great enthusiasm for 2 or 3 days and then having to scrap the lot because I find on mature reflection that it simply won't do. At the same time, I am cheered by the obvious fact that some of those who apparently seem able to go on, oblivious of anything and to create successes for themselves, do so regardless of any semblance of self criticism.[47]

The martyrdom of the creative artist tortured on the rack of self-doubt can be sensed here. Yet the inviting prospect of retiring – giving up – is never seriously contemplated:

In view of present activities and inspirations, it would be on my conscience if I were to retire as a writer. I have had letters from various unknown people that my music, the Symphony especially, not only gives them pleasure but is a comfort to them when they are feeling down and out.[48]

From this it can be seen how necessary to Moeran was the stimulus of approval. Some composers seem to be able to work on without this stimulus, as if in a vacuum; the examples of Havergal Brian or even J.S. Bach suggest themselves. Others, such as Wagner, seem positively to feed and thrive on adverse criticism; yet others, like Britten, found professional criticism well-nigh intolerable. Moeran needed the occasional success, and relished it:

The second performance tonight was simply wonderful: the orchestra played in a quite inspired way and Lawrence [Turner, the leader of the Hallé] also was in first rate form . . . . the applause was so prolonged that J.B. made me come on . . . .

P.S. I hope you don't think I boast, but I think my Violin Concerto is lovely!
But wait until you play the cello concerto with J.B. That will be better still.[49]

---

[47] Dated 26 January 1945.

[48] In a letter to Peers – undated, but probably 1948.

[49] In a letter to Peers – undated, but marked 'Chez Rogerson'. He was probably staying with Haydn Rogerson, who was principal cellist of the Hallé Orchestra at the time. 'J.B.' was John Barbirolli, the conductor of the orchestra.

In sum, much of his earlier work, including some songs, church music and most of the piano works he tended to dismiss. But for the major works, from the Symphony through to the Cello Sonata, he retained an affection. It is a harsh judgement; many would be far more charitable to the piano music. Nevertheless, in essence it is right. Moeran's claim for greatness will rest, as he saw, on this handful of works.

XII. THE MOERAN MEANING

In attempting even an interim assessment of the significance of the work of E.J. Moeran, one problem remains to be resolved – if, indeed, a resolution of it is possible. This is the problem of the plethora of composers to whom Moeran responds. Does there ever appear an authentic individual Moeran voice, or does he habitually speak with the voice of others? Is it purely a question of manner and style, or does he have something to say which is so personal that it transcends idiom?

Music affords numerous examples of composers who flattered by imitation. Among the very greatest, Handel, Bach and Beethoven are obvious cases, and their present assured place in the esteem of both critics and public suggests that posterity, in its judgements, is less concerned with sources and models than with absolute standards of quality. Thus it is perhaps here necessary to begin to distinguish between matter and manner, and with this in mind it may be helpful to consider briefly the fortunes of another composer whose work in some respects shows parallels with that of Moeran.

In Great Britain, until at least the early 1950s, much criticism of the music of Mahler dwelt on its vulgarity, long-windedness and reliance on what was seen as a ragbag of fanfares, café waltzes, bird calls and marches, together with an over-indebtedness to such earlier models as Brahms, Schubert and Beethoven, to whose music it was seen as distinctly inferior. From our perspective today, it is possible to see that such 'criticism' has failed to perceive the 'stylistic counterpoint', the deliberate play on different levels of musical meaning, which is part of the substance of Mahler's musical language. Admittedly, the wide range of discernible influences in a Moeran work amount to a very gentle stylistic counterpoint when compared to Mahler, but the critical experience of Mahler may nevertheless justify us in considering first the message, or matter, of Moeran before we consider the manner. What aspects of experience does he attempt to explore? Can specific themes (not necessarily musical – although they are there and may be significant as such) be identified and seen to run throughout his work?

To attempt an answer to these and other questions is by no means easy, and in any case the problems are compounded by Moeran's exceptionally long maturation process. If we say that only in the later works is the individual voice heard, do we thereby dismiss those works created on the way as unworthy? To do so would be to lose much fine music, for in Moeran, as in many composers, the early work, while marred by technical limitations, has a careless rapture inevitably lost with maturity. It is undeniable that Moeran's life was subject to misdirection, time-wasting and taking wrong paths. Yet the growth process is important and in Moeran's case especially so, since it enables us to trace recurring imagery, and the refinement of those images.

The works written up to about 1930 are comparatively straightforward. Often based on honourable models, they are pleasing lyrical songs, genre salon pieces for piano, chamber music of some scale and vigour, and orchestral essays in rhapsodic style, soaked in the melodic idioms of folksong. On the whole, these works are untroubled, even having about them a sunny insouciance. But from about 1930 onwards a gradual but perceptible change begins. At first there are just inexplicable passages of obscurity in otherwise sunny, pastoral movements. An example would be that which occurs in the middle of the first movement of the String Trio (Ex. 20, p. 94). Later, in the Symphony in G minor, the overall ambience is troubled and dark, so that the scherzo appears as a small oasis of light. Later still, the Cello Sonata seems more disturbed than any other major Moeran work. The tendency towards pessimism does not encompass all Moeran's later music – pieces such as the Third Rhapsody and the *Overture for a Masque* are exceptions to a by no means universal rule. But such a tendency is undeniably there.

The significance of Moeran's war experience has not been accorded nearly enough weight in such comment on his work which has so far appeared in print. He lived through three years of its horrors, and carried the permanent effect of his head injury to the grave. He was 'an officer and a gentleman'; as such we would not expect much comment by him to be recorded – in words. Experience of conversation with veterans of the First World War – admittedly limited – has been that few will speak of it. Memory becomes dim with time, yet such memories must be traumatic. All experience – especially experience of horror and misery – must always be a source of inspiration to the artist. We have only to consider the work of the war-poets Brooke, Owen or Sassoon to see the truth of this. What is true for poets, novelists or film makers is likely also to be true for musicians.

Vaughan Williams' experience of the War (for which he volunteered in 1914 at the comparatively advanced age of 42) is reflected in such works as *Dona Nobis Pacem* or, as prophecy, in the Symphony No. 6 in E minor. He, with Moeran, felt deeply the death of Butterworth in 1916:

> I sometimes dread coming back to normal life with so many gaps – especially, of course, George Butterworth . . . .[1]

One composer, Ivor Gurney, went insane as a result of his war experiences. The rare position of Moeran is that he was one of a handful of young musicians (he was 19 in 1914) to experience the Western front, to be wounded, and to survive. But even among that small number, he was further distinguished by his creative gift, which was to transmute experience into sound imagery.

The second factor which must be taken into account when the matter or message of Moeran's music is considered is his alcoholism. It is arguable how far alcoholism is a symptom and how far, in turn, it is a cause. We may well agree with Michael Bowles' view that Moeran's war experience was, to an extent, responsible for it, and we may certainly assume his problem was exacerbated by the sojourn with Warlock. The point here is that, for whatever reason there was for it, alcoholism was an element of the man. By his own admission,[2] he led a grey, lonely

---

[1] In a letter to Gustav Holst, quoted by Henry Steggles in the *R.C.M. Magazine*, Vol.LV (1959), No. 1, pp.21–24.

[2] In a letter to Peers dated 19 October 1943.

life which seemed likely to be transformed when he met his future wife. The marriage was apparently not a happy one; this, and the greyness, the alcoholism and the War we would expect all to be reflected in the music, at various times.

Nature was the eternal solace. He took a proprietary interest in favourite places – to climb with Peers the Hergest Ridge, or to show off the Kenmare River to friends. So crucial was setting for his music that he could not work or even complete a piece if the surroundings were wrong. Thus we can readily identify Norfolk music, or Kerry music, or that of Hereford. The early 1930s were, of course, a back-to-nature time – 'I'm happy when I'm hiking'. There had been a tramp poet (W.H. Davies, 1871–1940); and one of Moeran's close friends, the painter Augustus John, glorified the gipsy life in much of his work. Moeran himself, according to *The English Folk Song Journal*,[3] lived with tinkers for a while. Certainly his normal life-style was that of a vagabond – moving from hotel to hotel, however, rather than from camp-fire to camp-fire.

These, then, were the principal elements shaping both his life and his work, elements which are channelled into his music by emotional reaction to nature and circumstance. Far from being a weak imitator of his English peers, it is probable that, with Moeran, we have to look elsewhere for the nearest musical parallels. While on the surface Vaughan Williams, Ireland, Bax, Delius or Warlock all at various times appear to be contenders for the position of what, for the want of a better description, we might term spirit- or soul-brother, closer examination reveals important differences.

Warlock showed little or no ability to work in the larger forms, and in any case differs from Moeran and the other composers above in showing almost no interest in nature as a source of inspiration. To be fair, all the other composers mentioned do share this interest with Moeran – but that is as far as the resemblance goes. Vaughan Williams was a public rather than a personal nature poet. Both Moeran and Vaughan Williams were sons of clergy – but Vaughan Williams had a strong streak of Bunyan-like puritanism about him. Further, he

---

[3] See Chapter IX, note 19 (p.220).

was to an extent a musician-prophet – some aspects of this can be seen in works like the Fourth and Sixth Symphonies. Prophecy necessarily involves strong public commitment. Even apart from this, Vaughan Williams all his life was involved in Kapellmeister activity – music festivals, music for amateurs, hymn books and committees. In contrast, Moeran held no public office, did almost no teaching, and took part in almost no public music-making. Nor did he go out of his way to write for amateurs – the few two-part and unison songs hardly invalidate this point when comparison is made with the vast amateur output of Vaughan Williams.

John Ireland's approach to nature is not always free from sentimentality (nor is that of Moeran in some of his early piano music) and his view was always that of an adoptive Londoner, despite the countrified accoutrements of windmill and wild brooks. Neither he nor Bax, in contrast to Moeran and Vaughan Williams, took much part in the folksong movement. It is true Bax wrote of the Happy Forest, and contemplated the sea from the castle of Tintagel, but the woods he dared to enter were enchanted, and the sea was the magic Garden of Fand. In other words, he transformed the real world of nature into his own fantastic sound world – and at times it was quite a terrifying world.

Of all the composers with whom comparison is made, Delius was the most self-assured and, indeed, self-sufficient. He was arrogant, hard, and untouched, apparently, by the vicissitudes to which his life was subject. Despite the passion and the ecstatic climax to which his work aspired, there remains about it a curious detachment – an objectivity learnt, perhaps, from the post-Impressionist painters with whom he spent so many of his formative years.

Each of the perspectives explored by these artists is valid and is a mirror of each man's experience; but that of Moeran is different again. For, at its finest, his is a deeply personal music, possessing a strong subjectivity found only rarely in the work of his contemporaries. Of the English composers, the nearest parallel would be Elgar, who wore his musical heart on his sleeve more than most. Among the continental composers, it has already been suggested that comparison with Mahler might be revealing; even closer in spirit is certain music by Tchaikovsky – whom we have already observed to exercise some influence on Moeran, particularly in one of his most personal works – the Symphony in G minor.

What is it that the four composers – Elgar, Mahler, Tchaikovsky and Moeran – share? It is a capacity, better developed than most, to transmute personal experience directly into music. The emphasis here is on the word 'personal'. For all four were, in various ways, disturbed and suffering. In no sense does this mean that Moeran falls into the pit of self-indulgence, as Tchaikovsky sometimes does. His range is considerable, from bucolic high spirits through rapt serenity to deep pessimism. But in the end, as with Elgar, there is an underlying thread of melancholy, always, as it were, lying in wait so that the passages of lyrical joyousness are liable at any moment to be clouded or distorted. The musical gestures are not, of course, as forthright as those of Tchaikovsky or Mahler. Moeran was, after all, an 'officer and a gentleman'. Nevertheless, in his mature work, his music is the music of vulnerability, instability and woundedness. Thus he will take refuge in the jollity and conviviality of the alehouse, or lose himself in the anonymity of the crowd. The middle movement of the Violin Concerto is eloquent testimony to this. Or he will find no refuge at all but a brave acceptance (the Cello Sonata). Or he will find only the ultimate depression of *Rahoon.*

The mature Moeran has not the lushness of Delius, the lurid hothouse exoticism of Bax, the brooding austerity of the mature Vaughan Williams, the innocence of Ireland or the sophisticated complexity of the mature Howells. These epithets were chosen to summarise the *superficial* character of the work of these composers; the somewhat devastating one actually applied to Moeran was 'homespun'. If applied to certain of the earlier works, the word may be justified. No justification exists for applying it to the best of the later music, which shows a very sophisticated technique.

Always his music is effective in sound. It is an outdoor music, in which open, unclogged textures abound, fresh as air. This clarity of texture is not necessarily a quality of his contemporaries, despite their many other attributes. Moeran's music is

always immaculately presented in terms of dynamics, phras-
ings, and general finish, as Sir Henry Wood had observed when
writing about the Violin Concerto,[4] and his self-criticism was
formidable. Only the best works survived.

The principal tool of his technique can perhaps be summa-
rised as interval control. Thus there is a lyric impulse subjected
to a quite rigorous discipline – the parent-cell technique. In
none of what we may call our 'control group' of English
composers is such discipline imposed on the ideas as that
imposed by Moeran in his best work. Since the impulse is
lyrical, it follows naturally that what happens to the lyricism
must also have meaning. Lyricism may be distorted, as happens in the first movement of the Symphony; it may be withdrawn altogether after a sudden burst of warmth. It may be
encapsulated, insulated, cherished in isolation. In these
instances, the lyricism is qualified by harmonic means – by the
use of unnatural, 'wrong' harmonies, for example, or by false
relation. The latter technique is, of course, rooted in the conflict
of major and minor, and particularly that of thirds.

Other characteristics include the use (rarely) of real folksong, of pastiche folksong, and of what I have called the
processional. Just as the isolation of specific beauty (i.e.,
concepts of beauty with specific significance for Moeran) by
key is a form of symbolism about the meaning of which one can
only speculate, so too is the creation of pastiche folk melodies
placed at strategic points in certain major works (the *Sinfonietta*
or Cello Concerto, for example). It would seem that they
represent for him a kind of ideal, or 'desired state' of natural
bliss. In the two cases where actual folksong appears to be used
(*Lonely Waters* and *The Shooting of his Dear*) it is arguable that in
each case the words are a clue as to the reason for the use of the
songs.

The processional, or a variant of it, occurs in various works
from the early Violin Sonata *via* the Symphony to the Cello
Sonata. One may speculate that this, too, is a symbol – in this
case a symbol in some way connected with the composer's war
experience. This seems to be particularly true of those exam-

[4] In a letter to EJM dated 18 March 1942.

ples in the Symphony in G minor, and especially that in the last movement – a grey, hopeless procession to nowhere. Whatever it means, it is a recurring feature of Moeran's music.

Finally, all those passages so readily identifiable in their derivation from the work of others must be confronted. This is a problem that Moeran commentators have at some stage to face, and criticisms on this score dogged him, from the somewhat snide (and anonymous):

Moeran certainly manages his derived tricks naturally[5]

to the much more sympathetic:

Certainly he was often derivative, and from time to time Delius, Vaughan Williams and Sibelius all held sway over his medium of expression. He wrote so fluently that he probably did not realise his occasional indebtedness to his predecessors.[6]

There is no more element of plagiarism in all this than there is in Beethoven's nod in the direction of C.P.E. Bach in his early sonatas, or Schubert's in the direction of Beethoven in the Great C major Symphony. I would nevertheless question whether Moeran's derivations are always unconscious. May it not be that, on occasion, a specific passage or event in a universally known work is used by Moeran as a point of reference to reinforce whatever meaning he wishes to convey? Such passages may well have acquired a definitive status in terms of the emotion or feeling they carry. Some of the works we have noted in passing as prime influences are now brought together below. Where possible, a generally accepted significance for each is noted.

			MOERAN
ELGAR:	*The Dream of Gerontius* (Angel's Farewell)	Peaceful serenity	Violin Concerto
BAX:	Symphony No. 3 (conclusion)	Peaceful serenity	Violin Concerto

[5] Review of a performance of the Symphony in G minor by the Hallé Orchestra under Dr Malcolm Sargent (date unknown).

[6] Sir Arnold Bax, 'E.J. Moeran, 1894–1950', *Music and Letters* Vol. XXXII, No. 2, April, 1951, p.126.

TCHAIKOVSKY:			MOERAN
	Symphony No. 6 (first movement)	Shattering of peace	Symphony (first movement)
MOZART:	Symphony No. 40 (first movement)	Controlled emotion	Cello Concerto (last movement)
DVOŘÁK:	Cello Concerto (last movement)		Cello Concerto (last movement)
MENDELSSOHN:			
	Violin Concerto (first movement; secondary idea)		Violin Concerto (first movement, secondary idea)

Any reasonably musically cultured and alert listener could discover all these and many more with little difficulty. Is it not possible that this is the point? In other words, that the emotional meaning Moeran wishes the music to convey is doubled in force by the added meaning of the model to which reference is made?

It seems as if Moeran does work through symbol. A number of composers have done so including, at random, Bach, Mahler and Vaughan Williams. If so, Moeran's symbols are of distortion, contrast of major and minor, significant melodic shapes, association of idea and, indeed, association of other composers. In this language, a pastiche folksong becomes a symbol of nature – the 'desired state'. Disturbance is symbolised by mixed triads, false relation, or alternation of major and minor. 'Greyness' or melancholy may be symbolised by the withdrawing or freezing of lyricism – a sudden memory, perhaps, of the way in which beauty can be tainted or corrupted (by war?). Thus Moeran would appear to use a *musical* symbolism – as opposed to the painting imagery of Delius, the poetic imagery of Bax or the Bunyanesque imagery of Vaughan Williams.

Thus is Moeran's special area of experience – unique in British music – expressed, at the last, in masterful technique. This is not to place him among the greatest composers. Those places will always be held by men who could sublimate their experience into unquenchable optimism, such as Bach, Haydn, or Beethoven. Moeran, of lesser rank, is yet one of those composers with whom, in his moods, we can identify.

Appendix 1

STRING QUARTET NO.2 IN E FLAT

The autograph score of this quartet was found among the composer's MSS by his widow, Peers Coetmore. The MS bears no date, but it is clearly an early work.[1]

The E flat String Quartet is considered here in an Appendix because there is as yet no evidence, other than intrinsic musical evidence, with which to date it. The work as published has two movements which are linked by an idea common to both. The first movement, an *Allegro moderato* in $\frac{6}{8}$ time, is in sonata form. It is the primary idea of this movement – a gentle pastoral tune – which becomes the agent of unity between the two movements (Ex. 99). The companion movement is a

Ex. 99

theme and variations – but so constructed as to comprise the essence of a slow movement, a scherzo and a boisterous finale. The theme on which the variations are built is another of those pastiche folksongs which have occurred with increasing frequency in Moeran's music from about the time of the Symphony in G minor onwards.

It is possible to see why the publisher, Novello, saw fit to issue this Quartet with the somewhat dismissive 'early work' label. The first movement has an almost embarrassing complacency about it, and there is a real inconsistency of style between the two movements, despite the attempt to link them. Of the two, it is the second which speaks of maturity, and it is this which suggests there are factors which might well justify a late dating for the work as a whole. It may well be asked whether the dating of a work matters – surely what does matter is whether or not it is a worthy work.

In my view, the dating of a work does matter a great deal. The description 'early work' may carry loaded implications – and im-perfections may be explained away by its use. Indeed, it may even carry the unspoken codicil 'and not worth bothering with' – and it is

---

[1] Introductory note in the Novello miniature score.

significant that of all Moeran's published works this Quartet has
suffered more than its fair share of neglect. The Quartet is by no
means a major work, but it is a very characteristic one by a musician
who had played much chamber music in his time and knew the kind of
work to delight chamber music enthusiasts.

The Second Quartet most nearly approximates in stature and
import to the *Fantasy Quartet* for Oboe and Strings – with which it
shares the two-movement form. There is no other instance in Moeran
of a two-movement structure, and the Oboe Quartet dates from the
middle months of 1946. The E flat String Quartet is simple, innocent
and childlike in style – adjectives which inevitably recall Moeran's
letter[2] to Peers in which he reluctantly accepts her (implied) criticism
of the Oboe Quartet as 'a bit naive and childish . . . and very likely not
the music of a grown-up person'.

There is about Moeran's music in the last period of his life a tension
between the music I suspect he would have liked to write and that
music he felt it behoved him to write – that is, a distinction between a
child-like (not childish) innocence and a sophisticated maturity. I
have a suspicion that the String Quartet is, in its naiveté and
openness, representative of a creative urge in him – paralleled and
distorted into near-vulgarity in the unfinished Second Symphony
(Ex. 98, p.228: 'all the Kerry tunes put together') – against which one
must set the altogether sterner stuff of the Cello Sonata. The one feels
no need to struggle for new idioms; the other is more the music of 'a
grown up person'. There is nothing unusual in this – did not Sibelius
relax between his symphonic utterances with light, inconsequential
suites?

Many creative artists seek ever more simplicity in their later work
(Beethoven and Britten are notable examples). The extant sketches of
the Moeran unfinished Second Symphony show passages far removed
from the sophistication of the Cello Sonata and the *Sinfonietta* – yet the
Cello Sonata at least was roughly contemporary with it. In my view,
therefore, the simplicity and innocence of the Quartet are by no
means inconsistent with other music on which Moeran was occupied
over the period 1946 to 1950. Of the two movements, the second
shows the more complete mastery of texture and, indeed, the more
confident inventiveness. It also shows the stamp of Irishness. While
the earliest work is not devoid of Irish characteristics, this is perhaps
supportive evidence that the second movement at least is of late date.

[2] That headed 'Ledbury, Thursday'. It is otherwise undated, but is thought to be
from the autumn of 1946; quoted in Chapter IX, p.201.

Certainly, it is this element which is at the root of the stylistic inconsistency between the two movements.

In 1950 Moeran published the *Songs from County Kerry*. While he had collected them at various times from 1934 onwards, the actual arrangements probably date from the late 1940s. The melodic parallels between certain of these songs and passages in the last movement of the Quartet are striking and give weight to the idea that this movement probably is not an early composition. Thus there is a two-movement work, of which one movement is decidedly Celtic in style and mood and the other is not. The Celtic movement shows the influence of Kerry songs while the idea of a two-movement work can only in Moeran be related with the period of the *Fantasy Quartet* for Oboe and Strings.

These factors lead me to think that the second movement is later than 1946 and perhaps even as late as 1949. It will be remembered (p.224, above) that Moeran, in May 1949, wrote of 'concocting another quartet'. The first movement is more problematical although this too reflects that serenity which seems characteristic of Moeran's Irish 'Haven', even if it has no obvious brogue. It may well be earlier than the second movement – possibly even pre-1926 – but as with the Symphony in G minor, an earlier movement may have been revised and pressed into service in a later work, to be bound to its companion by thematic ties.

Why did Moeran not pursue publication of the work? He tended, after all, to destroy work he regarded as sub-standard. Is it possible he declined to publish it precisely because it was not representative of the new-style Moeran of the *Sinfonietta* and the Cello Sonata? Because it might be thought 'childish'?

I would like to think that the joyous Irish dance (Ex. 100) with which the E flat Quartet concludes was Moeran's last word – his 'Es Muss Sein'.

Ex. 100

Appendix 2

CLASSIFIED LIST OF WORKS

WORKS FOR ORCHESTRA

		Date of composition	Publisher and date of publication
Orchestra			
1.	*In the Mountain Country*, Symphonic Impression 3(1).2.3(1).2/4.2.3.1/timps., perc./strings	1921	OUP, 1925
2.	Rhapsody No.1 3(1).2+1.2+1.2/4.3.3.1/timps., perc./strings	1922	Hawkes, 1925
3.	Rhapsody No.2	1924	Hawkes, 1924
3a.	Rhapsody No.2 (revised and re-orchestrated for smaller orchestra) 2(1).2(1).2.2/4.3.3.1/timps., perc., harp/strings	1940-41	Chester, 1941
4.	Two Pieces for Small Orchestra: *Lonely Waters* 1.1+1.1.1/1.0.0.0/cymbals/strings/voice *ad lib.*	1924?	Novello, 1935
	Whythorne's Shadow 1.1.1.0/1.0.0.0/strings	1931?	Novello, 1935
5.	Symphony in G minor 2(1).2.2.2/4.3.3.1/timps., perc., harp/strings	1924-37	Novello, 1942
6.	*Overture for a Masque* 2(1).2.3(1).2/4.3.3.0/timps., perc./strings	1944	Joseph Williams, 1949
7.	*Sinfonietta* 2(1).2.2.2/2.2.0.0/timps., perc./strings	1944	Novello, 1947

256

	Date of composition	Publisher and date of publication

8. *Serenade* in G
    2(1).1.2.2/2.2.3.0/timps.,
    perc./strings
	1948	Novello, 1953

Solo Instrument with Orchestra

	Date of composition	Publisher and date of publication

9. Concerto, for violin and orchestra
    2(1).2(1).2.2/4.2.3.0/timps.,
    perc., harp/strings/solo violin
	1937-41	Novello, 1950

10. Rhapsody No. 3, in F sharp, for
    piano and orchestra
    2(1).2.2.2/4.3.3.1/timps., perc./
    strings/solo piano
	1942-43	Chester, 1943

11. Concerto, for cello and orchestra
    2(1).2.2.2/4.2.2.1/timps., perc.,
    harp/strings/solo cello
	1945	Novello, 1947

Chorus and Orchestra

	Date of composition	Publisher and date of publication

12. *Nocturne* for baritone, chorus
    and orchestra.
    ('Address to the Sunset' from
    Don Juan Tenorio the Great
    by Robert Nichols)
    2.2+1.2.2/4.0.2+1.0/timps.,
    perc., celesta,
    harp/strings/baritone/SATB
    chorus
	1934	Novello, 1935

CHAMBER MUSIC

13. Trio in D, for violin, cello and piano	1920	OUP, 1925
14. String Quartet No. 1 in A minor	1921	Chester, 1923
15. Sonata in E minor, for violin and piano	1923	Chester, 1923
16. Sonata, for two violins	1930	Boosey & Hawkes, 1937
17. Trio, for violin, viola and cello	1931	Augener, 1936
18. *Prelude*, for cello and piano	1943	Novello, 1944

		Date of composition	Publisher and date of publication
19.	*Irish Lament,* for cello and piano	1944	Novello, 1944
20.	*Fantasy Quartet,* for oboe and strings	1946	Chester, 1947
21.	Sonata, for cello and piano	1947	Novello, 1948
22.	String Quartet No.2 in E flat (posthumous)	?	Novello, 1956

PIANO MUSIC

		Date of composition	Publisher and date of publication
23.	*Three Pieces* The Lake Island Autumn Woods At the Horse Fair	1919	Schott, 1921
24.	*Theme and Variations*	1920	Schott, 1923
25.	*On a May Morning*	1921	Schott, 1922
26.	Toccata	1921	Chester, 1924
27.	*Stalham River* (Ballade)	1921	Chester, 1924
28.	*Three Fancies* for Piano Windmills Elegy Burlesque	1922	Schott, 1922
29.	*Two Legends* A Folk Story Rune	1923	Augener, 1924
30.	*Summer Valley*	1925	OUP, 1928
31.	*Bank Holiday*	1925	OUP, 1928
32.	*Irish Love Song* (traditional Irish folksong; from *Folk Dances of the World*)	1926	OUP, 1926
33.	*The White Mountain* (traditional Irish folksong)	1927	OUP, 1927
34.	*Two Pieces* Prelude Berceuse	1933	Schott, 1935

MUSIC FOR VOICES

Songs for Solo Voice and Piano	Source	Date of composition	Publisher and date of publication
35. *Spring goeth all in White*	(Robert Bridges)	1920	Curwen, 1924
36. *Twilight*	(John Masefield)	1920	Paxton, 1936
37. *Ludlow Town* When Smoke Stood up from Ludlow. Farewell to Barn and Stock and Tree Say, Lad, Have You Things to do? The Lads in Their Hundreds	(A.E. Housman)	1920	OUP, 1924
38. *The Day of Palms*	(Arthur Symons)	1922	?
39. *When June is Come*	(Robert Bridges)	1922	Curwen, 1924
40. *Two Songs* The Beanflower Impromptu in March	 (Dorothy L. Sayers) (D.A.E. Wallace)	1923	Chester, 1924
41. *Two Songs from the Repertoire of John Goss* (included in *Seven Sociable Songs*; others are by Hubert Foss, C.W. Orr, S.F. Harris and R. Paul) Can't You Dance the Polka? Mrs Dyer the Baby Farmer		1924	Curwen, 1924

		Date of composition	Publisher and date of publication
42.	*The Merry Month of May* (Dekker)	1925	OUP, 1925
43.	*Come Away, Death* (Shakespeare)	1925	OUP, 1925
44.	*A Dream of Death* (W.B. Yeats)	1925	OUP, 1925
45.	*In Youth is Pleasure* (from *Lusty Juventus*, R. Wever)	1925	OUP, 1925
46.	*Troll the Bowl* (Dekker)	1925	OUP, 1925
47.	*'Tis time, I Think, by Wenlock Town* (A.E. Housman)	1925	Winthrop Rogers, 1926
48.	*Far in a Western Brookland* (A.E. Housman)	1925	Winthrop Rogers, 1926
49.	*Seven Poems of James Joyce* Strings in the Earth and Air The Merry Greenwood Brightcap The Pleasant Valley Donnycarney Rain has Fallen Now O Now in this Brown Land	1929	OUP, 1930
50.	*Rosefrail* (James Joyce)	1929	Augener, 1931
51.	*The Sweet O' the Year* (Shakespeare)	1931	Augener, 1931
52.	*Loveliest of Trees* (A.E. Housman)	1931	Curwen, 1932
53.	*Blue Eyed Spring* (Robert Nichols)	1931	Curwen, 1932
54.	*Tilly* (in *The Joyce Song Book*, pp.17-19; limited edition of 500 copies) (James Joyce)	?	Sylvan Press, 1933

		Date of composition	Publisher and date of publication
55.	*Four English Lyrics*	1934	Winthrop Rogers, 1934
	Cherry Ripe (Campion)		
	Willow Song (John Fletcher)		
	The Constant Lover (William Browne)		
	The Passionate Shepherd (Marlowe)		
56.	*Diaphenia* (Henry Constable)	1937	Winthrop Rogers, 1939
57.	*Rosaline* (Thomas Lodge)	1937	Winthrop Rogers, 1939
58.	*Four Shakespeare Songs* The Lover and his Lass (a reworking of the 1934 two-part song; see below) Where the Bee Sucks When Daisies Pied Where Icicles Hang	1940	Novello, 1940
59.	*Invitation in Autumn* (Seumas O'Sullivan)	1944	Novello, 1946
60.	*Six Poems of Seumas O'Sullivan* Evening The Poplars A Cottager The Dustman Lullaby The Herdsman	1944	Joseph Williams, 1946
61.	*Rahoon* (James Joyce)	1947	OUP, 1947
62.	*O Fair Enough are Sky and Plain* (A.E. Housman)	?	Joseph Williams, 1957

		Date of composition	Publisher and date of publication

Folksong Arrangements

I   VOICE AND PIANO

63. *Six Folksongs from Norfolk*
    Down by the
       Riverside
    The Bold Richard
    Lonely Waters
    The Pressgang
    The Shooting of
       his Dear
    The Oxford
       Sporting Blade

| | | 1923 | Augener, 1924 |

64. *The Sailor and Young
    Nancy*
    (see also II
    UNACCOMPANIED
    CHORUS
    (SATB):72.)

| (Norfolk) | 1924 | OUP, 1925 |

65. *Gaol Song*   (Dorset)   1924   Winthrop Rogers, 1931

66. *The Little Milkmaid*   (Suffolk)   1925   OUP, 1925

67. *O Sweet Fa's the Eve*   Burns   1925   OUP, 1925
    (see also II
    UNACCOMPANIED
    CHORUS (SATB):
    71.)

68. *Six Suffolk Folksongs*
    Nutting Time
    Blackberry Fold
    Cupid's Garden
    Father and
       Daughter
    The Isle of Cloy
    A Seaman's Life

| | 1931 | Curwen, 1932 |

69. *Parson and Clerk*   (Suffolk)   1947   Joseph Williams, 1947

			Date of composition	Publisher and date of publication
70.	*Songs from County Kerry* The Dawning of the Day My Love Passed Me By The Murder of Father Hanratty The Roving Dingle Boy The Lost Lover The Tinker's Daughter Kitty, I am in love with you		1950, although collected over a number of years	Augener, 1950

II UNACCOMPANIED CHORUS (SATB)

71.	*O Sweet Fa's the Eve*	(Norwegian tune; Burns)	?	OUP, 1925
72.	*The Sailor and Young Nancy*	(Norfolk)	1948-49	OUP, 1925
73.	*The Jolly Carter* (see also Unison Songs: 86.)	(Suffolk)	1944	OUP, 1949

III VOCAL TRIO

74.	*I'm Weary, Yes Mother Darling*	(Greek folksong; collected and translated by M.D. Calvocoressi)	1946	Novello, 1948

IV MALE VOICES

75.	*Sheepshearing*	(Dorset)	?	Winthrop Rogers, 1927
76.	*Alsatian Carol* (solo and male-voice chorus)		1932	Curwen, 1933

		Date of composition	Publisher and date of publication

Unaccompanied Chorus
I   SATB

77.	*Weep You No More, Sad Fountains*	(Herrick)	1922	Boosey, 1924
78.	*Gather ye Rosebuds*	(Herrick)	1922	Boosey, 1924
79.	*Robin Hood Borne on his Bier*	(Munday and Chettle, *The Death of Robin Hood,* 1601)	1923	OUP, 1924
80.	*Songs of Springtime*		1930	Novello, 1933
	Under the Greenwood Tree	(Shakespeare)		
	The River-God's Song	(John Fletcher)		
	Spring, the Sweet Spring	(Samuel Daniel)		
	Love is a Sickness	(Thomas Maske)		
	Sigh no More, Ladies	(Shakespeare)		
	Good Wine	(William Browne)		
	To Daffodils	(Herrick)		
81.	*Phyllida and Corydon* (Choral Suite)		1939	Novello, 1939
	Madrigal: Phyllida and Corydon	(Breton)		
	Madrigal: Beauty sat Bathing	(Munday)		
	Pastoral: On a Hill There Grows a Flower	(Breton)		
	Air: Phyllis Amorata	(Andrews)		
	Ballet: Said I that Amaryllis	(Anon.)		
	Canzonet: The Treasure of my Heart	(Sidney)		

		Date of composition	Publisher and date of publication
Air: Where she lies Sleeping	(Anon.)		
Pastoral: Corydon, Arise.	(Anon.)		
Madrigal: To Meadows	(Herrick)		

II   MIXED CHORUS WITH MALE VOICE SOLO OR SEMI-CHORUS

82.	*Blue Eyed Spring* (see also Solo Voice and Piano: 53.)	(Robert Nichols)	1931	Curwen, 1932

Unison Songs

83.	*Under the Broom*		1924	OUP, 1925
84.	*Commendation of Music*	(Richard Strode)	1924	OUP, 1925
85.	*Christmas Day in the Morning*	(trad.)	1924	OUP, 1928
86.	*The Jolly Carter* (see also Folksong Arrangements II. SATB: 73.)	(Suffolk)	1924	OUP, 1925

Two-Part Songs

87.	*Green Fire*	(W.H. Ogilvie)	?	Deane, Year Book Press, 1933
88.	*The Echoing Green*	(Blake)	1933	Deane, Year Book Press, 1934
89.	*Weep You No More, Sad Fountains* (see also Unaccompanied Chorus, I. SATB: 76.)	(Herrick)	1934	Deane, Year Book Press, 1934
90.	*The Lover and his Lass*	(Shakespeare)	?	Novello, 1934

		Date of composition	Publisher and date of publication

Three-Part Songs

91.	*To Blossoms*	(Herrick)	?	Deane, Year Book Press, 1934

Male Voices

92.	*Candlemas Eve* (madrigal)	(Herrick)	?	Novello, 1950
93.	*Ivy and Holly* (solo tenor and men's chorus)	(J. Keegan)	1932	Curwen (Apollo Club), 1933

MUSIC FOR THE CHURCH

94.	*Magnificat* and *Nunc Dimittis* in D	1930	OUP, 1931
95.	*Praise the Lord, O Jerusalem*	1930	OUP, 1931
96.	*Te Deum* and *Jubilate*	1930	OUP, 1931
97.	*Blessed are Those Servants* (unaccompanied four-part (SATB) anthem)	1938	Novello, 1938

UNPUBLISHED

98.	*Dance*, for piano	1913	MS
99.	*Fields at Harvest*, for piano	1913	MS
100.	*A Shropshire Lad* (Housman) Four Songs	1916	MS
101.	*Fanfare for Red Army Day*	1944	MS (whereabouts unknown)
102.	*If There be any Gods* (Seumas O'Sullivan), for voice and piano	1944	MS
103.	Incidental Music for *Hamlet* (Arts Theatre Production)	1946–47	MS (whereabouts unknown)
104.	*Rores Montium*, baritone, TTBB and piano	undated	MS
105.	Overture for Orchestra – in pencil short score only	undated	MS

	Date of composition	Publisher and date of publication

IN COLLABORATION WITH WARLOCK

106. *Maltworms* (Still)   1926

ARRANGEMENTS OF MOERAN'S WORK BY HIMSELF AND OTHERS

107.	*Cherry Ripe (Four English Lyrics)* arr. two-part song	Winthrop Rogers
108.	*When Icicles Hang (Four Shakespeare Songs)* (i) arr. TB male voices (ii) arr. Female voices	Novello, 1942
109.	*The Lover and His Lass (Four Shakespeare Songs)* arr. SATB by Basil Ramsey	Novello (*Musical Times*), 1948
110.	*The Jolly Carter* arr. two-part equal voices by Leslie Woodgate	OUP, 1950
111.	*The Sailor and Young Nancy* arr. SS female voices by Phyllis Tate	Novello, 1952
112.	*Serenade:* Air (i) arr. organ by Basil Ramsey (ii) arr. SATB as *Irish Elegy* with words by Laurence Swinyard, arrangement by Desmond Ratcliffe	Novello, 1955
113.	*Songs of Springtime:* arr. SSAA female voices by Basil Ramsey	Novello, 1958
114.	*Magnificat* and *Nunc Dimittis*: unison voices by A.W. Bunney	OUP, 1961

OTHER

115.	Contribution to *The Roundabout Song Book*	1929

Appendix 3

MISSING WORKS

Apart from juvenilia (including three string quartets and a sonata for cello and piano which, according to Peers Coetmore, were destroyed), there are references in the extant Moeran correspondence and other sources to a few works for which the scores are missing. These are the *Fanfare for Red Army Day*, music for a London Arts Theatre production of *Hamlet*, and a possible Second Piano Trio.

Meticulous in writing his elegantly laid-out scores, Moeran was as haphazard in storing them as he was in most other aspects of his life. Had any of the juvenile works survived, it seemed possible that they might have come to rest in the extensive archive of his Uppingham teacher, the late Robert Sterndale Bennett. Barry Sterndale Bennett, after careful search, has found no trace of any. Only one source (Hubert Foss) mentions a possible Second Piano Trio, and in the absence of any other supporting evidence, its existence must at best be conjectural. The *Fanfare for Red Army Day*, as shown in chapter VIII, did exist and was performed. But the BBC made no recording, and despite the hope that a score might be with other Moeran manuscripts in the archive of the Victorian College of Arts, Melbourne, the College does not seem to have it. The only facts that can be established are that its manuscript was one of those brought back from Eire by Arnold Bax when Moeran died and that, on the death of Bax, the manuscript passed into the hands of the late Julian Herbage. Somewhere between there and Victorian College the manuscript, and maybe others, became mislaid.

The evidence for any music for a *Hamlet* production is tenuous. Rhoderick McNeill, in a letter to the author dated 30 July 1981, mentioned the possibility of its existence, and there certainly was a production of the play at the Arts Theatre in London in the mid-1940s, with Alec Clunes in the title role. Enquiries to locate any Moeran music for it have proved fruitless, and it is likely that it was a project which was discussed for Moeran but, as with others at the time, never materialised for him.

Appendix 4

BIBLIOGRAPHY

ANON. (in fact by Peter Warlock), *E.J. Moeran*, Chester Miniature Essays, London, 1926.

SIR ARNOLD BAX, 'E.J. Moeran: 1894–1950', *Music and Letters*, XXXII, No. 2, April 1951, p.125.

ERIC BLOM (ed.), *Leslie Heward (1897–1943): A Memorial Volume*, J.M. Dent, London, 1944.

GERALD COCKSHOTT, 'E.J. Moeran's Recollections of Peter Warlock', *The Musical Times*, March 1955, p.128.

HARRIET COHEN, *A Bundle of Time*, London, Faber, London 1969.

IAN COPLEY, *The Music of Peter Warlock*, Dobson Books, London, 1979.

LEONARD DUCK, 'Inspiration: Fact and Theory', *The Musical Times*, January 1953, p.13.

EDWIN EVANS, 'Moeran's Symphony in G Minor', *The Musical Times*, February 1938, pp.94–99.

——, 'Moeran's Violin Concerto', *The Musical Times*, August 1943, p.233.

ALOYS FLEISCHMANN, 'The Music of E.J. Moeran', *Envoy: A Dublin Review*, IV, No. 16, March 1951, pp.60–66.

LEWIS FOREMAN, *Bax: A Composer and his Times*, Scolar Press, London, 1983.

HUBERT FOSS, *Compositions of E.J. Moeran*, Novello, London, 1948.

ALAN FRANK, *Modern British Composers*, Dobson Books, London, 1953.

CECIL GRAY, *Musical Chairs*, Home & van Thal, London, 1948.

DAVID GREER, *Hamilton Harty: His Life and Music*, Blackstaff Press, Belfast, 1979.

NINA HAMNETT, *Is She a Lady?*, Allan Wingate, London, 1955.

PHILIP HESELTINE, 'E.J. Moeran', *British Music Society Bulletin*, June 1924.

LIONEL HILL, 'Delius–Moeran–Albert Sammons', *Delius Society Journal*, January 1983.

——, *Lonely Waters: The Diary of a Friendship with E.J. Moeran*, Thames Publishing, London, 1985.

MICHAEL HOLROYD, *Augustus John*, two vols., Heinemann, London, 1974 and 1975.

FRANK HOWES, 'Obituary: Ernest John Moeran', *The Journal of the English Folk Dance and Song Society*, VI, 1949–51, p.103.

ARTHUR HUTCHINGS, 'Ernest John Moeran: 1894–1950', *Monthly Musical Record*, 81, No. 926, May 1951.

AUGUSTUS JOHN, *Chiaroscuro*, Jonathan Cape, London, 1952.

MICHAEL KENNEDY, *Britten*, J.M. Dent, London, 1981.

JACK LINDSAY, *Fanfrolico and After*, Bodley Head, London, 1962.

STEPHEN LLOYD, 'E.J. Moeran: Some Influences on his Music', *Musical Opinion*, February 1981, pp.174–177.

RHODERICK MCNEILL, 'Moeran's Unfinished Symphony', *The Musical Times*, December 1980, pp.771–777; and subsequent letter to *The Musical Times*, April 1981, p.230.

WILLIAM MANN, 'Some English Concertos', in *The Concerto*, ed. Ralph Hill, Pelican, London 1952.

W.J. MITSON, 'Moeran, Ernest John', in Walter Wilson Cobbett (ed.), *Cobbett's Cyclopedic Survey of Chamber Music*, II, OUP, 1963, pp.145–46.

E.J. MOERAN, 'Some Folk Singing Today', *The Journal of the English Folk Dance and Song Society*, Vol. V, No. 3, 1948, pp.152–54.

CHRISTOPHER PALMER, *Delius: Portrait of a Cosmopolitan*, Duckworth, London, 1976.

PETER PIRIE, *The English Musical Renaissance*, Gollancz, London, 1979.

COLIN SCOTT-SUTHERLAND, *Arnold Bax*, London, J.M. Dent, 1973.

RICHARD SHEAD, *Constant Lambert*, Simon Publications, London, 1973.

HEATHCOTE STATHAM, 'Moeran's Symphony in G Minor', *The Music Review*, I, No. 3, 1940, p.245.

R. STERNDALE BENNETT, 'Obituary for Ernest John Moeran', *Uppingham School Magazine*, LXXXIX, No. 631, March 1951.

ERNEST WALKER, *A History of Music in England*, OUP, London, 1952.

J.A. WESTRUP, 'E.J. Moeran', in *British Music of Our Time*, ed. A.L. Bacharach, Pelican, London, 1951.

STEPHEN WILD, *E.J. Moeran*, Triad Press, Rickmansworth, 1974.

——, *The Music of E.J. Moeran: An Assessment*, M.A. Thesis, University of Western Australia, 1966.

Appendix 5

PERSONALIA

Sir John Barbirolli (1899–1970): English conductor who, as conductor of the Hallé Orchestra, fostered the work of Moeran and gave the first performance (with the BBC Symphony Orchestra) of the *Sinfonietta*.

Sir Arnold Bax (1883–1953): British composer of tone poems, chamber music and seven symphonies. Master of the King's Music 1942–1953.

Michael Bowles (b. 1909): Irish conductor and composer, who studied at the Irish Army School of Music and University College, Dublin. Music Director of Radio Eire, 1940–48, and conductor of the New Zealand National Orchestra, 1950–53. Author of *The Art of Conducting* (1959).

Harriet Cohen (1896–1967): Pianist who specialised in Bach and in the music of her time. Her circle of friends was impressive and international; and the favour in which she was held is seen in *A Bach Book for Harriet Cohen* (O.U.P., London, 1932), to which many composers subscribed arrangements.

Désiré Defauw (1885–1960): Belgian violinist and conductor, who became conductor of the Chicago Symphony Orchestra in 1943. The First String Quartet is dedicated to him, and he took part in its first performance, given by the Allied String Quartet.

Aloys Fleischmann (b.1910): Distinguished composer, conductor and lately Professor of Music in the University of Cork. Champion of the music of both Bax and Moeran.

Hubert Foss (1899–1953): Manager and Musical Editor, Oxford University Press Music Department. Composer and author of books on music.

Sir Dan Godfrey (1868–1939): As conductor of the Bournemouth Municipal Orchestra (1893–1934), he brought forward the work of many young British composers, including, for example, Moeran, Brian, Wallace, Farrer and German, as well as that of better-established figures such as Parry, Stanford, Mackenzie and Smyth. As Brian wrote (in *Musical Opinion*, October 1934, p.17), 'During his years at Bournemouth Godfrey has produced music by 220 British composers, and of the 842 different works, no less than 116 were first performances'.

271

LEON GOOSSENS (b.1896): Distinguished oboist – appointed principal oboe of Henry Wood's Queen's Hall Orchestra at the age of 17. Dedicatee of the *Fantasy Quartet* for Oboe and Strings.

JOHN GOSS (1894–1953): Baritone singer of notable sensitivity, yet broad sympathies. Highly regarded by the Warlock/Moeran circle whose work figured frequently in his recital programmes.

CECIL GRAY (1895–1951): Composer and critic. Author of books on Gesualdo, Sibelius and Warlock. Also of a *Survey of Contemporary Music* and the autobiographical *Musical Chairs*.

NINA HAMNETT (1890–1956): Illustrator, portrait and landscape painter. Works include portraits of Walter Sickert and W.H. Davies.

SIR HAMILTON HARTY (1879–1941): Distinguished Irish composer, accompanist and conductor (Hallé Orchestra, 1920–1933). Knighted in 1925. He gave early performances of Moeran's first orchestral work, and the Symphony in G minor is dedicated to him.

LESLIE HEWARD (1897–1943): English conductor who graduated through posts as assistant organist of Manchester Cathedral and teaching posts at Eton and Westminster schools to the conductorship of the City of Birmingham Orchestra from 1930 until his untimely death. Conducted the first performance of and made the first recording of the Symphony in G minor.

ARTHUR HUTCHINGS (b.1906): Professor of Music at the University of Durham (1947–68) and subsequently at the University of Exeter. Author of books of Schubert, Delius and the Mozart Piano Concertos.

JOHN IRELAND (1879–1962): Composer of sophisticated piano music, fine songs and chamber music, and a popular piano concerto. On the staff of the RCM where Moeran became his composition pupil.

WALTER LEGGE (1906–1979): Music critic of *The Manchester Guardian*, 1934–38. Closely associated with the recording industry since he joined the HMV Company in 1927. He was Director of Music for ENSA 1942–45. Founder of the Philharmonia Orchestra and married to singer Elisabeth Schwarzkopf.

ANDRÉ MANGEOT (1883–1970): Violinist, conductor and chamber music coach. Leader of the International String Quartet.

ROBERT NICHOLS (1893–1944): Poet. Served on the Western Front in 1914–18 War as 2nd Lieutenant. Professor of English at Imperial University, Tokyo 1921–24. Volumes of poems include *Invocation* (1915), *Ardours and Endurances* (1917), and *Such was my Singing* (1942).

ALEC ROWLEY (1892–1958): Known chiefly as a composer of piano-teaching material, but he also wrote chamber and organ music and songs of note.

HEATHCOTE STATHAM (1889–1973): Organist and Master of the Choristers, Norwich Cathedral.

SIR JACK WESTRUP (1904–1975): Critic, conductor and musico logist. Professor of Music at Universities of Birmingham (1944) and Oxford (1946). Knighted 1960.

Appendix 6

THE SYMPHONY IN G MINOR

Moeran wrote the programme note for the HMV recording of his G minor Symphony, released in January 1943 on HMV C3319–24. It was reprinted on the sleeve of the recent re-issue of the work in the two-record HMV set, *The Art of Leslie Heward* (EM 29 0462 3).

This symphony was completed early in 1937 and received its first performance at a Royal Philharmonic Society concert at Queen's Hall, London on 13th January 1938 under the conductorship of Leslie Heward. It may be said to owe its inspiration to the natural surroundings in which it was planned and written. The greater part of the work was carried out among the mountains and seaboard of Co. Kerry, but the material of the second movement was conceived around the sand-dunes and marshes of East Norfolk. It is not 'programme-music' – i.e. there is no story or sequence of events attached to it and, moreover, it adheres strictly to its form. It is scored for a moderate-sized orchestra (double wood-wind).

I *Allegro*. The Symphony opens without any preamble with the principal subject of the first movement, given out by the violins. In the fourth bar of this there is a figure of four semiquavers which subsequently plays an important part. Special notice may be taken of the downward leaps at the end of the theme. Presently there appears a fanfare-like motive on the horns, with which is combined the first subject *fortissimo* on strings. This very soon reaches a slight climax, ending with the downward leap. The music gradually quietens and slows down, a good deal being heard of the semiquaver figure, and we arrive in B major for the second subject. This is a long-drawn-out tune of lyrical character. It continues unbroken almost to the double bar, just previous to which part of the first subject is alluded to on solo violin and horn.

The development is ushered in by the semiquaver figure on a clarinet. The tempo becomes *Allegro molto*, the pace is set by a rhythmic figure on the strings, over which the semiquaver figure, now inverted, is treated at some length on the wood-wind, later in combination with the first subject in augmentation on bassoons and horns. There is a big climax leading to what amounts to the return and recapitulation. This is brief and quiet, the component parts of the first and second subjects and the horn fanfare being dovetailed in succession contrapuntally.

A lengthy coda concludes the movement, during which the rhythmic figure from the double bar assumes importance on the brass, and the inverted semi-quaver figure now augmented to crotchets is further developed by a solo horn over string accompaniment.

II *Lento*. The slow movement, which is in B minor, is based entirely on four motives which are given out at the start in quick succession. The first is an undulating one on cellos and basses, the second follows immediately on low flutes and bassoons, the third in canon on all four wood-wind sections, and finally a three-bar motive on divided cellos. The foregoing material occupies the first seventeen bars. These four motives are subsequently developed and combined in various ways until the second of them gradually attains final supremacy in what may be described as a variation of it in the form of a broad twelve-bar melody, appearing unostentatiously first of all on cellos and basses against running thirds on the wood-wind. This is repeated on violas, cellos and horn, a climax is led up to by the fourth motive, in which the first is thundered out by brass and wood-wind in combination with the tail-end of the second on drums and brass instruments. The music quietens, and once more the broad melodic variation of the second motive comes back into its own, played by the upper strings with the first motive in the bass. The movement closes with a brief glimpse of the third motive on the clarinets.

III *Vivace*. The key is D major, the sunlight is let in, and there is a spring-like contrast to the wintry proceedings of the slow movement. The construction is so simple that detailed analysis would be superfluous. The main ingredients are the long oboe tune with which the movement commences, and the subsequent broader melody for strings with its appendage of a dancing or, more truly, jumping motive on wood-wind instruments. Eventually, a burst of sharp *crescendo* chords on the brass leads up to a sudden brief climax, after which the first oboe is left over and hangs on to recall a fragment of his original subject over mysterious murmurings on muted violas and cellos, and the movement comes to an end, 'snuffed out', as it were, by a passing cloud.

IV *Lento – Allegro molto*. The Finale is preceded by a slow introduction of twenty-four bars in which the downward leap from the beginning of the Symphony is much in evidence. The germ of the second subject of the Finale is heard on the horns and there is a serene and peaceful melody on the strings which provides complete contrast to the sudden wild mood of the ensuing *Allegro molto*.

Here the tempo becomes a quick three-in-a-bar, and violas give out the first subject proper, which is in the rhythm of a triple jig. This is worked up to a climax on all the strings, underneath which the trombones come in with a short passage of sharp rising chords of the sixth, at the close of which the downward leap appears for the last time, to be swept aside by the subsidiary first subject. This is a soaring motive on violins and violas treated canonically with its second half on cellos, bases and tuba, which last-mentioned instrument now makes its first appearance in the Symphony.

A rhythmic bridge passage makes way for a climax in which the jig-like first subject is heard in two forms of augmentation, first on horns against staccato chords and then further stretched out on trombones against rushing scales on the strings and wind. Another climax heralds the second subject, given out on oboes and bassoon over a monotonous pedal figure on drums, harp and basses. This alternates with a broad, march-like theme for strings and an attendant canon for horns and basses, but eventually tails off on violins and violas, the concluding harmonic progression forming the germ on which is built up a long, rushing string passage. Over this appears first the jig-like tune, then a persistent development of the subsidiary first subject, which now assumes ascendancy. Presently the second subject makes several tentative experiments and eventually, after what has been a combination of working out and return from preceding material, appears in its final recapitulatory position, now in seven-four time.

The tempo slackens and the coda or, more properly, the epilogue, takes place for forty bars, all of which, except the last two, are on the tonic pedal of G.

Here there is quiet retrospection of the march-like theme on the violas, introduced by its attendant canon on the upper wood-wind. The semiquaver figure from the first movement is recalled in its inverted form, a final *crescendo* leads to the conclusion, and the Symphony ends with a series of six crashing chords.

GENERAL INDEX

277

INDEX OF WORKS